It Spooks | Living in response to an unheard call

IT SPOOKS

Living in response to an unheard call

Shelter50 Publishing collective

for Ryan

without whom the notes for this song would not have been gathered

Conceived, initiated, brought to life, project managed & edited by
Erin Nichole Schendzielos

Published in 2015 by
Shelter50 Publishing collective
Rapid City, South Dakota, USA
For commercial purposes please contact:
Shelter50publishingcollective@gmail.com
www.shelter50publishingcollective.com

All contributors have donated their pieces and all proceeds from the sale of this volume are for the further development and vision of Shelter50 Publishing Collective

First Edition | Monochrome

Printed and bound in the USA

Art direction & design by @MicahPurnell, England.
Including cover & all non-credited illustrations.
www.micahpurnell.com

shelter 50 publishing collective

@Shelter50books | #ITSPOOKS

CONTENTS

FOREWORD

Books like this don't just happen.

While this seems obvious, the deep truth of that statement was likely lost on you immediately after you finished the sentence. The words, thoughts, art, lyrics, musings, and expressions which now sit before you are the culmination of a group of people (sparsely interconnected) who all said yes to an unconventional project. This book exists primarily because of the vision, insight, and persistence of one remarkable woman. As the Shelter50 publishing collective brainstormed what it wanted as an inaugural publication, we knew we desired to create something off the beaten path and which drew upon the voices of many. Several ideas were suggested before our aforementioned remarkable woman had the audacity to propose we simply write Jack Caputo and ask him to create an essay, to which people could then respond in various forms. After all, we had met him in person once, several months earlier, surely he would remember us! My personal reaction fell somewhere between disbelief and mockery, for one does not "simply" do such things. The great thing about visionaries however is their ability to remain undeterred by the skepticism of those around them, and so THE email was sent, encoded with the impossible proposal. What ensued was a series of astonishments as person by person not only agreed, but expressed excitement to become part of this project. Piece by piece everything began to fall into place-with only a handful of detours along the way-and we are extremely pleased with what has been created.

Inside this process an unending gratitude needs to be expressed to our editing team: Sarah, Michaelia, Carla, Greg, and Erin and to the person with the artistic brilliance to put into form our wild ambitions, Micah! Of course, this book also exists because of the amazing theologians, philosophers, artists, lyricists, and thinkers who have contributed their "voices." Thank you for believing in something absurdly unrefined, and for helping make it what it now exists as, our most sincere gratefulness to you all!

There are a couple other things to acknowledge about the book in your hands. First, while we sought to include a broad diversity of people in this project, there is still a very obvious lack of many minority perspectives. This "exclusion" is certainly not intentional, and it is our wish to both recognize and lament its reality.

Secondly, we asked the authors/contributors of this book to keep their reflections as "accessible" as possible, meaning that it would not drift too far into the academy and consequently leave many behind. Certainly some of the writings flirted with this line, but we are very pleased with the overall readability. If the reader finds a certain contribution too weighty, or simply not as engaging, just keep going as there is a wide variety of thoughts and expressions throughout.

And lastly, as stated, this is the Shelter50 Publishing Collective's first publication. We have learned a great deal in this process and are excited to explore other creative projects in the future. While we worked diligently on getting the best product we could, we accept there will still remain mistakes and we lean on the grace of the reader for those. Overall, we hope the reader enjoys this book as much as we enjoyed creating it, and finds something transformative within it.

The Shelter50 Publishing Collective was established for the hope of giving voice to authors with culturally subversive and revolutionary ideas and stories. Our hope is to put into print books with the potential to transform people and communities, leaving the world in a better condition than we were handed it.

RYAN SCHENDZIELOS
Shelter50 Publishing collective

JOHN D. CAPUTO

Grandparent
ponderer
spooker

THE FOLLOWING ARE THE MASKS JOHN (JACK) D. CAPUTO HAS BEEN KNOWN TO WEAR IN THE PUBLIC SPHERE:

In public, "John D. Caputo" is the Thomas J. Watson Professor of Religion Emeritus (Syracuse University) and the David R. Cook Professor of Philosophy Emeritus (Villanova University), a hybrid philosopher/theologian who works in the area of radical theology. He has pursued the notion of what he calls "weak theology" in a series of academic books Radical Hermeneutics (1987), *The Prayers and Tears of Jacques Derrida* (1997), *The Weakness of God: A Theology of the Event* (2006), and *The Insistence of God: A Theology of Perhaps* (2013). But he also reaches out to a wider audience in books like *On Religion* (2001), *What Would Jesus Deconstruct?* (2006), *Philosophy and Theology* (2006), and *Truth* (2013).

HERE'S WHAT THIS CONTRIBUTOR WOULD SAY ABOUT HIMSELF:

In private, I am Jack, a life-long academic, now retired, whose wife, Kathy, says she can't tell I'm retired. That means I'm spending a lot of time writing and lecturing. While continuing my strictly academic work, the works of the "right hand," I've also been spending more time on the work of the "left hand," where I imagine myself liberating crucially important ideas from their arcane imprisonment in the academy and putting them out on the streets. So in imitation of the master, who mixed with tax collectors and sinners, I have been spending as much time as possible working with the Creston Davis' Global Center for Advanced Studies, Tripp Fuller and Bo Eberle's "Homebrewed Christianity," Phil Snider's "Subverting the Norm," Pete Rollins' various disruptive undertakings, and other rogues of truth willing to listen to me. Kathy and I have three wonderful children, all married, and seven wonderful grandchildren.

Proclaiming the Year of the Jubilee:

Thoughts on a Spectral Life

Proclaiming the Year of the Jubilee: Thoughts on a Spectral Life

1

When Jesus announced his ministry he said he was anointed by the Spirit to bring good news to the poor and proclaim the year of the Jubilee (Luke 4:16).

That is a haunting thought.

Why haunting? Why not just inspiring, beautiful, holy? Nothing's simple with you.

I am not saying it's not inspiring, beautiful and holy. I am just saying that it has a kind of spectral quality about it. In theology, everything is haunted.

By what?

If I knew what, it would not be a specter. By something, I know not what. Let's just say by "it," with all the anonymity of "it." It's vague but "it" is "there."

Then why call it theology? "It" could be anything.

That's very true. But in theology it goes under-unless it is coming under-the name (of) "God," of the rule of "God," the year of God's favor.

But what's so spectral about that? Where's the specter?

It's like 50 is a lucky number. Jesus said this a long time ago and for all the world it still hasn't happened, but nobody has given up on it. Don't you find that strange? We never get to 50 but they still keep saying it. We do the math, we keep counting and we never get to 50. I'd say that's a very spooky kind of mathematics. It is always coming but it never quite shows up; it keeps getting postponed. Maybe next year. So in my view I'd say we're haunted by its coming, by its prospect, by the specter of its prospect.

Very fancy! And you? I suppose you fancy yourself an expert in this field?

Let's start again. I am giving you the wrong impression. Specters pay us unexpected visitations; they do not come by invitation. This is less something that I propose than something to which we are all already exposed. Specters do not wait upon our permission. We are always and already haunted, like it or not. The specter spooks, it spooks, under one name or another, under many names, and we are all subject to it. So it is not a question of being an expert but of experiencing spooks.

You have chosen a very strange profession.

It has chosen me. It never consulted me.

What has chosen you?

It. An insistent, incessant "it." It gives me no peace.

So what do you make of this saying of Jesus? What's going on here?

If it spooks, if it's all spooked, the whole thing—thought, being, God—the one big question I have is how to live with it, with "it," with whatever's spooking things. How to proclaim the year of the Jubilee even though it never comes? How to lead a spectral life?

It Spooks Thought

The Modern Philosophers, the Men of Reason, of the Enlightenment, thought they could save us. They thought their Thought could save us. (Hint: when I capitalize words, I am using "scare quotes" to spook them, or to suggest that "it spooks" them. I could, like the Germans, capitalize almost everything, but that would be impractical.)

Karl Marx, one of the greatest of them, said that the Critique of religion is the first and most fundamental form of Critique, the very paradigm of Critique, after which other forms of critique are to be modeled. That is because religion distorts economic phenomena and supports economic oppression precisely by mystifying reality with its otherworldly ghosts—a ruse which capitalism also perpetrates in its own way (like the "invisible hand" or the phantasmatic "commodity"). To do Critique then is to demystify, to replace mystification with reality, to dispel illusions with the cold truth, to get rid of the ghosts of religion and replace them with hard economic reality. To critique is to exorcise. Criticism is exorcism.

Derrida wrote a book about Marx and, in the "spirit of a certain Marxism" (SoM, 166-67), said exactly the opposite: thinking is not Critique but spooking; not exorcism but haunting. When someone offers us a Critique, furrow your brow and suspect something shadowy is going on. I am going to call Derrida's frame of mind, faute de mieux, "postmodern," even though I know better. Derrida scorned this word on the grounds of its excessive mediatization—including all the specters of virtual reality and the internet—and of its tendency to draw neat lines between historical periods. But, as I used to say to him, that may be true, but it is a very good way to draw a crowd. Deconstruction is a way of thinking but deconstruction is not Critique. Instead of replacing mystification (ghosts) with reality (presence), it displaces reality with specters. It shows that it spooks the whole thing, Modernity and Critique included. Deconstruction does not dispel ghosts; it offers them hospitality (SoM, 65). Derrida gets spooked whenever anyone starts speaking of Critique and has recourse to Reality or Being or Truth in a table-pounding way, without adding on one of his own famous grammatological ghosts—"if there is any" (s'il y en a) or "perhaps" (peut-être) or "as if it were possible" (comme s'était possible), which modalize, modify and attenuate these pretenders to the throne of Thought. Derrida suspects every position is spooked by one of these

Deconstruction is a way of thinking but deconstruction is not Critique. Instead of replacing mystification (ghosts) with reality (presence), it displaces reality with specters. It shows that it spooks the whole thing, Modernity and Critique included. Deconstruction does not dispel ghosts; it offers them hospitality (SoM, 65).

appositions, every ontology displaced by a hauntology. He worried about the mystification baked into what poses as Reality, about all the powerful, intimidating authority of Truth and Being. Talking about Being is never far from talking like the Powers That Be, which really scares the hell out of us, especially when the police of truth come knocking at our door (or hacking our computers).

Marx's concept of Critique is paradigmatic of Modernism and Secularism. It goes about its business by arguing that x is "nothing other than" y, nothing but a disguised or distorted form of y, for which critical thinking steps forth to supply the undisguised, unvarnished, undistorted truth. (Hint: whenever you hear the words "nothing other than," head for the door, you may be next—that's deconstruction in a nutshell.) Religion, on this accounting, had been dragged before the executioner several times over in modernity. Religion is nothing other than the distortion of economic relations (Marx); nothing other than the desire for our mommy (Freud); nothing other than the will-to-power (Nietzsche). In short, nothing other than an illusion for which Marx and Freud thought they had the Truth—but not Nietzsche, who thought that Truth too was nothing other than an illusion. That is why Nietzsche's critique of religion is on the way towards becoming postmodern. Nietzsche's "death of God" unexpectedly re-opened the door for religion; but that's another and a complicated story I have addressed elsewhere.

What is it? What is the "it" that's so spooky in religion. What is the "it" that spooks? Maybe it's important? Perhaps.

If deconstruction were a World Historical Spirit (God forbid), I would say it has come into the world to spook the modernist-Enlightenment types. But the funny thing is that it also spooks the secular deconstructors. They are scared stiff that deconstruction opens the door to the return of (the ghosts) of religion, which from time immemorial has tried to scare the hell out of us (literally) by means of very powerful Sacred Spooks and very Holy Ghosts. That didn't scare Derrida, who liked to think against the grain. If intellectuals these days are all that spooked by religion, Derrida mused, maybe, just perhaps, there is something interesting going on there, and maybe "religion," if there is such a thing, does not mean just one thing. What is it? What is the "it" that's so spooky in religion. What is the "it" that spooks? Maybe it's important? Perhaps.

Take the case of Marx himself. The amusing thing is that Marx chased away or busted one ghost too many, the very one he most needed and relied upon, which we see in the opening line of the Communist Manifesto (SoM, 174). There Marx famously said that all of Europe is "haunted" by the "specter"(Gespenst) of "Communism." Communism, he and Engels said to Europe, is coming to get you. Now, in this book, after the collapse of the Soviet Union, Derrida is saying to us, do not think that Marx is dead. Marx was trying to spook old Europe, and as anyone who has even driven by a synagogue knows, this is a spook of a vintage "messianic" variety. Everything in Marx turns on calling for the coming of the "messianic" specter of radical justice. So it turns out that, like any Jewish prophet (SoM, 41-44) worthy of the name, Marx too was proclaiming good news for the poor and the year of the Jubilee! Marx had a lucky number! What is more scandalous than that? Marx—who we recall descended from a long line of rabbis—at the weeping wall praying for the year of the Jubilee? Is this a general rule? Whenever anybody has anything important to say or to do or to make, even and especially if this is supposedly a purely "secular" matter, there's a spook afoot, and maybe even a "religious" one. It's spooking them. There is spooking going on. Perhaps.

Or take the case of the Enlightenment itself. Much as the Men of Reason deny it, if we listen very closely to the cool dulcet tones of Reason in

Religion is nothing other than the distortion of economic relations (Marx); nothing other than the desire for our mommy (Freud); nothing other than the will-to-power (Nietzsche).

the Enlightenment we can hear a call, a command, a solicitation, an injunction, a little ghost or maybe a big one whispering in its ear: sapere aude, have the courage to think, the courage to ask any question. Behind all this Big Brave Talk about Critique, a little ghost! Beneath all the ontotheological bluster, a quiet prayer. There it is! I knew it. An invisible spirit was encouraging the Men (sic) of the Enlightenment to have courage, to have the heart, cor, to use their head, as it took a great deal of courage to question a murderous church and king. So however postmodern you may feel in the morning, do not be ungrateful to the Enlightenment as the day wears on. Behind their veneer of cool rational macho talking heads lies the passion of a whole body at prayer. We Men of the Enlightenment, Kant said, have come of age; we are the adulthood of humankind—but they are all praying for the courage to think. Just like old Marx they were all praying like mad but they will not admit it. They are praying for "emancipation," which it turns out is not a "metanarrative" but a prayer. Emancipation is a promise not a program, Derrida says (SoM, 75), which is why Derrida says it is the last thing in which he would have "incredulity." The only courage they lacked was the courage to admit that they are praying for courage. They were terrified of being called "spirit-seers," fearful of what Kierkegaard called the comic incommensurability of the body of a grown man at prayer, sunk to his knees, eyes closed, praying and weeping—like an old woman, they feared.

The only courage they lacked was the courage to admit that they are praying for courage.

Now take the case of the ongoing debate about religion. In modernism, the supernaturalism of religion is challenged by the naturalism of its critics; fideism, the access of faith to a higher reality, is contested on the grounds of the rationality of scientism and materialism. But the two sides share the same presuppositions. "-Isms" aplenty, a war of "-Isms," two sides of the same coin, competing versions of the same thing, two varieties of the same Real-ism, or Reality-ism, of pure Ism-ism—two versions of what Derrida (following Heidegger) called the "metaphysics of presence." Each side competes for the high ground of Presence, of what is really real, declaring the other side an illusion, or—the nuclear option—"nihilism." Two big bruisers itching for a fight, each making an endless "so's your mother" war on the other. In this corner, the ens realissimum, the really real and really Big Being, where the material world is finite, created and mixed with a dose of unreality. That emboldens John Milbank to denounce materialists as nihilists (in the name of "peace," of course), because without God matter is nothing at all. Only when matter is sustained by God can matter's reality be maintained; that's the True Materialism. In the other corner, no less big and mean, materialists making matter the only thing that matters, the only reality, while religion is the tragic illusion of thinking that real life begins only after you are six feet under. In short, nihilism again.

One has God on its side; the other has the material universe, two very Big Deals. One looks up unctuously to Heaven, the other squints through its telescopes at the heavens. Each side thinks it has reality on its side and the other side is bedeviled by nihilism, so they each want to drive the devil out of the other. This is what Kant called in his cool transcendental terms an "antinomy," meaning a debate that drives the rest of us crazy and will conclude (without conclusion) only when an expanding universe puts an infinite distance between the parties to the debate so that (mercifully) they can no longer hear each other shouting. Sometimes I wonder even if entropic dissipation, which brings the universe itself to an end (perhaps!), will be enough to shut them up. The one thing that just might be immortal is this debate itself, which is why we should be sure to bury the combatants in separate cemeteries, lest their ghosts continue their hostilities even after death and disturb the rest of everyone around them.

But do not be mistaken. Deconstruction (if there is such a thing!) has not come into the world to mount a new postmodern defense of religion, to offer a postmodern apologetics, which is what I like to call "postmodernism light." It is acutely conscious that God and religion have been our best alibi for oppression, exclusion and murder. Its distrust of religion, which is without limit, goes back, I would venture to say, to the bit of indigestible two worlds dualism religion has swallowed, the residual Gnosticism of Christian Neoplatonism it unfortunately ingested back when it was getting its intellectual sea legs, which all came to a head in Augustine's City of God. This soft Gnosticism transformed purely spectral phenomena into pure spiritual entities, mistakenly reifying them as inhabitants of a realm of Immaterial Being. It allowed Greek philosophical distinctions between eternity and time, the supersensible and the sensible, soul and body to command the interpretation of the Kingdom of God. The Christian Neoplatonists realized that there was something odd about the year of the Jubilee, that its time was out of joint, but instead of meditating upon its spectral annularity, its strange and messianic mathematics, instead of appreciating that it belongs to another more haunting, haunted temporality, it abolished its temporality altogether. It turned the year of the Jubilee into the timelessness of eternity. By thus confusing the Kingdom of God with a metaphysical realm beyond space and time, it turned the call for Kingdom into an economic chase here on earth after celestial rewards in the hereafter, where we are assured we will flit about in maintenance free bodies doing God knows what for all eternity. That dualism deserves all the abuse, suspicion and incredulity it gets, and I will come back to it at the end.

The Christian Neoplatonists realized that there was something odd about the year of the Jubilee, that its time was out of joint, but instead of meditating upon its spectral annularity, its strange and messianic mathematics, instead of appreciating that it belongs to another more haunting, haunted temporality, it abolished its temporality altogether.

The postmodern style of thinking about religion is quite different. Religion is not refuted with a table-pounding argument; it is not bombed into oblivion.

Deconstruction does not confuse thinking with a drive-by shooting. Instead, such dualism is dealt with more peacefully, with a yawn, with what Lyotard very precisely called, and no doubt after much research, "incredulity."

Such religion is unbelievable. We don't believe it and there is no need to discredit it as it is making itself unbelievable all by itself, with every billboard it puts up attacking the theory of evolution, global warming, the emancipation of women and same sex marriage. With each passing day it makes itself more unbelievable with the "dare to think" set, although, as Lacan points out, it will probably last forever in the Bible Belt (where they don't dare). The "new atheists" should have spared themselves (and us) the trouble. They are trying to break down a door that is wide open, and besides they are not nearly as good at discrediting religion as is religion itself. Even the believers inside religion, the ones who struggle to believe, who believe that they believe, as Vattimo says so deftly, do not believe this religion.

So it is not that postmodernism finds nothing objectionable about religion, but that by virtue of its suspicion of Big Reductionistic Stories, it resists saying "Religion"—it resists the insistence of the capital letter—is just one thing, just one Big Diabolical Thing or (the other side of the same coin) just one Big Holy and Celestial Thing. Instead, it thinks, it suspects, something spooky is going on here, which is both a promise and a threat; we never know about spooks. This is spooky business and the question is, what spooks? So having shown the door to both the Big Strong Men of Reason and the Big Strong Men of Theology, who are out to exorcise each other, it sits down to listen for the spooks, to attend to the multiple, conflicting and still small voices of religion, if there is such a thing. It is feeling around for something going on in it, for something playing more quietly in the background, something more elusive, that is not drowned out by the noisy war conducted between the Faithful and the Atheists, something that is complicit with neither secularism's dismissiveness nor religion's anxiety, superstition and violence, something thought-worthy, something spooky, something oddly, eerily there.

That is what the figure of the specter provides. The specter is neither simply present nor simply absent; it is neither simply living nor simply dead. Specters are neither theists nor atheists, neither black nor white, neither leftists nor rightists. Specters are highly egalitarian; they disturb everybody. The specter leads a shadowy insubstantial life, the demi-life of the living dead, of the undead, a penumbral life, from paene umbra, "almost a shadow." Not a full-blown shadow but almost, an exquisite Latin formulation. (Hint: add the fabulously precise imprecision of "almost" to Derrida's list of spooks). So to proclaim the year of the Jubilee is to say, it's almost 50, that it has a special asymptotic annularity, a spectral temporality. The specter makes its presence felt without being actually present, but its apparitions are not mere hallucinations. We do not simply believe or disbelieve specters. We do not know what to believe. We are too uneasy to just believe them but we are too unnerved to suspend our disbelief. These apparitions are not realities but they are not simply illusions. If "it" is spooky, this could be it, or almost. If we try to give the specter respectability in the academy, we could propose offering a course entitled spectrology, or spectral hermeneutics, or the phenomenology of the spectral. Its subject matter is not ontology but hauntology; not onto-theology but haunto-theology; not theo-logy but a theo-poetics. We might even propose the creation of a whole department of Penumbralogy. As the curriculum committee would no doubt find all our proposals very elusive, we would, as a last resort, recommend that it be run as an interdisciplinary course and sent over to the Humanities Center where they are always looking for courses on the "wholly other."

If we try to give the specter respectability in the academy, we could propose offering a course entitled spectrology, or spectral hermeneutics, or the phenomenology of the spectral. Its subject matter is not ontology but hauntology; not onto-theology but haunto-theology; not theo-logy but a theo-poetics.

We can now distinguish two ways to be critical of religion. The first is (modernist, reductionist) Critique. It has a firm ground external to religion, an external point of leverage (materialism), a secure base from which it launches missiles aimed at the heart of religion, dropping the bombs of Reality upon the villages and towns of religious illusion, aiming at the simple destruction of religion. The second lacks all such external leverage, has no firm and unshakeable ground, and has not even the wherewithal to lay down its head. It engages in a weak and quasi-transcendental scrutiny—deconstruction can be very critical of religion but it is not a Critique of Religion—which takes up residence within religion, like a war correspondent embedded in a military unit from which it makes all its reports. It undertakes a meticulous, internal reading of multiple religious texts, traditions, institutions and practices, engaging in a micrological exposé of the internal tensions that inhabit and constitute the multiple phenomena of religion. It takes the side of religion in such a way as to get inside it and feel about for what is going on in religion, for what's spooking it, looking for traces of the events convening there. The aim is not the destruction of religion, but its deconstruction, indeed the exhibition of the auto-deconstruction that is taking place in religion, where the expositor is doing nothing more than expounding what is already exposed, already going on in religion, like the first reporter on the scene.

...deconstruction can be very critical of religion but it is not a Critique of Religion-which takes up residence within religion, like a war correspondent embedded in a military unit from which it makes all its reports.

The aim is not to destroy religion but to "repeat" it, which means to re-read it, to re-invent the events that already inhabit and constitute religion, by exhibiting all the ghosts by which these texts, beliefs, traditions, practices and institutions (am I omitting anything?) are haunted. The aim is to open or re-open religion to its future, to let it tremble with a future it cannot see coming—and also with a past it would rather forget. Whenever anyone says this is x, where x is some entity, creed, program, proposition or proof (am I omitting anything?), the hauntological, penumbralogical, micrological reader suspects that a closer study will reveal ghosts in its closet. Whenever someone says "Religion," deconstruction behaves as if it has seen a ghost, asking in wide-eyed disbelief if there is such a thing, just one thing called "Religion," in the singular, in western Christian Latin. It turns the table on the table-pounders who say, I am a believer, say, a Christian (or I am certainly not), with the sly suspicion that a closer examination will show that they are haunted by many other competing voices which they will not allow themselves to confess. Whenever pressed about whether he is an atheist, Derrida would say "I quite rightly pass for one," that is what they say about me and they are probably right, but I do not know. I am haunted by many ghosts and they give me no rest. Believers will find no better formula for their belief than that. Whenever anyone says, this is a strictly "secular" matter the hauntologist suspects it is haunted by the ghosts of "religion," by a little prayer, by an implicit theology or "unavowed theologeme." Just so, whenever people say, this is a strictly "religious" matter, the hauntologists suspect several secular spirits are hidden up their sleeve, which is why his reverence prefers his long robes for official functions.

—2—

It Spooks Being

You are forgetting the most ancient and venerable principles of philosophy. Being is; non-being altogether is not. Thus spoke Father Parmenides.

Almost.

That's the point! There's no almost here, no shadowy quasi-nothings, or quasi-beings, which are the illusions with which mortals, two-headed, fill their empty heads.

What is eating you?

I am just following Parmenides, the name of the Father

of Philosophy and of the Thought of Being.

Well, the name of your Father is making you awfully anxious. Loosen up.

Parmenides thought that Being could save us. A long line of metaphysicians—I can see Plato and Aristotle, Augustine and Aquinas up at the front—marches loyally behind him. But Being, on our hypothesis is spooked. But by what?

We all know that ghosts come back from the dead. The French call them "revenants" (from the Latin re-venire, "to come back"). They are the undead, who have come back to pay us a visit because the business of their life is unfinished and they are demanding that we finish it for them—like the ghost of Hamlet's father, which is the point of departure for Derrida's analysis, or like the ghost of "Christmas past" tormenting miserable old Scrooge. Ghosts have unfinished work, unkept promises, frustrated hopes, dreams gone wrong, unrequited injustice, and they have come back to see that these matters are redressed. That is why Walter Benjamin turned the idea of the messianic inside out and said that we are the messianic generation. That gets our attention. Nobody is going to save us; we are going to have save the dead. We are the ones the dead were waiting for—which is an eerie thought—to make right what was done to them. We are responsible to the dead. So Being, if by Being we mean Presence, the Present, is haunted by the wounds of the past, by what Metz called the "dangerous memory" of the dead, whose death it is up to us to see was not in vain. In this amazing soteriology, that would mean that the death of Jesus did not save us, but that we have to save Jesus, to see that his death was not in vain. Instead of billboards saying "Jesus Saves," we need new ones saying "Save Jesus."

But the reason—if ghosts need or even have a reason—ghosts come back from the dead ultimately has to do with the future. Old Marley wanted Scrooge to avoid making the same old mistake he did; he wanted Scrooge to have a future in what time was left to him. Scrooge after all had an infinite advantage over Marley; he still had time. So this ghost come back from the past had the future on his disembodied mind. The same thing goes for the King who wants Hamlet to make right his murderous usurpation. It is the future that can be different, the future that holds a promise, the future that lures us on—as we proclaim the coming of the Kingdom, or the year of the Jubilee—even as the future is also menaced by the threat that the worst will happen, since, when it comes to ghosts, no one is guaranteeing anything. So the present is exposed to the arrivants, to who or what is coming, as well as to revenants, those are coming back. We live in messianic or spectral time, responsible to both the living and the dead, both the living and the still to come, to the whole community of saints. We live in the space between a memory and a promise.

Old Marley wanted Scrooge to avoid making the same old mistake he did; he wanted Scrooge to have a future in what time was left to.

Being then is haunted, broken open, by the past and the future. Being is unhinged by time. If I ever could get up the nerve to write a book entitled Being and Time, I would defend the thesis that Being is spooked by time and that time is out of joint. It's time that has spooked them all, metaphysicians, theologians, the whole lot. Hamlet said the time, Denmark at his time, is out of joint. But the point is general: time itself is the out-of-jointedness of Being.

It's about time you came clean. You are saying time is

it. "It" is about time. The

"it" is time.

Almost. Be careful. Don't rush to judgment. Take your time.

Time doth make cowards of us all.

Put it this way. "Time," if there is such a thing, is "it," if there is such a thing. And then add what that famous metaphysician Bill Clinton said when he found himself in a tough spot: it all depends on what the meaning of "is" is. Be that as it may, they're all unnerved by time, by the coming to be and passing away of things. To the poetizing of Parmenides' great poem on Being I would oppose a little verse by Robert Frost entitled "The Span of Life" that tidily sums up what is unnerving them:

The old dog barks backwards without getting up.
I can remember when he was a pup.

The first line is haunted by the second line, by the temporal shift to "was," which is what really spooks us. Time is what is eating at us; it is consuming us. Time doth make cowards of us all. So when Parmenides said time is not Being but illusion, Plato thought the old man was going too far. Feeling called upon to rise to its defense as best he could without engaging in open patricide, Plato pleaded that it is a copy of being, a little bit false, that's true, but also a little bit true, too, not simply false and we even need to use the appearances of things in time to ascend up to the true timeless world. Plato was damning time with faint praise, of course, but he was saying to Father Parmenides, please, be reasonable, it is almost real, apparently real and we philosophers have to account for appearances and live with them. Or, as Derrida might have put it, of course the past and future are not simply present, "of course they do not exist—so what?" (SoM, 174).

Think of the classical metaphysical picture of Being as Presence as a blurry photograph suffering from a double exposure—to a past that will not let us forget it, to a future that will not stop calling upon us. Far from being full and well rounded, solid and plenitudinous all the way through, as Father Parmenides dreamed, the present is destabilized and discontent, porous and permeable, in a word deconstructible. When you're haunted—and when are you not?—the time is out of joint. What passes itself off as present is inwardly disturbed and disjoined. There is no such thing as a well-joined time, a tranquil temporal "now" imitating an eternal restful now.

Whenever a belief or a practice, an institution or a tradition, steps forward claiming the authority of Being, which allows its officers to pass themselves off as the powers-that-be, the idea is to spook it, or show it is already spooked, that the "it spooks" is already doing its eerie work there. That will not destroy it but give it a future, which too often it does not want—the one percent, for example, can do without the Jubilee Jesus had in mind—because the future is dicey business. Just consider what an unnerving thing, or non-thing, or quasi-thing time is, if it is. The future is the "future present," the future that we can more or less foresee and anticipate, and for which we can reasonably prepare. That is important and requires a lot of hard work, and things may go terribly wrong with our best laid plans. That is because of the "absolute future," the absolutely unforeseeable and unprogrammable future, which takes us by surprise, which blindsides us, for which we cannot prepare.

time is out of j o i n t

It's about time you came clean. You are saying time is it. "It" is about time. The "it" is time.

Almost. Be careful. Don't rush to judgment. Take your time.

Anyone who calls for the coming of a new day needs the hardiness to say yes to the coming of what they cannot see coming. It may turn out to be a day in which you should never have gotten out of bed.

And it gets worse than that. The future is not only the future of the future; it is also the future of the past, what Benjamin and Derrida call the promise of the past, our hope in the past, the coming back again of something simmering from time immemorial, which will also take us by surprise. These joint specters, of the absolute future and the absolute past, see to it that Being, the Presence of the Present, is spooked by time, disjoined by haunting specters taunting it from either side, by both prospective and retrospective specters, from before and after, giving it no rest.

So what old Parmenides called unchanging Being we Penumbralogists say is a blurry double exposure, luring us on, unnerving us, unsettling us, asking us to screw up our courage, just like old Scrooge, who has these two ghosts to deal with. I have not forgotten the third one, the ghost of Christmas Present, the very spirit who was speaking to him right there and then while he stood on his bed all atremble. That is what Kierkegaard and Heidegger called the "moment" of decision, which passes through the ordeal of undecidability. The moment in which we are haunted is not the "now" of Platonism and Christian Neoplatonism, which tries to reassure itself that the temporal "now" is a poor imitation or a copy of an pure unchanging now by which it is constantly monitored and kept safe. The calm Neoplatonic now is actually quite a bit of violence against time and the moment. It is a bit weak-kneed and timid; it has no heart for the future, which is chancy, and it prays for this "moment" to pass—instead of giving it a chance. If only being would hold firm, it thinks, in pure, perfect, compact, complete, leak-proof presence, we would not have to deal with the spooks of undecidability; no ghostly spirits could seep through its cracks. We wouldn't have to talk to them! That's another important point about specters. Notice that when it comes to specters, we cannot be content to just be spectators. We cannot just "look at" (theorein) specters. We must, like Hamlet and Scrooge, hear them out and engage them in conversation, address them as well as allowing ourselves to be addressed by them, finding out what they have on their eerie minds, discovering what they expect us to do. Specters expect something. They expect something to change! Specters have high expectations; they shatter the settled and limited horizon of expectations with which we comfort ourselves. When we say, you can only do what is possible, or no one could be expected to do any more, specters expect more.

Notice that when it comes to specters, we cannot be content to just be spectators.

But what do they expect? Do they expect the impossible? Why are they bothering me? I was sound asleep in my bed. I did not ask for this trouble. Who invited them? Who asked them to come, to disrupt these quiet midnight hours with their disturbing visions and voices, with such uncanny, fetching, dangerous, insolent, insistent solicitations? Am I even awake? Am I dreaming? Was this a nightmare? What does this specter expect of me?

—3—

It Spooks God

So according to you, it's all spooked-Thought and Being. But what about God?

God is that than which nothing greater can be conceived.

Almost.

God is the ens realissimum, infinite and perfect.

If there is one.

God is our Savoir.

If he shows up.

God is what He Is, Who will be what He will be, who will always be faithful to His people.

Maybe, but you cannot count on it.

Surely, if ever anything were "it," God is it. God always was and always will be necessarily-it.

Perhaps. It depends.

Theologians think that God will save us. God rises up as pure Being above all becoming, as the eternal above the temporal, as most really real of all above the shadowy quasi-realities of the created world. God is the Pure Spirit who eludes this game of ghosts by which we are held captive down here below.

But that's just it! If, as we have been saying, nothing is present without being haunted, that nothing has Being unless it trembles with may-being, peut-être, that nothing is real unless it is destabilized by the irreal, that goes for God, for God above all, the ens realissimum, the most really real of all. God does not get a pass. God does not stand above this fray. God, God above all, is the most spectral phenomenon of all! God is the most really spooky of all, the specter par excellence, the most suspicious, ghostly ghost of all. God is not only a spectral figure but the very figure or paradigm of the specter, ens spectralissimun, if we could say such a thing in Latin, which of course we cannot. It's barbaric Latin but you see the point: God is that than which there is nothing spookier, nothing more haunting, nothing more haunted. That's why we would be hard put to find a better case of spectral phenomena than religion, which is a concentration, a celebration, a mélange, an elaborate orchestration of ghosts, even and especially very holy ones, which is why Marx put religion at the top of his (hit) list.

Just look at the historical record: God is that than which there is nothing more perfectly present or even omnipresent—yet is nowhere to be found; nothing is more prestigious than the "word of God"—yet what is more biting than the silence of God when evil surrounds us on every side? Nothing is more luminous that the light of God—yet nothing more hidden; nothing more saving—yet nothing more likely to leave us in the lurch time and again; nothing more powerful—yet seeming never to lift a finger on our behalf when we need help the most. The track record of God coming to the rescue of suffering innocents is so bad you have to wonder why the long robes keep bringing it up.

Just go down the list of divine names and every time you'll find a ghost. I think we need a new list.

Is God it? Is God there? Not there? Was that God, in that moment—or, as Nietzsche somewhat cynically suggests, a bit of undigested beef disturbing our sleep? Was that the ghost of the King, Hamlet keeps asking himself, or a hallucination? This spectral undecidability is the insubstantial substance of one of the greatest masterpieces in the history of English literature. But it pales (like a ghost) in comparison with, unless it draws its power from, the divine undecidability whose visitation leaves us shaken to the bones. Was this God or some malicious specter bent on deceiving me, Descartes asks in a fit of epistemological anxiety. Outside epistemology, out on the streets, in actual life, we have a parallel anxiety. Is that God or the Evil One leading me into the worst violence? Is that the living God or something undead stalking me day and night? Who is calling, or what, and how am I to speak of such an elusive spirit? But then again how can I not?

He or she or it, I know not what, one or many, real or unreal, saving or dangerous, whoever or whatever this is, will not leave me alone.

Whoever said God is dead must have been smoking something. God is the most undead of all.

If I were reincarnated as a medieval theologian, as sometimes happens in my dreams, I would launch my career by announcing a quaestio disputata, a (highly) disputed question, in which I would defend the thesis that the essence of God lies in God's para-existence, God's spectral persistence, God's purely penumbral presence, in short, that the essence of God lies in God's insistence. Back at the friary, I would daily pray, at matins and at vespers, for God to rid me of God, for God to send the God of Pure Being, Pure Light and Pure Truth packing. God give me purity but not now, in fact, now that I think about it, not ever! I prefer impure thoughts.

This strange and uncanny somewhat, this insistent and unsettling specter, this anonymous disturbance, this "it" that comes and goes under the name (of) "God" has pursued me down the long corridors of time, all the way back to grade school nuns hovering over us like specters leaving us to wonder if there were real bodies beneath these black veils, all the way up to old age, springing up in the unlikeliest places, breaking through the tiniest crevices of quotidian life, breaking in at moments of high drama, seeping subtly into my daily routine, stealing upon me unawares, looking back at me in the mirror in the morning, hailing me from high atop a frozen mountain peak, calling me to set sail upon the deep, out beyond the horizon, where the land is out

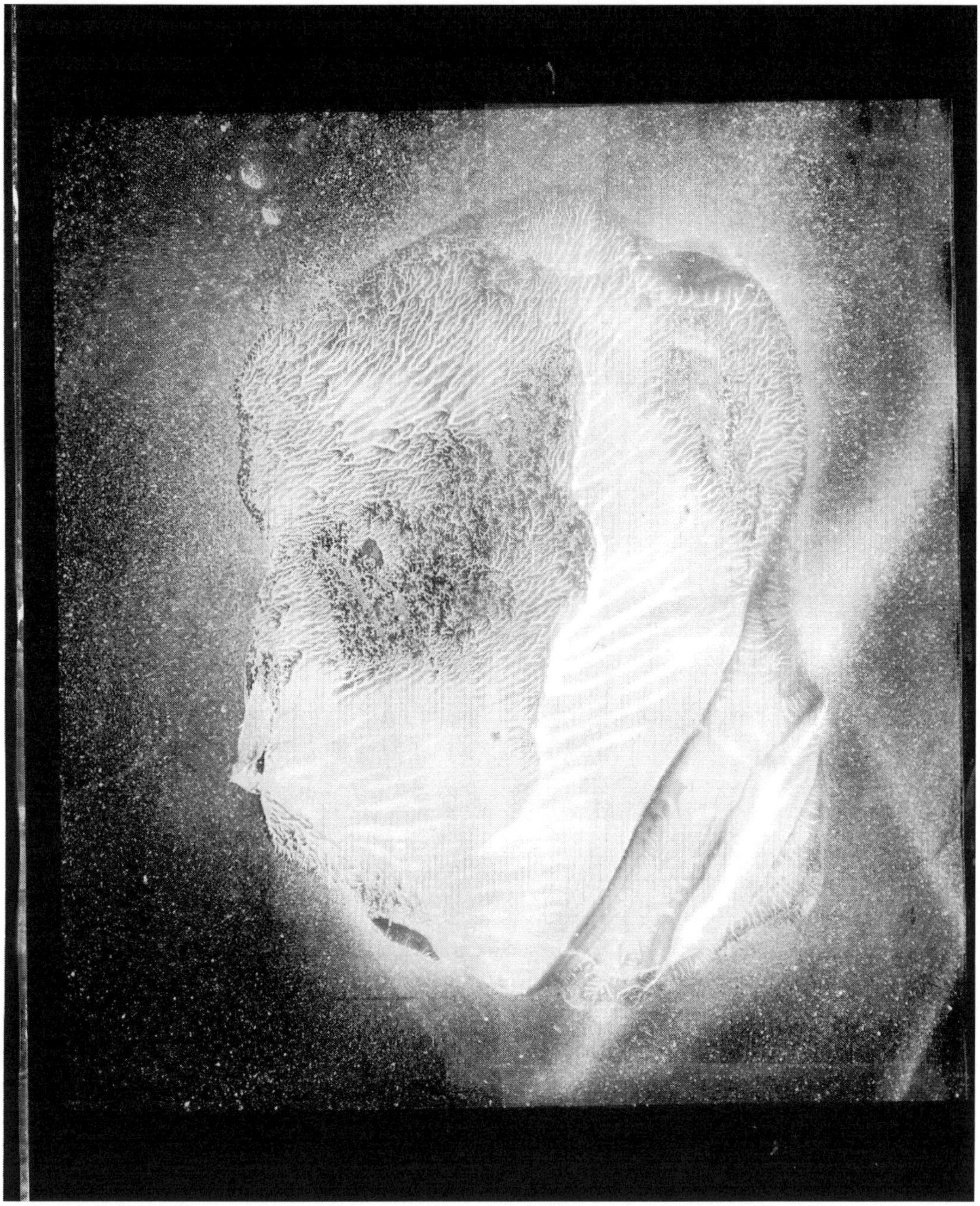

of sight, knowing that there I would be alone, unprotected from its insistent, incessant solicitations. Everywhere I turn, high or low, north or south, desert or oasis, I am disquieted by these unsettling visitations, pursued, questioned, accused, exhilarated, caught up short, overcome by the coming over me of something, I know not what.

What does this spirit, this specter of all specters, expect of me? I am addressed, summoned, called upon, called out, interloqué, poor me, in the accusative, my cowardly "I" having long fled this scene of accusation.

What was that strange noise that sounded like someone's voice?

"God," they say, and maybe they are right. God, perhaps. The specter of God.

This is a serious case, one for the specialists, the expert hauntologists, ones who have mastered these phenomena and have the latest spectrological equipment, if only I can find a directory of such physicians of the soul. I need the best. It is not simply that there is a hauntological effect here, in the name of God. My situation is much worse than that. I am being disturbed by the very paradigm of the specter, not only the spookiest specter of all, but the very figure of the specter. Whatever this is that has gotten inside my head, inhabited my heart, gotten under my skin, I have to deal with it. I have somehow drifted unawares into dangerous and uncharted waters, or wandered across a border into a lawless land, somehow found myself in a perilous place, at the very heart of hauntology. This place is filled with spooks, everywhere I turn.

This uncanny spirit, let us say "God," perhaps, if only to make an infinitely long story short, does not exist. If God existed, if a name and address could be supplied for the impossible, then the impossible would be possible. Were it ("it") either an existent or a non-existent, then everything would be easier. Then at least there would be a diagnosis and we could look for a cure. But at the moment I do not even know what kind of doctor I should see. If the question of God were a question of existence, I might be able to settle it, to prove it one way or another, to disprove it one way or another, and then I would be able to move on. But the trouble with God, and God is trouble, believe me, infinite trouble, giving me no peace at all, is that God is neither present nor absent, neither simply given nor entirely hidden. God is neither a saturated phenomenon, as Marion tries to assure us, nor a total illusion, as the cool handed rationalists, no less assured, tell us, but a strange and fluctuating phenomenon, a soliciting, incessant, insistent apparition, a specter. God is not an entity out there who answers to the name "God," but a call calling to us in a certain uncertain voice, in and under the name (of) "God," delivering an obscure message, leaving us restless for something, I know not what, eliciting a desire not just for this or that, but a desire beyond all desire, for a knowing without knowledge, reducing us to prayer, to praying like mad to an unknown God, where we pray God to rid us of God.

But the trouble with God, and God is trouble, believe me, infinite trouble, giving me no peace at all, is that God is neither present nor absent, neither simply given nor entirely hidden.

I am haunted by this voice. "God does not exist; God insists." That is what I hear day and night, running through my mind like an annoying jingle I cannot turn off. I wake up with a start in the middle of the night, bolt upright in my bed, pupils dilated, looking all around. I could swear there was a voice in the room. I distinctly heard it say: "You know it but you will not say it. God does not exist. God insists." But I look under my bed, open all the closets, look out the window into the night and there is no one to be found. Is this an inspiration, a visitation by a friendly angel in my dreams—or am I just being spooked? Were I a Rationalist philosopher and of a more sound mind instead of a spirit-seer, I would make this assertion my axiom, my first

God does not exist, I insist on this, but that does not mean-and everything depends upon this-there is nothing to God. Far from it.

principle, my ground. But that would be a rash and hypocritical undertaking for one as haunted and disturbed as am I, for one awash in tossing seas, in a tiny craft adrift over fifty thousand fathoms, who can offer in evidence only the groundless grounds of something I know not what. God does not exist, I insist on this, but that does not mean—and everything depends upon this—there is nothing to God. Far from it. If there were an easy choice between being or nothing, my life would be simple. I could make a choice with the full assurance that there is at least a fifty percent choice that I am right. I could condense the ambiguity of my life into a proposition, that proposition would in turn represent reality, and it would come accompanied by warranty. There would be a kit which would contain a proof for my proposition, along with an installation disk which includes an error check to make sure the program was properly installed and there were no miscalculations. What could be simpler than that? Then I could take the weekend off and have some peace.

Hegel began his lectures on the philosophy of religion by saying that religion is the Sabbath of life, the domain of eternal truth where all the riddles of the heart are resolved and all our sorrows comforted, a day of rest from the trials and tribulations of life, when the harshness of fate vanishes and everything dissolves into light and love. I love Hegel as much as the next fellow, but I have to ask, what was the great man thinking? What was he on? What was he sniffing? If I were Žižek, I would rub my beard, tug on my t-shirt, and exclaim in my best Slovenian accent, "my God, the truth is exactly the opposite!" Religion is the source of the greatest unrest and lack of peace. Religion, not the unbelievable one which is out to makes its enemies its footstools—in the name of the God of love, of course—but the thoroughly haunted and disturbed religion, the religion sous rature, religion crossed out and erased, but not so thoroughly that we cannot still read the writing underneath, still discern the word "religion" beneath the cross. Let us say, to make an another infinitely long story short, a religion without religion, which is also too simple, since we cannot simply do "without" anything. Whenever we try to do without something we will always be haunted by whatever we think we have left behind, whatever we mistakenly think we have left for dead, without appreciating that the dead are never just plain dead. Nothing is ever simply dead. It always comes back to haunt us, above all the living God, who is the undead par excellence, that than which there is nothing spookier. The more we say, God is dead, the more anxious we prove ourselves to be, looking over our shoulder to see who that shadowy figure is who seems to be following us, the more deluded we prove ourselves to be, the more we prove that something is eating at us—in short, the more we show our insensitivity to the spectral effect. Above all with God! The last thing we could ever say is dead, the last thing we can kill off and leave behind for dead, without a flicker or trace of life, is God! God is that than which nothing is more undead. What greater specter than the specter of God?

If I were Zizek, I would rub my beard, tug on my t-shirt, andexclaiminmybestSlovenianaccent, "my God, the truth is exactly the opposite!"

To get back to Hegel's point, maybe if I were a great German metaphysician back at the University of Berlin, maybe if I had seen the World Historical Spirit on horseback, maybe my religion would be the Sabbath of life. But as for poor me, a poor existing individual, as Kierkegaard like to say, my religion with/out religion—both with and without, neither with nor without, religion, if there is such a thing—gives me no rest. My religion is restlessness and disquiet; it leaves me in a state of permanent unease, never satisfied with anything other than dissatisfaction. All my religion does, this spectral haunto-theological counterpart to religion, is disturb the peace and violate the Sabbath laws with penumbral violations. In fact, the Sabbath, if there were one, in my religion with/out religion would not be one day set aside for rest but the restless industry of everyday life, perpetual unrest around the clock, 24/7. What was Hegel thinking?

—4—

This all sounds a little crazy to me. Maybe the problem I am having is that I really don't understand what you mean when you say "it spooks."

It's a metaphysical joke.

I fail to see the humor.

It's a riff, a poke in the ribs of Parmenides and Heidegger.

That requires a very strange sense of humor.

You have to be into stuff like this.

You have to be mad.

Perhaps, in a very precise sense. Almost.

It Spooks

The one thing that the long robes most dread hearing is someone say that they are spiritual but not religious. My idea is to give them still more bad news: God, too, is spiritual but not very religious. Actually the news is worse than that. When I say "spiritual," I mean spectral, spooky. It gets still worse. I am not saying that God spooks but that it spooks God. I am not saying that God spooks us, that God is the name of an infinite being who does the spooking and, being infinite, is really good at it. Instead, by saying that God does not exist, I am saying that God is not an agent who does things, like spook, and that God's infinity is of a rather in(de)finite sort. Grammatically, the name (of) "God" is a noun, but grammatologically, in my vocabulary, it is not the name of anything nominative or substantive; it is neither a substance nor a subject nor their synthesis.

When I venture to say that God does not exist, I am saying that God is not something present, a pure, perfect and complete presence, presiding over all, an omni-being who out-knows, out-wits, and generally overwhelms His (sic) creatures. I hasten to add, at this point, that I am not saying God is a "he" or a "He." I have spell checked this document, and every time I use the masculine gender for God, I do so on purpose. I am then referring to the testosterone-rich omni-macho creator ex nihilo spun out from a highly patrological patro-hierarchical theology so brilliantly put on the run by Catherine Keller. The more insistent, hauntological figure of God, on the other hand, the one who is haunting me, appears as best I can make out to be of multiple and fluctuating genders, certainly more than two, at least fifty, sometimes even shading off into neuter anonymous impersonal it-like tones. The "it" of "it spooks" is like the "it" of "it's raining," it's very hard to say what it is. If He started out as a He, He has been in virtue of his transcendence transgendered several times over into innumerable varieties. So what I am saying is very polymorphic and highly apophatic.

> I am saying that God is not an agent who does things, like spook, and that God's infinity is of a rather in(de)finite sort.

So here's the joke. The problem old Parmenides and Heidegger both faced was how to affirm the reality of Being without turning Being into a being, a particular, nominative, substantive, subsistent thing. So they both came up with more or less the same solution: of individual beings we can say that they "are" (or exist), but of "Being itself" we can only say "there is." A particular being is, but there is Being. In German, that would come out "es gibt das Sein," literally, "it gives Being," which like the French il y a is the idiom for doing what we are doing in English when we say "there is." So, the joke is in the German; instead of saying es gibt, we who are spooked by Being say "es spukt;" not "it gives" but "it spooks," not "there is Being" but "there is something spooky going on." If you spend enough time hanging out in the Humanities Center you will find this funny, but at the same time you will realize that it is really very serious. I would like to take credit for finding it, but we owe to Derrida who found it in Stirner, who said "es spukt in der ganzen Welt," the whole world is spooked (SoM, 136). This we can use as a general formula for the penumbrality of Being, for the way Being is spooked, with a completely straight face. Almost.

So of God I say the following. God does not exist but there is something going on in and under the name of God, something very spooky. God does not exist, but that does not mean there is nothing to God. There is a God-effect, or there are innumerable God-effects, but they are spectral. There is a spectral effect with God. There are spectral effects happening under the name (of) "God." Specters are not particular beings; they do not subsist and they are not agents. Nor are they Being, but there are spooky goings-on (events). Beings have gotten something going on with them called events. In this spookier way of thinking by which I am beset, the name of God is not the name of the First Being of ontotheology, to which Tillich said the proper theological response is atheism, which for Tillich did not spell the end of theology but the beginning. But neither is God the ground of being of Tillich, nor the hyper-being of mystical theology, to which I reply that the proper theological response is also atheism. I say this, once again with a proviso, that this is not supposed to be the end of theology or of mystical theology, but the beginning of theologizing otherwise. Let us say it is a hauntological theology or a spectro-theology or penumbra-theology, which is, to put it in the most affirmative way possible, at the very least something spectro-apophatic. That just means metaphysics must check its guns at the door when the hauntological marshal is in town.

In saying God does not exist, I am saying there is something going on in the name (of) "God" but it belongs to another order, producing effects on another register, neither theistic nor atheistic, neither ontological, me-ontological nor de-ontological—but hauntological. They are not going on outside space and time but in a special spectral temporality. Treating God like an existent entity is like imagining a virtual drink is going quench your thirst. God is not an entity, not a matter of spirit or of matter, not a matter of being or non-being, not a matter of entities, propositions, and proofs, not a matter of creeds, councils and candles (am I omitting anything?). God is not a Pure Spirit ensconced in an immaterial realm, nor is God Pure Matter, but a specter. God does not exist; God insists. God is neither presence nor absence but insistence. God does not subsist; God insists. God insists with the insistence of a call, like a very holy ghost calling for justice, mercy, compassion, forgiveness, hospitality, love, the year of the Jubilee in a time we cannot

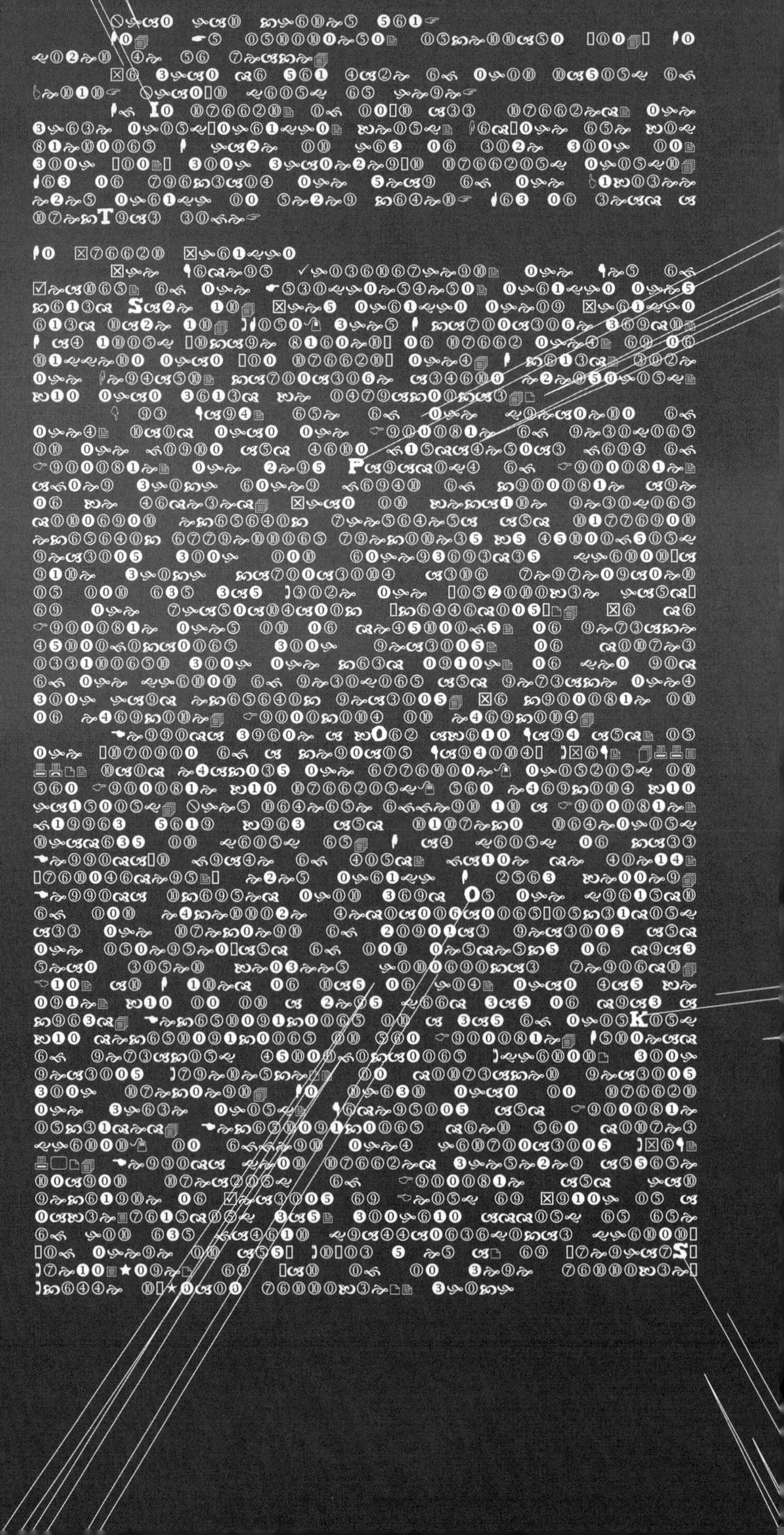

calculate but for which we pray and weep. But (there is always a but, which is another nutshell) that in turn means that, spook that God is (spooked as God is), we always risking the worst violence in the name of God's love or justice. Praying God to lead us not into temptation is a bit hypocritical; the name (of) "God" is temptation, and to pray is to expose ourselves to temptation, which is why we should take care what we pray for and why the first last and constant prayer is to pray God to rid God of God, as we learn from the mystics. I have a taste for the mystics, for their joys and plaints and pliant strategies for wrestling with the nameless. I love everything about the mystics except for the one thing I do not love, their Neoplatonism. That is my lover's quarrel with them.

God insists with the insistence of a call, like a very holy ghost calling for justice, mercy, compassion, forgiveness, hospitality, love, the year of the Jubilee in a time we cannot calculate but for which we pray and weep.

Now it is well known that "insistence" is a pathological matter. I admit that. But by admitting that I do not admit that I advocate an obsessive drive that makes us sick and dysfunctional. On the contrary, I am trying to rev up the intensity of life by setting out the prolegomena to a penumbral life, an active salutary spectral life which communicates with the living dead. I am admitting that we are all mortally wounded souls, suffering from an incurable condition called "life." But I regard this as a kind of salutary pathos that is the condition of a passionate life, of the intensity of life, of a kind of élan vitale that pulsates through our bodies and gives us joy even if it keeps us awake half the night. So in speaking of leading a spectral or penumbral life I do not mean a dispassionate spiritual one, but one full of passion. If insistence drives us mad, it is with a madness for what is coming, which is highly exhilarating. In spectro-theology we are calling for the year of the Jubilee, for the coming of the Kingdom, which means being mad for justice, mad with loving our enemies, forgiving the unforgiveable, being holy fools for the Kingdom. At the same time, I admit that a force this spectral, this uncertain, this insistent and solicitous, may lead to the worst violence, the worst persecution and the madness of murder. When it comes to specters we are required to be discerning. So if I am declared mad by the Inquisition or by the Enlightenment my defense will be that there is more than one madness, that madness does not mean just one thing. There is no such thing as Madness, in the singular. After all, madness is a spectral thing, if ever there were one, just as spooked as anything else and maybe more. So the association of madness and insistence has a perfectly sane explanation. What more rational explanation of a certain madness, a certain folly, than the insistence of God?

—5—

I am surprised that you dared to mention God's infinity. That if anything should put a stop to this craziness. God's infinity means God is complete, whole and perfect. Why would you even bring that up?

In my spare time, on my days off, I have been working up a new list of divine names. Right now I am working on "infinity," which I think may take a long time to finish.

By infinity I have in mind not an ontological but a hauntological

The to-come is itchy because it is never satisfied with anything. It is always calling, insistently, unconditionally, say, for justice, saying, praying "come" to what is to-come, hoping to making the truth come true, in the world, in the flesh, to give existence to its insistence, to make up what is lacking in the body without flesh of insistence.

name; not a mathematical way of counting but a penumbralogical one; not an infinite being in the nominative, which ontologizes God, but the spectral open-endedness of the "to-come" in the infinitival. As I have been saying, in a penumbral theology, Being is spooked by time. Being wants to be tight and well-joined but time pries it out of joint. Time is the magic potion in penumbralogy, just a touch of which changes the whole solution. With just a single droplet of time, Being and full presence start to boil over (ebullitio was Meister Eckhart's word in his Latin works) with the open-endedness of the to-come. The reason this is maddening—if madness has a reason, if there is a reason in this madness—is that it is like a Messiah who never shows up. Or if someone whose lucky number is 50 comes along and announces good news for the poor, shelter for the homeless, and the year of the Jubilee, the year the one percent are going to have to pay their fair share, someone else announces the Jubilee has been postponed. Maybe next year. The time is out of joint. It is coming, to-come. The year of the Jubilee never arrives, structurally. It is an arrivant, but it never arrives. If someone proclaims the year of the Jubilee, and it does not show up, that does not mean it was a bad prediction, or that we have to crunch the numbers again and see where the calculation went wrong. It means it is not about mathematics and prophets are not meteorologists. That would be the ham-fisted way the Men of Reason hear this saying, with no ear or eye for specters, since they are terrified of being labeled spirit-seers. What Men of Reason miss is that the year of the Jubilee belongs to hauntological time, not to chronological time. It belongs neither to eternity nor to calendar time; not to the realm of eternal infinite being but to a spectral and infinitival time to-come. In hauntological time the calculus is incalculable, which is very strange. You keep counting but you never get to 50. It is always almost 50, but not yet, and we cannot get that far, even if that is what we desire, affirm, pray for and weep over, all day, every day, year after year. 50 is not a matter of mathematics; it is a matter of hope.

When I say that the maddening thing is that the "to-come" is "structural," that means it is by design, not a design flaw. Structural means that is the way it was built, its factory condition; it's not temporary problem with that will go away later on, with more time. The "to-come" refers to an unconditional promise that is never kept, to the in-finity of the un-finished, of the un-defined and un-definable, to the unconditional open-endedness of the future, which is the very word for the future in French and German, where they speak "the to-come" (l'avenir, die Zukunft). The force of the infinitival infinite is that of a broken, hyphenated force, unstably pieced together by a hyphen, deprived of full presence, disjointed, out of joint. The to-come, which makes time out of joint, has come to drive you mad and it has a maddening make-up. It is a "weak force," with all the force of a call but without an army to enforce what it calls for. The to-come is like the old line in politics: you campaign in poetry but you govern in prose. We live in the distance between poetry and prose, between the to-come and the situation in which we find ourselves, the space of time called the moment. The to-come is itchy because it is never satisfied with anything. It is always calling, insistently, unconditionally, say, for justice, saying, praying "come" to what is to-come, hoping to making the truth come true, in the world, in the flesh, to give existence to its insistence, to make up what is lacking in the body without flesh of insistence. No, no, this is not the Messiah, or justice, or the year of the Jubilee. No, no, not yet. Maybe next year. Furthermore, it warns us, the whole thing may be a disaster; what looks like a holy ghost must turn out to be wholly ghastly. It may be the worst year of your life. The to-come refers to the coming of what we cannot see coming, which can be nasty business.

(Another hint, a useful methodological tip, a little rule of thumb, one that will help you see the method in my madness: Ontologies consolidate; hauntologies hyphenate. Ontologies confidently speak of democracy or justice, God or the kingdom of Jubilee; hauntologies cautiously speak of a hyphenated democracy-to-come, justice-to-come, kingdom-to-come, a coming God, the Jubilee to come, and so forth. "And so forth," of course, means there are more-to-come, infinitely more. The hyphen is the diacritical mark of spacing and timing, of différance, a little reminder that we are woven from the warp of space and the woof of time, that we are warped and woofed by différance. Even God cannot pretend indifference to différance. The whole world is spooked.)

I said I have a taste for the mystics, whom I love quite madly, above all Meister Eckhart, who said something very pertinent to this little discourse on the "it spooks:" God needs us, he said, and the hornets of the Inquisition swarmed all over him. There may be something saving about God but we in turn have to save God, in just the way Paul said we have to fill up the things that are lacking in the body of Christ. God, being merely infinitival, needs concrete finite bodies, troops on the ground, to conjugate this infinitive. The unconditional to-come is asking us to come to its aid, to fill up what is lacking in its spectral body, soliciting us to gives its spectrality reality. Specters expect us to give their insistence existence, to give their weakness strength. God needs us and we are the ones God is waiting for. Specters expect everything, the impossible. We are the ones this specter expects and, being infinitival, what it expects knows no limit. The name of this spectral call we call God is the name of a call to which the only testimony is the response, the only evidence is the answer, the only proof is the action. What I call religion, if there is such a thing, is like answering a call we never heard. Everyone in earshot asks, who are these people talking to? They must be mad.

No, no, this is not the Messiah, or justice, or the year of the Jubilee. No, no, not yet. Maybe next year.

In my spare time I am also working on a new translation of Augustine's Confessions. I have decided to translate his cor inquietum as "haunted heart," a heart made restless by the specter of what is to-come. When Augustine hears God calling him through the voices of the children playing the tolle, lege game, in my edition I take the liberty of having him open the New Testament to the word "come" (Rev 22:20), which is the penumbral, penultimate verse in the New Testament. It's only fair that I should be given such liberties with the text. I am kept up half the night, my room full of spooks, and I should be able to make a profit on my discomfort. The insistence of God reduces me to tears, to saying, praying "come" in response to an obscure and coming spirit, calling "come" in response to a fetching if elusive call, which is getting itself called in and under the name (of) "God." This specter pays me clandestine visits, sometimes dressed in rags, asking me for a cup of cold water, sometimes coming with an unexpected rapping on my door in the middle of the night, which could be trouble. There's nothing riskier than having commerce with the unknown, the unexpected, the unforeseen, with calling for the coming of what we cannot see coming.

So to make these shady matters as clear as day, let me say this. God does not exist; God spooks. But God is not an infinite being who uses his infinite power to spook us. Es spukt, "it spooks," as in "it rains," of uncertain gender, number and agency. The infinitive "to spook" conjugates into the finite form, third person impersonal, "it spooks," where "it" stands for anything, the whole world, anything and everything is spooked. There is spooking going on everywhere, especially in and under the name (of) "God." Something

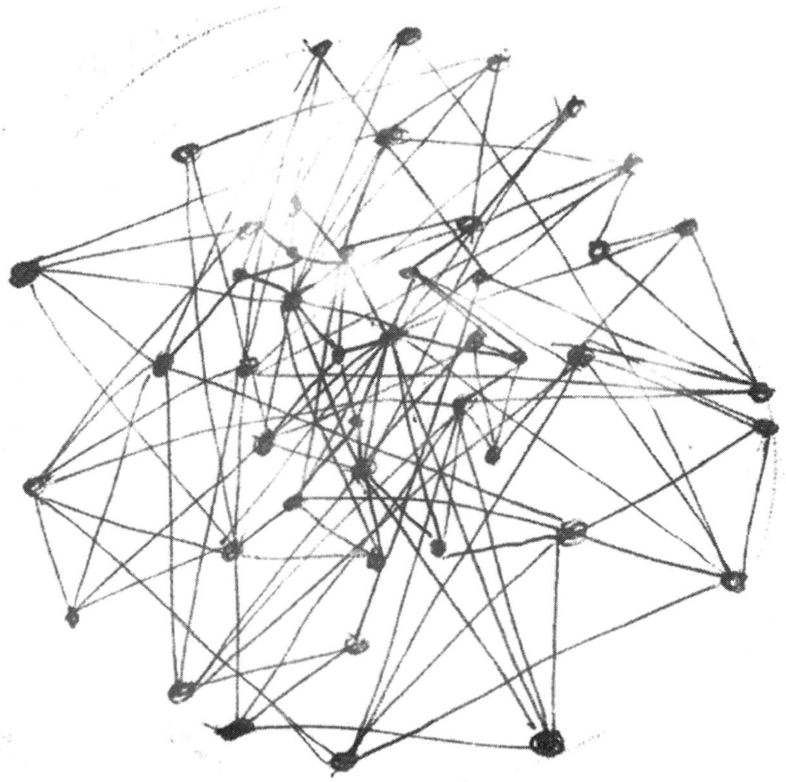

There's nothing riskier than having commerce with the unknown, the unexpected, the unforeseen, with calling for the coming of what we cannot see coming.

is getting itself called, something is being called for, asking to be recalled, something insists, in the middle voice. I can neither say God does it nor that this is "nothing other than" my own projection (Feuerbach), that these spooks are all in my head, either of which would finally finitize and decide my infinitival unrest and exorcise this uncertain specter. At the very moment I can say, this is what is spooking me, the spook disappears and is gone forever. At the very moment I say, this is the living God, or this is my resentment, or my unconscious, or my social environment, or my Mommy, the spook would be completely exorcised and I would be in the clear, in the black-and-white clarity of being and non-being, no longer in the accusative, I would be innocent as the driven snow. The very structure of a specter, and therefore of a call, is that we cannot identify the provenance of the call or make out exactly who or what is calling or being called for, so that the responsibility falls upon me, in the accusative, which is the decision of the other in me. Otherwise, without this spectrality, I can always say I was just following orders. God, the Law, the Party, the Cause, the Church, my mommy, the nuns, made me do it. Don't blame me. I have an alibi. I just work here. I don't make the rules.

—6—

It sounds to me you are just pulling this out of your hat.

On the contrary, it is pulling at me.

It's all in your head.

It's heading right at my head.

I think you are just making it up.

On the contrary, I have the highest authority for it.

You mean, it is in the Scriptures?

Almost.

On the Divine Names

God, I like to say, is not a projection but a projectile headed straight for my head. It is nothing I have imagined. I can even point to text and verse.

God, although in the form of God, did not think existence something to be exploited, but emptied himself of existence, and took the form of insistence, humbling himself and being content with weakness, with the weak force of a call which calls upon us in the form of a slave (Phil 2:6-8). The call rises up from the bodies of ta me onta, the nuisances and nobodies of the world (I Cor. 1:1-2), the wretched of the earth, the homeless, the displaced and deported, the least among us, the slum dogs who never become millionaires.

Think of this as the audacity of God—another divine name for my list. The audacity of God is to dare to not exist, to dare to disappear into the world and to reappear only in spectral form. The audacity of God is to leave the existence to us, which is risky business. God only knows, God may come to regret it (Gen 6:6). That is the most audacious moment in the Christian tradition, which corresponds to the audacity of the God of the Tsim-Tsum, the divine retraction in the Kabbalah. There God entirely disappears in order to make room for the appearance of the world; the divine being shrinks down to an infinitesimally small point in order to let the universe expand out infinitely in every direction. If I were a contemporary physicist, I might be tempted to make something of that, especially one who thinks the process is endless.

The audacity of God is to empty out the robust and intimidating being of the First Being, of the ens realissimum, of the Hyperbeing, into the quasi-being, the penumbral being, the fluctuating, uncertain, undecidable para-being of a specter, which leaves everything to us, which calls upon us to respond, which puts God in the position that God needs us. God's audacity is to throw the responsibility for God, for God becoming God, on us, which is the height of audacity.

If I am reincarnated as that medieval theologian in my dreams, the other thing I would do is a treatise on the divine names, a new de divinis nominibus, which I would sign Reb Derrisa, a pseudonym I would concoct to throw the hounds of the Inquisition off my scent, hoping they mistake it for the work of some obscure Kabbalahist, by then long dead. In my treatise, I would treat the divine names not as attributes of full blown presence but as their weaker spectral counterparts. In my version, existence would be weakened into insistence; Spirit into specter; the eternal into the momentary; omnipotence into the weak force of a call; necessity into the perhaps; infinity into the infinitival; divine providence into the risk of an unforeseeable future; perfection into the promise of the world; the all-good into the hope that it works; God's glory into the audacity to not exist; divine transcendence into a way to name the varying intensities which charge the plane of immanence with the anarchic energy of the to-come. Then I would pray for a speedy re-reincarnation somewhere else before the Inquisition decodes the whole thing and tracks me down, as none of this is far from their flames.

—7—

But if the whole thing's spooked, Thought, Being, God, then what are we to do? Are we not just left paralyzed?

In a hauntology, that's when we're really on the move.

But it seems impossible to do anything.

By the impossible everything begins.

If God does not exist, what good is God?

Everything depends on God's inexistence.

What Do Specters Expect?

The question is, as J.F.K. would have said, ask not what you can you expect from a specter but what specters expect of you. Ask not what good can specters do, but what kind of life specters expect us to lead. That is why my bumper sticker would read not "Jesus saves" but "Save Jesus," which is up to us.

Let's start with the words of ghosts, which are very special. These uncanny visitors have not just dropped by for an idle chat. They have no time for that; they mean business. Their words are meant as pressing injunctions, exhortations. Specters have great expectations, raised expectations; they expect things to happen. Specters expect change, transformation. They have interrupted their rest and put themselves to considerable trouble—after all it cannot be easy to come back from the dead—because of unfinished business, business they themselves cannot conduct, having been since deprived by death of the necessary credentials, stripped of their worldly papers. These ghostly bodies without flesh lack the material embodiment to affect the bodies of flesh and blood in need of help, and it is with these bodies in need that their business is to be conducted. So the words of ghosts are meant to be transformative, not merely informative; they are not merely passing on a bit of information to correct the historical record of what happened some time ago. Specters expect to transform lives; they do not expect spectators but deeds. They want to touch afflicted bodies, to disturb lives in easy drift, to provoke action in an indifferent world in which they, pure spirits that they are, are ineffective.

Specters insist, but it is we who exist. Specters call, but it is we who must respond. Specters come to us because we are the only ones who can help. They need us; they have been waiting for us.

When Kierkegaard had Johannes Climacus say that the name of God is the name of a deed, he got the whole idea.

The name (of) "God" is the name of call to which we are supposed to be the response. Without the response the name is a dead letter. The real death of God is to ignore the call, to let the specter expire, to let it draw its (really) last breath. For all the world, the only thing anyone can see, and the only thing that exists, is the response. The only witness to the call is the response; the rest is spectral, invisible, ghostly. To the rest of the world those who are moved by God look like dancers where no one else can hear the music.

Specters expect the truth; they expect us to make the truth come true. Truth here does not mean what it means back in the departments of (modern) philosophy, propositions inside our head picking out objects in the world outside our heads. Instead, truth means facere veritatem, making the truth, doing the truth, making our lives into a work of truth.

When Meister Eckhart says God needs us, he got the whole idea. Without us, the name of God is a reed blowing in the wind, a tinkling cymbal, just talk.

When Paul said we are to fill

up what is lacking in the body of Christ, he got the whole idea.

The earthly body of Jesus had taken its leave of the world and now it was up to us to heal the sick he left behind and proclaim the year of the Jubilee.

When the author of the Fourth Gospel said the Word must become flesh, he got the whole idea. The disembodied spectrality of the call must be incarnated in the world of flesh and blood. The call must become a response. The word must take the form of transformed flesh.

When Marx said that up to now philosophers have been content to interpret the world, now the time has come to change it, he got the whole idea.

The idealism of insistence must be transformed into the materialism of existence. But Marx should have been kinder to "interpretation." Interpretation goes all the way down, into action, which is why I like to speak of "radical" hermeneutics. Marx should have understood that there is no such thing as a purely inactive inoperative interpretation. If it is not engaged in the world, it is not an interpretation but an idle thought, a free floating fancy. To understand anything at all is to interpret, and to interpret is to have settled into the minute interstices of the concrete world, to have engaged its forces, so as to see what this idea is doing, what it is demanding, what is happening in it, how it is to be played, what disturbance it creates. That, as they say back in the Humanities Center, is what an interpretation "means." There is no such thing as an uninterpreted fact of the matter, no such thing as interpretation that floats above the world in pure weightless inactivity. We do not have an interpretation except in the response to what is addressing us in the concrete situation and calls for action. The call is heard only in the response. Without the response, the call remains just a ghost.

To the rest of the world those who are moved by God look like dancers where no one else can hear the music.

When Eckhart has Jesus' "Martha, Martha" mean that Martha had two gifts, both the vita contemplativa and the vita activa, he got the whole idea.

Without the response, the call is like Eckhart's "Mary," languishing at the feet of Jesus, too anemic to act. Martha's hospitality, her preparation for the coming of Jesus, for his most basic and "unmentionable" bodily needs, does not distract her from her unity with Jesus; it constitutes it, providing existence for the insistence of the event that takes place in and under the body of Jesus.

That is what specters expect.

But is this expectation not unrealistic? Is it not impossible? Has it not been utterly undermined with this talk about God's spectral inexistence? If God is not a transcendent, omniscient, omnipotent superbeing in the sky, who can hold back tsunamis before they reach the shore, cure cancer, and come to the aid of the home team in a crucial game; if God cannot help us in our hour of need, answer our prayers, and be there in the first place to answer our prayers—if God is not all that, what good is God? What good is God's inexistence when existence is what we really need? If God cannot separate sheep from the goats, reward his friends and punish his enemies, what good is God? If God merely insists and does not exist, what good can God be? If as we have said God is not an agent/entity and does not "do" anything, what good can He (sic) do?

My main response to these questions is another question: if that's the "good news," what's the bad news? My perversity is to think that there is no greater obstacle to the event that stirs within the name of God than to reify that event into an existing being with such super-powers. The name of God is not the name of a super-hero, an existing, super-existing Superbeing, swollen an excess of existence and phallic power, who ultimately—He bides his time and plays His cards smartly—squares all accounts and orders all the disorders that break out down here in our disjointed time. That deserves our unreserved atheistic unbelief, unconditional incredulity. It is the worst paganism. There is nothing that so thoroughly erodes action and distorts life than expecting to be saved and rewarded by a Superbeing, nothing more at odds with the kingdom of God than this cynical economy of rewards and punishment which demeans life into a means to an end, that turns life into a coupon redeemable for an eternal redemption, for an eternal reward, and the love of God into credit in a celestial bank. As Meister Eckhart said, some men love God the way they love their cow, for its milk. The year of the Jubilee is not the reward in the hereafter for sticking it out here below. The year of the Jubilee is the infinitival to-come to be realized in time, always coming, always calling, almost here, never quite. It is not eternal rest but the restlessness of a call for what is coming that intensifies temporal life to the limit.

The spectrality of God is to disappear into the promise of the world and to leave existence to us, not to promise heavenly interventions that will sweep down from the sky and put terrestrial life down below in order; not to stand over the world as a divine accountant keeping track of the credits and debits heaped up by a hapless humankind down below. God is not an infinite immaterial solution to finite material problems. God is the problem of which we are expected to be the solution. God is not the "answer" but the question to which we are to be the response. (I am never going to find bumper stickers like this. I am going to need to find a company that does custom work!) God is not a necessary being but a suggestive possibility, an almost impossible one, of which we are to be the actualization. God is a spirit, a specter, a call, a plea, an exhortation made to us to transform insistence into existence. Nothing perverts God more profoundly than to reify God into an infinite immaterial entity residing in an immaterial realm, who being eternal has a long memory, who does not forget those who have served and those who have offended the divine order; who, having infinite might at His command can right any wrong that He has a mind to correct, just so long as He feels like it. A being of such Big Might is a Big Mystery, remember, so sometimes He does not come through! Chalk off the infant mortality rate in undeveloped countries to The Mystery of Divine Providence. He knows what He's doing, even if we don't, or so they say. Tell that to their parents.

What more perfect mystification of an event, what more perfect perversion of the year of the Jubilee than to make it the year that God will make his enemies his footstool, separate the sheep from the goats, rewards his friends with eternal happiness and punish his enemies with insufferable suffering, and perhaps drop by if time permits—after all, He's a busy Man—to shrink an inoperable tumor. What greater perversion than to make the year of the Jubilee the year God inflicts insufferable suffering upon the enemies of God? Such a God would be the envy of Nero—the maximum of pain while being guaranteed the impossibility of death. That would make the sufferings of a Roman crucifixion, lasting but a few mortal hours, small potatoes. Mel Gibson should me a movie about that! As T.J.J. Altizer's Blake asks, what difference is there between this Transcendent Power and Satan?

What more perfect perversion, what more perfect storm, than to enlist the Year of the Jubilee into a Neoplatonic economy that cashes in works of mercy for eternal rewards? That is rather a lot of corruption for people in the business of earning incorruptible bodies! While they were otherwise taken in by Neoplatonism, the mystics saw right through this ruse. That is why they called for a life "without why," without the Eternal Reward in the Sky, and why Marguerite Porete called for bidding adieu to virtue, to cease making the virtues "fat" so that your celestial pension payments will be fatter still. The spectral inexistence of God undermines a life spent trying to heap up eternal rewards, which is the only condition under which the year of the Jubilee is possible.

—8—

You will have a hard time selling this in the churches.

How many ways can I say this? This is not about selling anything.

It Spooks but does It Preach?

I was once was asked whether I thought this whole thing I was doing with the weakness of God, the inexistent insistence of God, could "preach." It spooks but does it preach? Can the "it" which "spooks" be preached? I was struck by the expression. To say that something will "preach" means it can

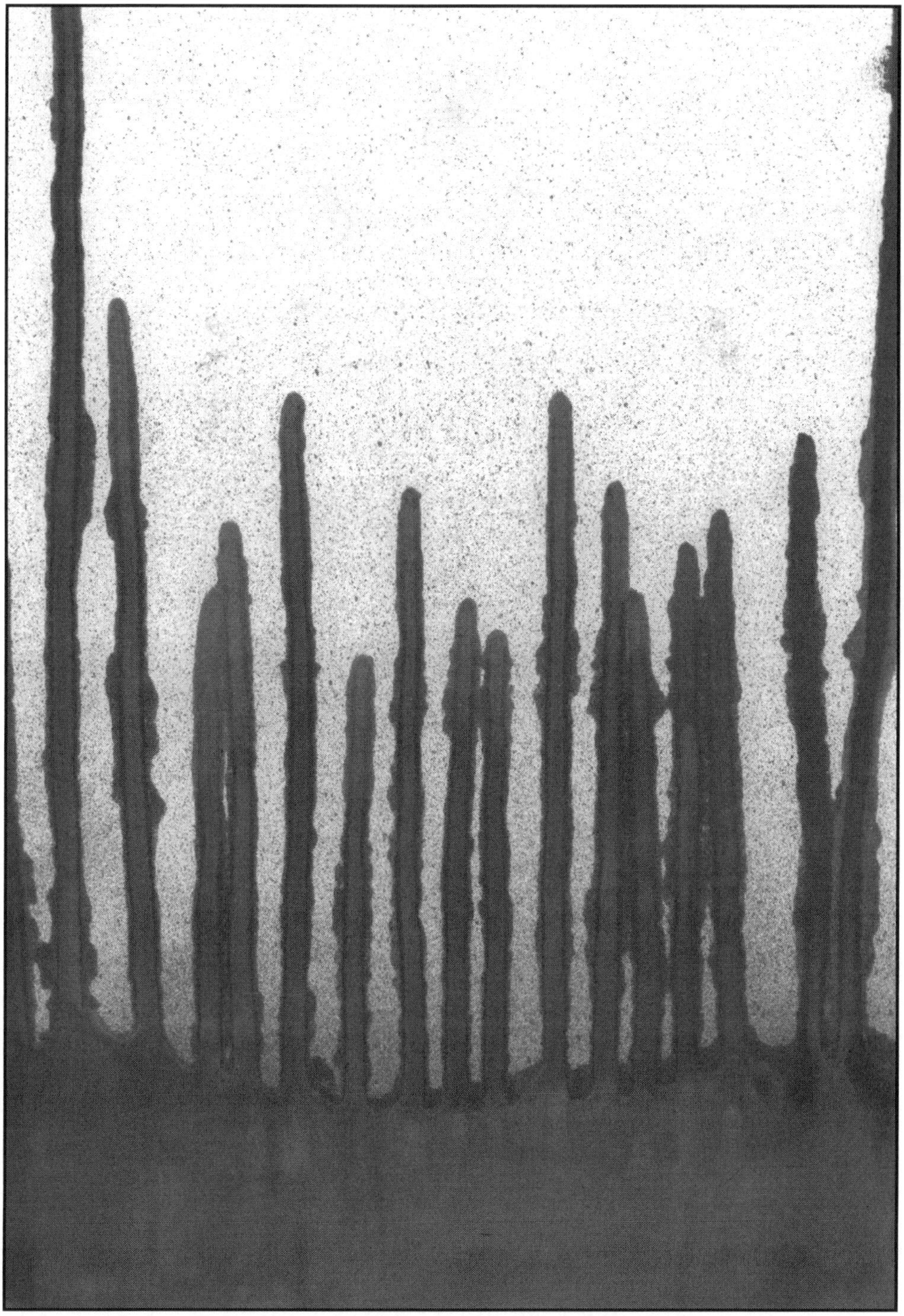

There is nothing that so thoroughly erodes action
and distorts life than expecting to be saved.

touch lives, issue in action. It is a magnificent locution for penumbralogists who love the middle voice. It allows the "it"—something being preached, something getting itself preached, where the agency remains anonymous—to assume the active voice.

My answer is that the spectrality of God is the only thing that can preach. Otherwise preaching is a sales pitch and it is trying to pitch celestial snake oil. It is trying to sell the faithful that they can get something eternal for almost nothing (time), when it should be saying that you get nothing for doing everything, that it's not about getting something. Preaching must dare to make its way out into the deep, where the land is no longer in sight, risking the perils of being lost at sea, daring to preach the Kingdom of God without rewards. It must dare to preach of expenditures that have no return; of gifts that do not get reciprocated; of hospitality that puts itself at risk without expecting a heavenly mansion in return. It must dare to preach the insistence of God where God is not a being who packs a punch and can punish his enemies and reward his friends. It must dare to preach a God who does not just step in to do the heavy lifting for us, which only mystifies life with supernaturalist fantasies. The insistence of God requires us to assume responsibility for our lives, to respond to what is pressing in upon us and demanding action, to stand up not as an autonomous I but respond in the accusative, and to do so not because there is celestial money in it for us, not because we will be rewarded in the year of the Jubilee. But because the year of the Jubilee (if there is any) which is both always coming, always to come, is also today, and it presses in upon us here and now, urgently, in the "moment." The to-come is not a distant time in the future; it is the urgency of the moment.

God is not the "answer" but the question to which we are to be the response. (I am never going to find bumper stickers like this. I am going to need to find a company that does custom work!)

My own perversity is to say that the meaning of the name (of) "God" is what gets done for the least among us, even if (especially if) the name (of) "God" never comes up. Attending to the bodies in need that populate the Scriptures is the "body of God," to employ Sallie McFague's excellent expression, with or without the name (of) "God." Lord, when did we see you hungry, thirsty, or imprisoned and come to your aid? That beautiful story (Matt 25) perfectly embodies the spectral life, the spectrality of action, personal and public, ethical and political, because everything in the story depends upon the invisibility of God, the inexistence of God, the spectrality of God. In this story, the only thing that exists are these bodies in need and tending to these bodies. But as soon as the veil is lifted, as soon as the anonymity is removed, as soon as the Lord steps forth and is plainly visible, as soon as we get to the punch line of the story, the whole thing is annulled. It turns out that this moving story is framed with the terrifying threat of the coming of the Son of Man on the last day to separate the sheep from the goats, rewarding the former and visiting unspeakable suffering upon those who get out of line. Talk about a "punch" line—it beats the kingdom of God senseless!

Preaching should be a call to make the name of God come true; it should be preached without promising celestial cash rewards, eternal credits for temporal works, without threatening punishment, and without promising timely supernatural interventions to step in just in time when it has all become too much for us; it's about Calvary, not the cavalry.

Comforting the sick and dying should be just that, holding the hand of the afflicted and sitting up with them through the night, without the tasteless assurances of heavenly banquets for people on feeding tubes or whose terminal condition means they are past eating. Comforting the sick and dying already is the year of the Jubilee, the life of God in the world, the Kingdom of God, with or without God. It already is the word of God made flesh, its

The sheer purity of that inexistent solicitation shook a very strong woman to the bones and, while it rattled her "beliefs," it did not lay a glove on her deeper "faith" in the event, under whatever name it addressed her.

realization, enfleshment, incarnation, carnal realization. The existence of God is the companionship offered to the dying through the night, God being there wherever two or three gather under the name of God.

The works of mercy are just that, ways of letting the name of God take place in the world, letting the event that stirs within the name of God happen, letting God's insistence acquire mundane existence. God is not eternal; God is momentary, made actual only in the moment, happening only in the moments of mercy and compassion. Otherwise the works of mercy are works of mercenaries with the gleam of eternal rewards in their eye. Serving the wretched of the earth is reduced to a terrific bargain, the best possible way to heap up rewards for the hereafter while still here on earth—and to make a lot of converts in the process. There is no such thing as a free lunch, especially in religion. Works of mercy are a plus-plus, good business, a great deal, a great way to heap up the coin of the realm in the kingdom of rewards and punishments.

Praying in secret is good advice, but please do not pray in secret so as to not to forfeit the eternal rewards due to you later on in heaven, as the tax collector has Jesus say (Matt 6:6). Prayer is not a matter of delayed gratification. We pray in secret because praying, whether in secret or collectively, is a way to keep ourselves open to a quiet call that is easily drowned out in the booming buzzing boisterousness of life. Praying has nothing to do with rewards at all, here or hereafter. Prayers are not IRAs that we are advised not to cash in before retirement, which incurs a penalty. Prayers are really prayers when we do not know if there is anyone there to hear them or to whom we are praying or for what. By the impossible everything begins.

Marguerite Porete called this perverse economizing on God the "Little Church," a petty and pusillanimous way to treat the year of the Jubilee. To this she opposed to the "Big Church," where the Kingdom of God is not a matter of following the celestial money but a more magnanimous way of living and loving "without why." For her trouble, the Little Church, which was swollen big with Big Men in long robes who carried a Big Stick, burned her at the stake. In speaking of a "religion without religion," the religion inside religion that struggles to twist free of the constraints imposed by the religion on the outside, I have a parallel distinction in mind. So if the Inquisitors show up at my door I will blame the whole thing on Marguerite. "The mystics made me do it!" is the last thing you will hear me shouting as they drag me away.

My perversity is to think that Mother Teresa's finest moment is found in the doubts she expresses about whether she "believed" any of the teachings of the Church, whether she even "believed" in "God," which is what she called this spectral solicitation emanating from the faces looking back at her on the streets of Calcutta, a solicitation she had been answering all her life. What she never doubts is her work, because her work is the Kingdom of God; her answer to the call is the only reality enjoyed by that call. In her moments of doubt, of "incredulity toward big stories," I think, the name of God is purified of existence and the sheer insistence of God, the call to make the name of God come true, is disclosed. The sheer purity of that inexistent solicitation shook a very strong woman to the bones and, while it rattled her "beliefs," it did not lay a glove on her deeper "faith" in the event, under whatever name it addressed her.

A Spectral Life

It spooks. It preaches as it spooks by calling for a spectral life.

Everything depends upon the spectrality of God, upon the inspiration of this spectral spirit, upon the promptings of this specter, which expects a transformation of our lives.

Everything depends upon the audacity of God, who not thinking existence something to be prized, and being humbly content with spectrality, empties God of God without remainder into the promise of the world, daring to leave existence to us.

Everything depends upon us, who must have not only the audacity to think, sapere aude, and who must never leave off thinking, which was the specter that inspired the audacity of the Enlightenment, but still more a second audacity, uttering a second yes to what is coming, yes, yes, come, viens, oui, oui. That is the audacity to hope in and for the coming of what we cannot see coming, which is a dicey business requiring a high tolerance for risk.

So if someone comes proclaiming the year of the Jubilee, the year that is always coming but never quite comes, that does not call for calculation, that calls for hope. Hope is the air, the ambiance, the element of a spectral life. To live a spectral life is to lead a life of hope.

Dare to hope.
Sperare aude!

CARRIE BORCHARDT

WONDERER
APPRECIATOR
EXPRESSER

THE FOLLOWING ARE THE MASKS CARRIE BORCHARDT HAS BEEN KNOWN TO WEAR IN THE PUBLIC SPHERE:

Midwestern born, Recent Graduate of a Liberal Arts University in Indiana, Registered Nurse, World Traveler, Spanish Speaker, Closet Writer (until now!), Mission Trip Leader, Feminist, Avid Volunteer, Brazilian JiuJitsu Novice, Current Resident of Austin, TX, after a gap year throughout Europe.

HERE'S WHAT THIS CONTRIBUTOR WOULD SAY ABOUT HERSELF:

My life could be characterized by wanting to try everything, meet everyone, and rest never. I was raised along with my six siblings, just outside of Milwaukee, WI, in a homeschooling religious community before moving to Indiana for college. The greatest thing I've ever done for myself was walk into the counseling department and ask for an appointment. Since that time, vulnerability, authenticity, introspection, and empathy have become driving forces in my journey. Dostoyevsky's Brothers Karamazov is the book I cannot live without. My favorite job I have ever worked was serving at a bar. I have lived short-term in six countries, am an active member of the Couchsurfing community, and initiate spontaneous friendships often. I get asked if I am under the age of 18 at least once a month.

10/15/09

You are beyond description. The way You work in so many different lives so diversely is unbelievable. Why You would lower Yourself to this level is so indescribable that it could never be praised enough-not with all the people created singing for a thousand years, and certainly not in my own lifetime.

10/24/09

I was just thinking about everything I struggled with in middle school and high school. I had so many feelings of depression and anger I thought I would never come out of it, and yet somehow managed and that is all byYour grace. Thank You so much for helping me out of that pit; it was the worst thing I ve known. I admit I still have moments of weakness-moments of anger, moments of dependence on things other than You, moments of impurity. Please help me decrease these distractions. Allow me to receive full healing.

05/13/10

I also feel a bit lost in my relationship with God. I don t know if He wants to open up to me. It makes me sick thinking about it. Sometimes I just want to go up to heaven and have everything be perfect and not deal with reality. Hopefully I will reconnect soon.

05/21/11

I want You to be my sole comfort, my only desire. Please help me to rely on You for my entire life and for every need. I adore my times of dependence on You.

10/26/11

I cannot wait to meet You face to face. I long for your presence. Only You can satisfy. To You alone may my Spirit yield.

01/12/12

I thank You so much for Your consistency despite my emotions. You truly are so faithful. Please bless me with Your presence especially when I feel so lonely. You are the only One that fulfills.

09/13/13

I know Your love but I still forget to act out of that freedom. Are You frustrated yet? Please meet me here, accept my apology. I am sorry for separating myself from You because of something I believed about You. We love each other and have so much history. I need to start trusting You more.

12/3/13

I want open house with You. Break the wall between my spirit and my soul and burst forth.

05/08/14

I don t want a faith that hangs on the condition of me avoiding a single thought. I don t want a hope that forces me to dehumanize and criminalize the other. I don t wish to take part in a community that excludes others and sees the world I live in as a horrifying place. If the cure to my doubts is to give up my mind s wrestling match, to deny the existence of other avenues of thought, ignoring their logic and refusing to see their value, over-simplifying them, or making them an automatic evil, I don t want a cure. I would rather lay prone on my deathbed, overcome with the confusing worlds which collide in my head than sit in simplicity and feigned confidence of the hopeful and deluded.

What value can a faith have if it shies from anything that threatens it? While it claims brilliance and power, man s words contain the potentiality to intimidate its greatest proclaimers with the reading of a wrong book, a glance at the wrong essay. It exuberates confidence, but its readiness to prove and to point shows an insecurity of belief much deeper than the certainty it boasts.

I don t want a god that protects me from myself. I don t desire a king who offers an escape from a reality, just a more acceptable addiction that keeps me from looking in the mirror, keeps me hiding my ghosts from my own eyes. I don t want a sacrifice which allows me to scapegoat all the ugly parts of myself onto something else, covering up my internal poverty with hasty praises and disowning every confusing part of me on a savior. I don t want a parent who allows me to come, but not everyone else with their beautiful stories of brokenness. I don t want a judge with whom I m terrified to reveal my inner thoughts, sure that with one incorrect phrase, my eternal fate will be determined. I don t want a lord who dulls me to this world, who stifles me with my own almost knowingness and blindness.

I don t want a meaning that includes ostracizing my friends. I don t want the falsity of goodness to humanity and the need to role model my beliefs to stand in the way of health and wellness and self-respect. I can t believe in a liberation that only applies to few based on predisposing conditions.

I don t want a group that fancies other beliefs as disrespectful to god, as a group who are willing to deny any evidence and continue on in ignorance just to spite this deity. I don t want a family who withdraws when they discover new parts of me, who endeavor to hush my ponderings with their facile responses.

I refuse, not due to hardheartedness or a choice to spit in the face of the divine after acknowledging this presence my whole life, not because of anger or rebellion. Because I believed until the point that it hurt, until the point that I was forced to view it from another angle. I saw some loose strings and I tugged. And it unraveled so quickly and easily. And now, I stand with a heap of formless ugly yarn, and yet, I couldn t be more thankful. I don t need it to take form anew or be organized. I would rather it look like this with a full journey ahead instead of acting perfectly content yet simultaneously suspecting that even one staggering thought, one wrong move- and it might all unravel.

05/18/14

If You don t exist, I should feel free, self-actualized, and the owner of my own life. But I feel hardened, less empathetic, less joyful, and I miss You. I miss feeling enlightened and inspired by You. I miss crying to You, feeling Your presence, trusting Your promises, worshipping. I miss assuring myself of Your life. I miss the redemption story. I miss trusting You would make every wrong thing right. Perhaps, I just miss consistency.

06/23/14

Six months ago I left my house and everyone I knew and flew into an unknown, a question mark on the map which has quickly and intimately been colored with faces and sentiment and memories. I left with concepts and ideas and a code written on my heart that I was sure the world respected and abided by, even if it manifested itself in a disguised and unfamiliar way. I entered unsure about the specifics, but confident of the general scheme, a framework that had always provided some continuity in the enormous chaos of the world I had just left. If this framework had carried me through my dysfunctional childhood, my adaption from homeschooling to a more diverse world, my progressive internal enlightenment, and my previous travels, I was confident and ready for all my experiences to be stored away in this same comforting framework.

I ve become more enthralled with this world I live in and captivated, disheartened, mesmerized, and confused. And my small and few experiences enlighten me to a lifetime of deepening my understanding through admitting my small fraction of wisdom makes little difference in the world and is only a small dent in my sphere in the universe. I ve given up on lofty goals of making a difference and embraced allowing the world to change me. Perhaps it s I who needed changing more in the first place.

Six months ago, I stood on a bridge I anticipated would last through any turbulence. And I watched how easily and completely it dashed apart with external pressure- even by the small pocket of my mind that permitted the fantasy of other beliefs. I fell into the water expecting to be swallowed up by the dangers I d been preached about my entire life. I found myself instead at a pleasant temperature, able to float, and marveling at the navigation of the unknown. I fell in love slowly, then all at once with the marvels and hazards of a life unchartered.

11/18/14

When I cannot name the It which bids me back and back again, I feel powerless, unidentified, unnamed. But when I try to box it in with any parameters, I find it bears no weight to me. It loses its power and I attack Its statues as soon as I name them. In this tension It seems to almost survive and lurk on. And so I move forward, imagining some beautiful there with an It more comfortable and defined. And that someday I will be there . And when this doesn t work, I give way to frustration and apathy, muttering that no one has a clue anyways, but it d be nice for everyone to just admit it.

Struck by an indifference that never occurred to me in my sureness, and simultaneously feeling level with the world, humble and open to its oddities there are moments of excitement and inspiration from this haunting and the beautiful places of love and an almost illusiveclarity that sheds light on all the shadows of the past. And there are other days I envy my perceived piety and certainty and wish taking a step back were a plausible option.

I reflect on my own sapere aude journey, how for years I stifled my doubts with reverence and how life itself had to strip me of my pride of sureness before I dared asked the Other who It was and what It s shadowy motives are. And still, I feel terrified to verbalize aloud this journey, as in the past. You left the confident place you once sat, for this indecisive and ambiguous place? What could be the reason? And how can I explain, that the experience of life itself stripped me from that place- especially to those whose view of these struggles is that I have chosen to ignore God. The journey was harsh and unforgiving, but also sincere and in a strange way, almost kind.

When I was invited to write this piece, I felt an overwhelming hesitancy. Revelation of my journey means more deconstruction, from myself and from others. And how can I publish my own misunderstandings and blunderings right along with the brilliant journeys of others? And how can I, after having been inspired and exuding confidence and enthusiasm for these very subjects a thousand times before, now expose my indifference and confusion and my view of life ahead with my timid and exhausted wheels still turning over and over again?

And yet, here I somehow sit, willing to be seen, spooked by my own spectrals

A five year old, staring eerily at the ceiling fan, struggling through the description of eternity provided by a proud Sunday School teacher. Forever? And then more time after that? And so young and terrified of the world I knew so little about, I begged that God would save me, but secretly whispered that even heaven would be hell to me. Because eternity is a hell of its own, and no one had to teach me that the boredom of purposelessness and the exclusion of any population is a nightmare no matter what they call it.

A seven year old, frightened to stillness, trying to listen and not listen simultaneously to a drunken father singing to the night, and gripped by a stripping shame and guilt that overwhelms all sense of identity. I am mortified, sure that I will never tell anyone of this vomitlike sensation for the rest of my life. I decided to pray, to release it all to the One who cares and hears and protects. It almost gently cradles me to sleep that night.

A nine year old jotting down her secret lists, detailed documentation to ensure every perceived duty is accounted for and no allegations could be made that day, a prescription for how to ensure God is satiated. I cross off the daily prayers, the time attempting to apply the confusing texts in a way that makes sense in a child s life, and the effort spent lending time to family. I pray that God is honored by my duty, but secretly, I am praying that I am not condemned for being myself and for the times when I m not holding every thought captive, the feelings of hatred and resentment that swim up. I quickly convert them to self-loathing, which I m sure appeases the Divine.

An eleven year old laying in a panic attack, overwhelmed by the upcoming divorce and the demands newly required of her and feeling utterly terrified of the unknown. I decided to tell all to the One who brings the tranquil and comforts. I listen to my breaths space out and my heart stomp more softly and thank the One who hears and sees and knows.

A fifteen year old exhausted at the end of an unhealthy relationship, but with a heart unwilling to give up this attachment. I asked to be mended by the great Healer who wanted to listen for hours.

A nineteen year old dehumanized by anger, striking the person who epitomized every hurt, backing slowly away, appalled by her own monstrosity. I beckoned the great Creator for a remembrance of my own person, and I felt urged forward tenderly to seek help, to begin the long process toward vulnerability and forgiveness.

A twenty-one year old broken-hearted from the rejection by the emotionless face she d so learned to love and trust and lying tormented by a seemingly eternal ocean of pain that hollows her insides. I cried out to a Counselor who provided wisdom and introspection a thousand times during those long, monotonous months of loneliness.

A twenty-two year old, traveling alone and encountering the world in a new way, unsure how the beliefs that formed her entire perspective could change so rapidly with exposure to an unfamiliar world. I whispered to God, begged him to be alive, to be listening, to validate every previous ghost.

A twenty-three year old, standing in Europe, but gazing out at Asia, in front of a body of water so majestic and intimate and universally appreciated, It causes an abrupt pause. Transcendence must exist or the water could not bring up such a inward stirring. I praise the Almost that draws me near.

And I m a haunted being; I think I am at peace, and then these past spectrals come a knocking. The beautiful and terrifying ghosts do not leave me to sleep easily these nights. Is this my complex psyche or my friction with the Divine?

And this It is something I am pushing or pulling and am rarely content with Its current state. When It seems almost absent, I beg for its calmness, its reminder of transcendence, its shadowy illusion to true meaning. And when It feels almost present, I am overpowered by my lack of control and beg It leave me be. The paene umbra never leaves enough evidence to convict It, but never leaves so little to hush my suspicions of Its mysterious visit.

It spooks. And I believe I will be haunted my whole life. Some moments I beg release from these spirits, imagining peace if it abandons me. I am Captain Ahab, obsessively deluded that the killing of the great whiteness will cure me of my insanities. I know that a true release from them would be the death of this tension that keeps me so apt to feel, so willing to experience the rawness of life.

And so I wrestle them. I am Jacob with a limp and a peculiar struggle with the Great It that engages me, baffles me, and provokes me forward. I continually feel compelled, almost involuntarily, to explore this hauntingly beautiful Mystery that spooks my past, present, and future.

T A D
D E L A Y

P S Y C H O A

T H E O

P H I L O S

T H E O L

P U B

S C H

THE FOLLOWING ARE THE MASKS TAD DELAY HAS BEEN KNOWN TO WEAR IN THE PUBLIC SPHERE:

Psychoanalytic theorist. Philosophical theologian. Public scholar.

HERE'S WHAT THIS CONTRIBUTOR WOULD SAY ABOUT HIMSELF:

Tad DeLay is a public scholar, advancing psychoanalysis and critical theory as methods for analyzing religion. Both as an academic researcher and a provocative theorist for actually-existing religious communities, his work focuses on the personal aspects and political functions of belief. The psychoanalytic theology explored aims to unsettle traditional theologies by speaking indirectly against their sources in compulsive repetition, social relations, and unconscious anxiety. Having studied psychology and theology, DeLay is currently a doctoral student of philosophy of religion at Claremont Graduate University. He recently published a book on psychoanalytic theory and radical theology, and he lives in Los Angeles.

N A L Y T I C

R I S T

P H I C A L

O G I A N

L I C

L A R

Orthodoxy's Anxiety and Ideas that Fail

It seems dismissive to say that "today everything is theological, with the exception of what the theologians talk about." But this observation from the German legal theorist Carl Schmitt is the type of thing no theologian will read without immediately feeling a resonance. Theology speaks at something indirectly, but we are seldom rewarded for anything more than repetition of a tired formula, for as John Caputo agreed, "In theology, everything is haunted." Or perhaps we should say that if theology is not haunted, then it has nothing to say. This chapter is a protest against ideas that fail.

Caputo once defied the gatekeepers by pleading, "Don't give religion to the theologians. Don't let them have it. It's not theirs. They don't get to build their fence around it. You have to keep the police away from literature, and keep them away from religious questions, too." As a theologian, I take our field's formation and study very seriously. But at the same time, I agree with Caputo: "Religious authorities are terrified of genuinely thinking about religion in a deep and probing way, because they know that will expose all the uncertainty in religion and the fact that nobody knows just what's going on. The stronger and the louder you shout your confessional faith, from my point of view, the more insecure you prove yourself to be." The ego attaches to an idea, and we fear our worlds will shatter if the idea becomes jeopardized.

How does one respond to an unheard call? This ostensibly religious problem is no different than the whole pattern of our lives. We often act and repeat as automatons according to the demands placed on us by nobody in particular, we strive to please gods who are not judging us, we serve vocations that were not demanded, and we retroactively craft our justifications. We attach ourselves to things because they remind us of the Thing, the transcendent security of a lost-object we never manage to recover. What never existed is difficult to re-find.

Art and religion have a curious relationship to a haunting void. Art expresses a void precisely by covering over it like so much paint on a canvas, too precise a caption reduces expression to narrow propaganda. Religion is a language that edges right up to the ineffable. A confessional theology explains the void as something shallow, expressible, and dependable. A radical theology embraces the anxiety of unknowability, and it risks the heresies just the same as subversive art risks a misreading.

In this book's opening chapter, Caputo took a page from Lacan, a provocative psychoanalyst my work centers upon, to say that religion—of the Big Reductionistic Stories variety—will likely last forever. For what it's worth, Lacan also observed reductionistic "ecumenism only seems to have a chance if it is grounded in an appeal to the feebleminded." If your theology preaches easily, there is always the chance you are underestimating your hearer's capacity to hear. Psychoanalysis is a theory of trauma, and it concerns itself only with what does not work. The only thing more anxiety ridden than self-destruction is the serious work involved in addressing our sabotage so that we might heal. Sometimes the gods that haunt us provoke thinking and healing; most of the time our gods demand we continue our repetition ad infinitum. The quote Caputo referenced came from an interview in which Lacan characteristically evaded a direct response to a series of questions until one was asked that required no such equivocation: what of the war between psychoanalysis and religion? Religion, he said, "will triumph not only over psychoanalysis but over lots of other things too. We can't even begin to imagine how powerful religion is. Religion, above all the true religion, is resourceful in ways we cannot even begin to suspect."

Religion will outlast a great many things. The anthropologists tell us religion began with early shamans oscillating between the roles of priest and politician, for we apparently developed a need for one peculiar representative to occupy the voice of gods and ourselves. Critique of religion always causes anxiety when it infringes upon either of the two things religion does best: personal meaning and tribal cohesion. The gods never die, but they change forms and spook us under a different guise. We like to think we choose our beliefs, but they choose us. We never asked to believe or doubt. Doubt is a response to anxiety, but what exactly is anxiety? It is not quite what it is so popularly reduced to, a fear wholly without object. Anxiety is a response to something happening, whether real or imagined, perhaps stirring from a barrier we feel slipping away. We do not choose to doubt the theologies handed to us; it simply happens or it does not at our first intuition that we no longer need to maintain an idea that does not work.

We are told we should fear heresies. The Jewish theologian, Abraham Joshua Heschel, once said that it is hypocrisy rather than heresy that leads to spiritual decay. When we feel doubts rising, we have two—and ultimately only two—options: 1) we redouble our efforts with penance to assuage guilt (or however else we creatively opt to maintain repetition), or 2) we transgress the beliefs that do not work. The "big Other" is a way of speaking indirectly about a need we have for a subject-supposed-to-know; the big Other can manifest as any number of gods—parents, politics, a God on occasion—but the imagined entity to which we declare fidelity is arbitrary. Freud once observed that if our options are either guilt or anxiety, most people choose the simplicity of guilt. The big Other's confessional theology depends on it, for to realize that no big Other is judging us will dissolve our world. As Caputo writes, "nothing is real unless it is destabilized by the irreal." Anxiety is a signal, and it is a signal that something in the Real is simply not working anymore.

If your god cannot die, your protests against the decline of theocratic culture will be as loud as your insecurity. If your god cannot die, a faith that kills its god just as his faith waivers will not sit well. The maintenance of impotent orthodoxies and resistance against our suspicions tells us we would prefer to keep our beliefs that do not work. If we believe fully without doubt, it is because we have turned the temple veil into an iron gate.

The statisticians tell us my millennial generation is the least religious ever recorded, supposedly a result of our higher education rates, or because we told ourselves we are spiritual-but-not-religious, or because of the misfortune of our parents never putting to death the gods of bigotry, racism, patriarchy, and war. This abandonment is true even in the Bible Belt where I was raised, which Caputo describes as the place where religion persists because we dare not think. Indeed, it is not that people choose foolishness but rather that foolish gods chose us and demand our allegiances, for as Caputo says, "God does not exist; God insists." It is similar to a claim I want to make: the unconscious big Other does not at all exist but instead insists—on the repetition of what does not work—all the same. Deconstruction and psychoanalysis have very different meanings in mind for such similar language, but perhaps placing radically different theories side-by-side will allow us to speak indirectly.

Orthodoxy is what we obstinately maintain when we have nothing of value to say regarding the doctrine itself. We know an answer does not work, but repetition settles easier than admitting the big farce. Orthodoxy cannot handle spooks. Orthodoxy can handle the bureaucratic university theologians, those who maintain and repeat, but it cannot handle provocateurs with eyes to see. To say something cryptic enough to be meaningful will also be ambiguous enough to be misinterpreted. Orthodoxy is often the insistence on repetition of what does not work. Our theology does not work and we know it, so we hide in the safety of spaces we have been before. We do this because we know our gods are dying.

The big Other faces no threat at the death of our gods, for gods will always resurrect with a vengeance. It is not the least bit uncommon for my co-millennials who have supposedly abandoned gods to ask one last question that presents itself as tempestuous for the gatekeepers of orthodoxy. That the non-religious millennial should care for the gods' opinions should not be shocking in the least—again, the gods never really die. They simply take on a new guise and continue to spook like a plague. We have done this ever since we, as infants, first suspected the reflection in the mirror was our own and, all too unsure of ourselves, turned round to verify our suspicion with our m(O)ther. Our earliest moments of individual reflection—and every moment since—required the big Other's affirmation. We seek the ratification of our positions not because we are insecure but because we are humans who developed a need for an(O)ther's ratification.

My experience has been that everyone engaging the field of theology with serious reflection—which, to be sure, is an unfortunately rare occasion—does so to work out something about themselves. Somewhere far back, an idea worked its way into us and will not let us go. Our discourse is getting at something, but we are unsure of what our language aims to designate. Orthodoxy—and by that I mean the discourse that has nothing to say of the doctrine itself—designates the territories to police. As Caputo put it, we need to replace our deontologies with hauntologies. Theologies that have something to say—and by that I mean the honest heresies of our inquiry—speak indirectly. The indirect hauntology speaks not at what does or does not exist but at what spooks and insists.

For Caputo, God is what never ceases to spook and haunt and demand our attention. For Lacan, the big Other is the demand that we maintain patterns of repetition that do not work. Let us place these two versions of insistence side by side in the domain of folk religion and identity politics. More than ever, if we are not to play the part of a fool for some knave willing to take advantage of our naïveté, we need to think about the ways in which all our beliefs—from the traditionalist's pietism and theocratic politics to the secularist's dismissal of religion—are co-opted alike by the role of the cynical knave. The knave, whether priest or politician, knows the game and must keep the rules out of sight.

A long while back in our history, calling the king a fool was a capital offense. Of course, if losing one's head was a serious possibility, peasants naturally guarded themselves by an ever-expanding network of taboos that kept them as far as possible from treason. They ended up spending a lot of time thinking about how to avoid saying or even thinking that the king was an idiot. The Inquisition exposed the church as an idiot, but more broadly this expansion of taboo is how all confessional theologies construct themselves. We end up with dubious ideas that only exist to support the slightly less dubious idea we began with. We rearrange the ideas to maintain the stability of our unconscious demands, and we leave the sources of our anxieties untouched even as we convince ourselves we have unveiled the world. But again, all this does is draw attention to the plain and simple truth of the matter: the king really is an idiot.

Caputo describes insistence as partly pathological, but it is not entirely the obsessive's excessive drive. If Caputo and I diverge in our views on this matter, it would result from what we each mean by this word drive. For religion in particular, I find Freud's distinction between instinct and drive particularly helpful, the former being anything that conserves and the latter being excessive (whether for better or worse). Christianity, whether in the form of folk religion or many confessional theologies, is traditionally more on the side of instinct—it conserves its domain and polices its boundaries. For theology to be more than an instinct, more than some peculiar facet of evolutionary adaptation that kept our ancestors functioning, we need to think of theology as a death drive. The drive is the insistence on excess, whether destructive or creative. It is what cannot be accounted for as a simple adaptation. A drive is the space of creativity and the resistance of boundaries, and by calling theology a drive I am explicitly saying there should be no boundaries our thought should fear to transgress once we suspect a doctrine does not work.

Radical theology is not the Big New Thing; it is a suicide pact. Deconstruction and psychoanalysis create overwhelming pain on the pathway from what does not work to what just might work. Radical thought—like the activism from which it should emerge or which it should incite—is an intermediary moment, a protest that can and should live only as long as the matter it arose to protest. The history of protest movements tells us there are two—and ultimately only two—possible endings: 1) the protest succeeds in transforming its socio-economic space, or 2) the protest is co-opted and subsumed into one of its predecessor positions. Hegel described the sublimation to a new social position as requiring 1) a heightened state of antagonism that 2) sublates to a new position while 3) preserving the knowledge of the previous antagonisms. When our cultural awareness of economic antagonisms has not sufficiently risen to the level required for transformation, movement will be successfully repressed. It is the same when we engage in a theological debate (and this is all too often the trouble with discussing confessional theologies) where terms cannot be stated in a fashion direct enough to foster and sustain a real debate of ideas. What will be the fate of radical theology?

Radical theologies spook because they say this: all your closely-guarded suspicions, they are right on the mark. Repression is never simply suppression; repression always returns as something. Doubt is a response to anxiety, and anxiety is not without object. Radical theologies will not appeal to those who censor their doubts. If religion is an adaptive instinct and God is Being, the inquiry is easy. The correct answers are all predetermined, for foolishness has to be nourished, and the big Other is not spooked by our creatively new defenses for ideas that do not work. If religion is a creative/destructive drive and a hauntology that insists, the inquiry is difficult. One mode is a repetitive bureaucracy and the other is (perhaps occasionally) incisive analysis. At any rate, everything is theological today, except for what the theologians discuss.

What does a response to an unheard call look like? Do we think we have a choice about whether or not to respond?—the truth is that we respond to an unheard call with every moment of our lives. The unheard call insists, which all too often leads to orthodoxies and the repetition of what does not work. The alternative, as Caputo rightly says, will not preach well; it is also the only thing that can preach. The choice is not so much between whether or not to respond to unheard calls; it is whether to maintain orthodoxies or to opt instead for the radically freeing, dangerously heretical, and ultimately the only honest path: we must always be willing to put to death ideas that do not work.

LIN ELIZABETH PREISS

DISRUPTOR COMFORTER SEER

THE FOLLOWING ARE THE MASKS LIN ELIZABETH PREISS HAS BEEN KNOWN TO WEAR IN THE PUBLIC SPHERE:

artist, chaplain, explorer, devil's advocate, wife and mother.

HERE'S WHAT THE CONTRIBUTOR WOULD SAY ABOUT HERSELF:

One of the most soul-resonating moments in my early adult life came, ironically, by the most ordinary means of a bumper sticker: Disturb the comfortable; comfort the disturbed. This balance of faith and challenge speaks to my understanding of the Divine inaugurated by the event of a particular god-man 2 millennia ago. This disruptive balance frames my passion for chaplaincy, theology and art alike.

As I bear witness and advocate for those whose worlds are turned upside-down, I am made steady by a weathered Love that turns the world inside-out. My own chaos is comforted when I can sit with others amidst the unanswerable questions that come from physical, emotional and spiritual brokenness. I am sustained by audacity and hope in a companioning G-d who is not threatened by honesty and doubt.

In that vein, my artwork focuses on the coexisting tension between disruption and hope, pain and healing, beauty and brokenness. As both a chaplain and artist, it my passion to utilize aesthetics and shared space to encourage spiritual encounter through the arts in sacred-profane settings. I love getting my hands dirty, working with the stories, materials, limitations and possibilities around me and see what comes from these juxtapositions. My failures keep me from taking myself too seriously and the absurdity of my endeavors keep me grounded.

Pay no attention to the Man behind the Curtain - 1

PETER ROLLINS

Living
Dying
Trying

THE FOLLOWING ARE THE MASKS PETER ROLLINS HAS BEEN KNOWN TO WEAR IN THE PUBLIC SPHERE:

Author, speaker and community organizer. I promote Radical theology as a disruptive theory and socio-political practice that can help individuals and communities embrace more healthy and helpful forms of life. I've gained degrees in Scholastic Philosophy (BA Hons), Political Theory (MA) and Post-Structural thought (PhD). My most recent books are *The Idolatry of God* and *The Divine Magician.*

HERE'S WHAT THIS CONTRIBUTOR WOULD SAY ABOUT HIMSELF:

I am a tiny fragment of the universe perceiving itself for a moment.

Spectral Technologies. Turning Poltergeists into Holy Ghosts

What we Bury in the Day, Will Return in the Night

In Charles Dickens' *A Christmas Carol* we read of a covetous old miser entombed in a self-made prison of bitterness, greed and hatred. The story begins on a cold Christmas Eve with the old miser, Ebenezer Scrooge, turning down a dinner invitation, refusing to give alms for the poor and begrudgingly letting his clerk have Christmas day off to spend with his family.

But that evening, his former business partner, who had died seven years earlier, appears with a solemn message: Scrooge will be visited by three spirits in the dead of night. If he listens to them, he will find a new life, but if he closes his ears, he will be condemned to carry chains for all eternity.

The transformative figures in this narrative are the ghosts. These uninvited guests are messengers with good news for a deeply flawed figure.

Therein lies the power of ghosts.

Ghost are difficult figures to grasp, they blur the boundary between presence and absence, between existence and non-existence. They mark something gone, but not yet past. They are a type of ripple left in the wake of an event.

The word "wake" carries with it another meaning, beyond its obvious one. For a wake not only connotes the after effect of a happening, it also relates to an old Celtic ritual surrounding death. A wake used to name a custom in which people would keep watch over the body of a loved one until it was buried.

To participate in a wake required one to be alert.

Perhaps to the fact that the dearly departed don't have one-way tickets. They return to us when we least expect it. They might be dead, but they're not gone. In the spirit of Freud, we might say that what we bury by day, returns by night.

Like Scrooge, we all have our own ghosts, whether we acknowledge them or not. We are haunted houses, even though few of us are brave enough to hunt out what dwells there. And, like Scrooge, these ghosts have the power to offer us salvation if we listen to them, and damnation if we don't.

What I want to do then is explore what it might mean to become awake to our ghosts, not just as individuals, but as participants in religious and political structures. For, as we shall see, ghosts haunt systems as much as they haunt individuals.

Poltergeists or Holy Ghosts

In order to better approach the nature of ghosts let us imagine a situation in which a family have lost their son/brother. Let us also imagine that the family have attempted to bury the memory of this trauma as deeply as they can. Each Sunday they all get together for dinner and talk about their week. But no one ever mentions the one who is missing from the gathering. While those gathered around the table might be thinking about the family member they lost, it is also very possible that no one is. In other words, they are not merely avoiding talk of the loss, they are avoiding thinking about it. Yet just because the loss isn't being brought to the surface doesn't mean that it isn't making itself present. Indeed, it is precisely because this loss is not being talked about that it is present. Present in a spectral way.

In situations like this it can seem like the lines of communication are bending around some traumatic core, a traumatic core that no one wants to address for fear of evoking a crisis.

The problem however is that the crisis isn't in danger of arising, the crisis is already there, it is simply being repressed. And it is precisely this repression that makes the ghostly presence so dangerous. For if we do not find ways of bringing these things to the surface, they will manifest themselves in more problematic ways. Perhaps coming up in stress, physical illness, depression, bursts of anger, drug abuse or any other number of seemingly unrelated ways.

To take a different example, we might imagine a marriage in which two people have gradually grown apart. On the surface they attempt to keep up the pretence that everything is good. They continue to act as if nothing has changed. But things are not what they appear.

Over time a whole subterranean network of acceptable transgressions have been created to make sure that the surface remains undisturbed. While both agree that bitterness, anger, resentment, and emotional affairs are out of the question, there is a tacit agreement that these are acceptable as long they are never brought up. The couple, as well as the children, are dimly aware that all these things are going on under the surface, but no one brings them up for fear of what might happen. Yet, once again, ignoring these ghostly realities doesn't prevent a crisis from happening, but merely prevents the crisis from being confronted. A strategy that ensures the repressed truth make its voice heard in other ways. Like in the behaviour of the children in school, the amount of hours worked by the woman, or the time spent out with friends by the man.

Or take the phenomenon that I've heard from a variety of people living in the Bible Belt of America who, on visiting their religiously conservative parents, go to church, even though they don't attend at any other time.

While there are no doubt many who do this to hide the fact that they don't go to church, the people I've met often confess that their parents know fine well that they don't otherwise go. In these situations all the relevant parties know that the church attendance is a mere pretence, but everyone keeps up appearances regardless.

No one is actually being fooled by the game, but everyone keeps playing it anyway.

This game is usually carried out in the name of peace. As long as no one brings up the truth, calm remains. Yet beneath the smooth surface, turbulence exists. Once again the strategy of keeping things in the depths only serves to cause explosions elsewhere.

In each of the above examples we glimpse how haunting works. More than this we see how ignoring our spectres makes them into poltergeists. Knocking things around, disturbing the daily run of our lives and making our existence more painful that it needs to be.

For when we cannot carry out a wake on behalf of what we bury, when we cannot tarry with them, mourn them and make our peace with them, they make sure never to give us peace.

Yet, there is an alternative to ignoring what spooks us. For, if we allow these spirits to speak, they become holy ghosts. To turn our poltergeists into holy ghosts a séance is needed. One must summon the spirits, and let them be heard.

In the unhealthy marriage mentioned above, it's only when the unspoken is brought to the surface that real and substantive change can happen. When this happens there are basically three possible outcomes.

They attempt to bury everything again

They decide to end the marriage and pursue different journeys.

They engage in work that would lead to a more healthy and fulfilling relationship

If things can't be buried again the unhealthy relational system will find itself unable continue in its old way. It will either fall apart or undergo substantive change. Either way things can't remain the same.

What we witness here is the traumatic and terrifying insight encapsulated in the saying, "the truth will set you free." An insight that we reject in a variety of ways.

Of course we reject this idea for good reason, because we think that facing the truth of what's going on beneath the surface of our individual lives, sexual relationships and families is the very thing that will bring about some apocalyptic end.

This is true in that facing the ghosts brings an end to the old. But in doing so it also opens up the possibility of the new. It frees us from oppressive realities and opens up paths to healthier lives. The new arrives in such a way that we can only call what we once knew "the old."

Ghosts in the Ideological Machine

A Christmas Carol is not simply the story of a selfish individual, for it is an allegory telling us something about the political and economic system of the time. Scrooge acts as a metaphor describing how cruel, harsh and oppressive Victorian England was to poor workers. In this way, we are faced with the idea that wider political systems are also haunted by truths they would rather ignore.

To see how this operates at the level of national politics lets take the example of Love Makes a Way, an Australian activist movement born from outrage at a federal policy that resulted in almost a thousand children of asylum seekers being held in detention camps.

This was not some covert act being hidden from the population; it just wasn't gaining much national attention. In response Love Makes a Way encouraged religious leaders to address this by engaging in illegal sit-ins at the offices of key political figures. The first protest led to arrests and charges, but it also meant that the issue became major news.

This caused serious political embarrassment to the Government, all the more so because the leaders were exonerated and commended by the judge. The ugly truth was firmly brought to the surface and policy changes were made.

But systems seek equilibrium and thus they try to keep the dead buried. In this case the Government learned and adapted. It realised that charging the religious leaders was a bad idea, so the next time they quietly arrested the protestors and let them go. In attempting to avoid a confrontation with an internal crisis, the system adjusted to the resistance movement. It sought to avoid confronting the ghosts in the machine.

The more that a system has invested in the status quo the more it will do to hide the spooks and spectres that haunt the corridors of power. The more a given system holds up an ideal of itself as good, pure, whole, and true, the more that it has to hide anything which contradicts this. Any self-proclaimed city on a hill will have bodies buried in the ground. The higher the hill, the more skeletons you'll find beneath it.

This is what happened in the events surrounding a popular religious network in America called Mars Hill. On the surface everything was polished, professional and on point. Slick speakers, skilled musicians and a message informing those involved that they where bringing truth and light to the world. Yet the less such an ideal self image admits of its faults, the more those faults must be repressed, and the worse things get.

In the case of Mars Hill there was a whole subterranean network of disavowed activities including plagiarism, misogyny, manipulation of book sales, unfair dismissal of staff and totalitarian leadership structures. Some of these were only known by few, others where known to almost everyone involved, but they remained largely unspoken. It was as if people had agreed to abide by an unspoken pact. Yet the ghosts didn't remain silent and the effects of the repression came to light via the mistreatment of individuals. It was only because many who left Mars Hill became increasingly vocal about the abuse that the implicit constellation of acceptable transgressions within the Mars Hill edifice were brought to the surface, an act that fundamentally undermined the system.

While the leader of Mars Hill, Mark Driscoll, said that he had wished the problems had been dealt with internally (rather than in the "court of public opinion"). The problem is precisely that these transgressions were already known internally. For real transformation to happen resistance needs to occur in a way that isn't endorsed by the system it critiques.

Politically speaking, this can help us understand the importance of protests taking place in Ferguson after the shooting of Michael Brown. What we have witnessed there are protestors who are finding ways to bring to light the systemic racism operating within the political system itself, a resistance that is drawing to the light of day the ubiquitous, normalized violence operating in disavowed ways.

Effective protest involves courageously and creatively finding ways of bringing the unspoken truths of a given system to the surface, confronting it with its own disavowed truth, it's own undead and unwanted phantoms.

Not the problem, but the solution to a Problem

The point here is that the unspoken subterranean truth is not a problem, it is rather a solution to a problem. It is precisely here that the figure Judge Dredd can prove illuminating. Dredd is a law enforcement officer working in a dystopian future ravaged by radioactive waste. As a Judge in Mega City One he has the authority to arrest, sentence, and execute criminals at the scene of a crime. The judgments are harsh, immediate, binding, and given without considering the wider context.

At a superficial level this system would seem to express the most concrete form of judicial system imaginable. A Judge comes to the scene of the crime, assesses what has happened there and pronounces a sentence. This could then be contrasted with what we might call a system that abstracts from what is happening. Asking broader questions about the conditions that encouraged the person to commit the crime in the first place.

This description of abstract and concrete is however very different from the more philosophical understanding of these terms. From this perspective Dredd can be seen as the ultimate example of enacting an abstract system of justice. Instead of taking into consideration the complex network of concrete conditions that would be required to properly understand and deal with the crime, Dredd abstracts the act from its frame and treats it as a type of isolated monad. He sees it as a cancer that must be removed, rather than a symptom that speaks of a deeper issue.

For Dredd, a crime is a problem that must be punished rather than the sick solution to a problem that must be dealt with.

When crime is abstracted in this way we fundamentally fail to see how it is intricately connected to the society from which it arises. For instance, if the prison system is full of people who lack education, who've experienced severe poverty, or who have faced long term unemployment, then this signals that we live within a broader political context that is failing people in these ways. The prison system then becomes the solution. In order to cover over this failure we attempt to hide what arises as a result of it behind iron bars.

It's easy for us to support prison ministry when we see ourselves as morally upright individuals helping criminals. This view maintains the dominant ideological perspective. The problem comes whenever we consider that the prison system might be the result of a criminal system that we participate in. The disturbing thing about criminals then becomes the way that they might, if taken seriously, expose our own participation in, and support of, a criminal system.

By abstracting prisoners from wider society we protect ourselves from this disturbing reality and effectively inoculate ourselves against confronting the problems that exist within our world.

This is, of course, a disturbing activity to engage in. For in doing so, we are no longer able to maintain the fantasy that we are a type of hero helping poor, unfortunate people. Rather we realize that we need to do this work in order to discover how poor and unfortunate we are, and how violent the structure we participate in is for some people.

Spectral Technologies

The hidden truth that haunts a given system cannot be done away with; it can only be avoided or tarried with. The former is the path of death, creating poltergeists that wreck havoc, the latter is the path of salvation.

Healthy systems, whether personal, religious or political involve keeping a wake, staying alert to the ghosts. In light of this we need to help systems to encourage this alertness.

In terms of religious structures I wish to outline four practices that can help us locate and listen to the ghosts that haunt. These acts can be called decentering practices in that they are each involved in the process of surprising us and knocking us off course.

Each of these spectral technologies take into account the idea that outsiders are often helpful when attempting to locate what haunts us. As an example, I recently shared an ancient Buddhist parable that told of a young, unwed, girl who gave birth to a child. The story went that some family members abused her until she gave up the name of the father. She confessed that it was a Zen master who lived on the outskirts of the village. The villagers denounced the master and demanded that he look after the mother and child. In response he simply said, "very well, very well." His name was ruined and his disciples abandoned him. After a year the girl could stand it no longer and confessed that she had lied. The real father was her neighbour. The villagers apologised to the master and prostrated themselves at his feet to have the child back. The master returned the child while saying, "Very well. Very well."

I told this parable to illustrate a point I was trying to make about accepting lies that are told about us. However it was only when a couple of people challenged me that the parable used the abuse of a young woman as a prop, that I realized how I hadn't questioned what was the most disturbing part of the story. Not that the Zen master was being lied about, but that a young woman was mistreated for having a child out of wedlock. At this point I had three choices. I could just ignore the criticism, defend myself, or apologise and make amends. But without someone else pointing this out I would have done nothing at all.

The practices that I will outline here are designed to bring the light of an outside perspective into actual existing religious systems. The first is The Last Supper and involves a group of twelve people meeting together once a month for a year. Each event involves inviting a guest with different beliefs and practices to participate in a dinner. During the meal the guest is symbolically placed in the seat of Christ, to symbolise that they are the bringer of truth. In addition to this it also plays off the idea that this was Christ's last meal, and might be theirs as well.

Over the starter the guest is invited to talk about what they believe, during the main course questions are encouraged, and over dessert the question is asked, "What's your critique of us?" The idea is that through listening to the other person one will start to see things within one's own system that were previously ignored. While very little will likely happen over one evening, over the course of a year it becomes difficult to avoid discovering aspects of one's own system that might be disturbing.

The Evangelism Project is similar to The Last Supper and involves setting up visits with different religious and political groups to be "evangelized." While part of the visit involves listening to what the other group believes, the evangelism of the title occurs whenever the question is again asked, "What's your critique of us?"

Both of these practices create a situation analogous to a factory creating pollution as an indirect result of its manufacturing process. In order to address this problem the factory owners need to be made aware of the pollution. Something that often involves those people who are directly affected, bringing it up. Those in the factory might be dimly aware of the pollution, but they will likely ignore it until they are confronted with the negative impact it's having.

The final two practices are Atheism for Lent and The Omega Course. The first takes some of the most perceptive critiques of Christianity, breaks them into small blocks, and uses them as Lenten reflections. The point is not for those engaging in the course to judge the material, but to let the material judge them. Thus exposing oneself to insights that may expose destructive and problematic elements of one's own worldview.

The Omega Course takes a similar approach, but this time by looking at people who self-identify as part of the Christian tradition. It plays off the well-known evangelism program The Alpha Course. The Alpha Course creates a space for theological discussion, but ultimately advocates an evangelical view of the world. The Omega Course asks many of the same theological questions as The Alpha Course, but it attempts to show how there are numerous conflicting ways of addressing those questions within the Christian tradition. Ways that draw out both the importance of debate within the tradition and the fluidity of orthodoxy.

On Not Knowing Where We're Going

The reason for bringing up the ghosts that haunt our various social, religious, and political systems lies in the transformative power of the act. What's interesting in this approach is that one doesn't need to articulate a clearly defined alternative to the existing system, but simply draw up the antagonisms already existing within it.

This type of reformation doesn't require the presentation of a ready-made alternative. For the problem with attempting to define a truly new system is that we're generally so immersed in a given ideology that we can't even imagine a genuine alternative. What we imagine is generally just an innovation within the current system rather than a way of fundamentally reconfiguring it. Instead of carefully constructed alternatives the revolutionary figure begins by attempting to expose the repressed crisis that already exists within the system itself.

To return to the earlier example of people attending church whenever they stay with their parents, we can imagine one of the people involved in the pretence deciding to call it out. If they are persistent then this act will either force a split in the family unit or cause a change in how the family relates.

One can't chart in advance what will happen, and one needn't know in advance what a positive outcome might look like. What is required is simply the courage to bring the repressed to the surface. The more carefully and considerately this is done, the more likely a positive outcome will be. But there will be no guarantees concerning what will happen.

In terms of religion, the reformation of Luther is an interesting example of this process. Luther didn't want to create the Protestant Church, he simply wanted to bring to the surface the problems that where existing within the institution at the time. His work was initially resisted and so a new type of church was gradually birthed. Yet he also had a dramatic impact on the system that rejected him. It gradually had to face the problems Luther had exposed and reform itself in light of them.

Protestantism was not some pre-conceived system that Luther had planned in advance, it was the unexpected outworking of his attempt at internal reformation. An internal reformation that involved bringing up the unspoken transgressions of the system he was part of. And that brings us to another important point, the new is not safe against making its own ghosts.

Everyone wants to create their own form of Eden, a place where the ghosts don't exist and the darkness is dissipated. But this is nothing but a dangerous and destructive fantasy that leads to unhealthy, destructive systems. There are better political and religious systems, but these are systems that are open to the other, welcoming of their ghosts, and desirous of ongoing transformation.

The spectres that we've been exploring here are not neutral creatures, depending upon whether we listen to them or not they will be guardians of the status quo, or an invitation to new life. In short, they will be poltergeists, or they will be holy ghosts.

And that brings us to another important point, the new is not safe against making its own ghosts.

R Y A N

SCHENDZIELOS

S t o r i e r

Improviser

U n d o n e

THE FOLLOWING ARE THE MASKS RYAN SCHENDZIELOS HAS BEEN KNOWN TO WEAR IN THE PUBLIC SPHERE:

Pastor of The Well, lead in his 5th grade melodrama, "believer" of his own stories, seminarian, gym rat, pseudo self-doubter, urban hermit, and hopeful nihilist.

HERE'S WHAT THIS CONTRIBUTOR WOULD SAY ABOUT HIMSELF:

Everything I could say here is just a story (or series of them) that I would like you to believe about me, and therefore can never be trusted. I live most days in the in-between, weaving in and out of various narratives and trying on new and well-worn identities. Some days I find what could be called joy or delight in this, and some are like spending the day watching continuous reruns of past Bronco Superbowls (the ones they lost!) while being force fed coleslaw. I am thankful for the former days!

The Dancing Medley of Light

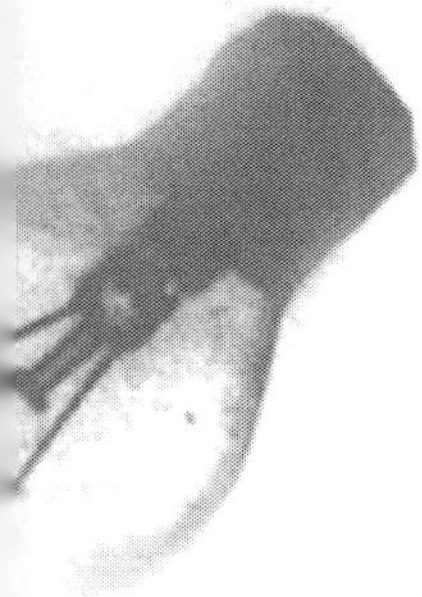

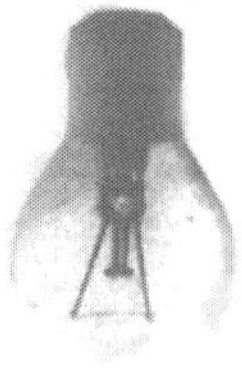

By all measures the village of Chiaroscuro was as ordinary as they come. Those who comprised the village were hard workers and took pride in the society they had created. Each member embraced a specialized role in the community as a tranquil rhythm flowed through their shared life. None of this was strictly coincidence or the product of great societal planning however, for the people of Chiaroscuro had a secret. Whenever relational tensions arose between people, dark forms would appear known as "the shadows." Much more than just folklore, these shadows embodied the anger, frustration, and hurt created in the discord between people, and their presence echoed out waves of fear and anxiety. They would hover and haunt the village, seeking to magnify the disharmony created. The people were not frightened of these shadows, however, for just beyond the village's edge, on the forest hillside, there lay a horn of extraordinary power. The horn was magical because whenever tension occurred and the shadows appeared, all the people had to do was journey to the horn, think upon the event which brought the shadow, inhale deeply, and then blow their deepest breath into the horn. If this was done, out of the wide end of the horn there flowed a dancing medley of light, which scattered the shadows and restored the tranquil rhythm of the community. And so, the horn held the hope of the village, reassuring them of their safety and that there was always a way to reconcile the wrongs done. It was esteemed as a gift from the gods, always keeping at bay the potential unraveling of culture. Stories were written, statues carved, and songs sung of the security provided by the horn. It was inside this comfort Chiaroscuro lived. It was also for this reason that panic spread so quickly when it was discovered one day the horn had gone missing. At first, people only began to disagree about what might have happened to it. Did someone take it? Was some kind of trick being played? With each argument and quarrel, however, more and more shadows appeared, and the village began to spiral downwards. Neighbor turned against neighbor and even friends found themselves in postures of struggle. After a week, shops closed and people rarely went outside their homes. By month's end the once peace-filled village was blackened in shadows as people raged and fought in chaotic dissension. Hope had drained from the air and despair for the end crept into their collective mind. The fighting boiled to a breaking point one afternoon at the village square as now rival groups clashed in opposition. Inside of the screaming and shoving, a young girl, Asha, found herself swallowed by the mayhem. She squeezed and pushed and stumbled her way through the entangled mass until she stood overlooking the whole scene from atop a staircase. Tears formed in her eyes as she took in what had become of her once beautiful village. While all this stirred and tumbled inside of her, Asha suddenly burst out in a piercing scream. The sound shattered the havoc below and all heads turned, fixing their gaze upon her. Stunned by the reaction, Asha frantically searched for what she would say or could do. After several eternal seconds, and still desperate for a response, she did the only thing she could think of. Imagining all the turmoil which had brought about these events, she drew in a deep breath and blew it out with every ounce of her being, and from her lips there flowed a dancing medley of light!

Photo by Al Waller

MICAH PURNELL

authentic fraud

In-love

THE FOLLOWING ARE THE MASKS MICAH PURNELL HAS BEEN KNOWN TO WEAR IN THE PUBLIC SPHERE:

By day Purnell is a graphic designer offering a bespoke service to the creative industries including album artwork, book design and outdoor campaigns of an alternative nature amongst other enjoyable pastimes.

Micah is from Manchester, England.

HERE'S WHAT THIS CONTRIBUTOR WOULD SAY ABOUT HIMSELF:

By night Purnell is a text based conceptual artist debating contemporary ideology in a public place. He works to strip down text to a pithy core in order to create a hook that illuminates more complex, offbeat ideas. Prints of his work are available but (as a rule) usually once they have been strategically placed in public settings such as billboards, fly-poster sites, custom made street signs, pubs/bars and lamp posts with the use of posters, stickers, beer mats and badges. His book, *These Thoughts of Ours*, (available via his website) is his collection of over 80 sayings covering issues of identity, generosity, integrity, consumerism and visual culture, to name but a few.

My prayer for you : produced publicly via *Print Up Paste Up* specifically for *It Spooks*

WING
YIP
Chinese &
Oriental
Groceries
80
Stagecoach

JOHN HARDT

W e i g h t e d
Wasted
W o u n d e d

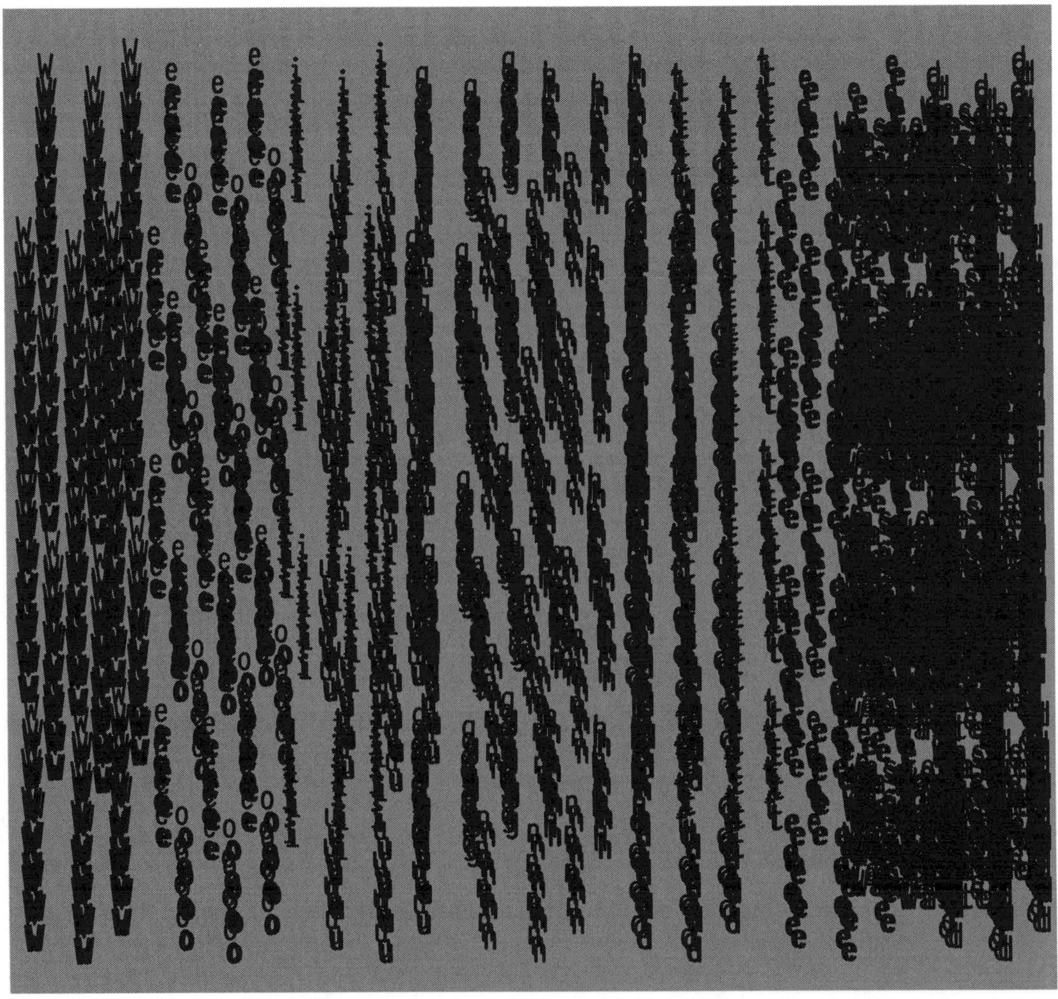

THE FOLLOWING ARE THE MASKS JOHN HARDT HAS BEEN KNOWN TO WEAR IN THE PUBLIC SPHERE:

Musician, Pastor, Facilitator of a Broken Liturgy

HERE'S WHAT THIS CONTRIBUTOR WOULD SAY ABOUT HIMSELF:

Nothing, usually. I don't like talking about myself. But being forced by the publisher of this book to put down a label, I would say that I am an agnostic community leader with Christ-like tendencies. A theology nerd drawn toward radical practice and thought. A husband seeking to love myself in order to better love my wife. A coffee snob. A music snob. An art snob. And I like bourbon.

let it blow

she came to me in the dead of winter
she came to me in the dark of night
she told me that jesus was coming back soon
and i'd better stay away from the light

i begged her to tell me the hour
i begged her to give me the day
but she disappeared like a thief in the night
and i covered my head to pray

oh, let it blow

now i sleep with one eye open
i sleep with the lamp on and yet
i'm haunted by the ghosts of yesterday
and a tomorrow i'd rather forget

you see, the stars have all fallen from the sky
the stars have all fallen down
the vultures gathered around the dead
and we're waiting for that trumpet to sound

oh, let it blow

keep watch for the day is coming
keep watch for the night is here
one will be taken and one will remain
be ready for the end is near

oh, let it blow

SARA WILHELM GARBERS

Feminist, Ethicist, Intuitive, Leader, Partner and Friend (I cheated that's like seven words, sorry,

not sorry)

THE FOLLOWING ARE THE MASKS SARA WILHELM GARBERS HAS BEEN KNOWN TO WEAR IN THE PUBLIC SPHERE:

Doctoral Student at Loyola University—Chicago—Integrative Studies in Ethics and Theology
Preaching Team Member of First Covenant Church—Minneapolis
Background in Higher Education Administration (former Director of Admissions at Luther Seminary and Associate Director of Admissions at Bethel Seminary)
M.Div. from Bethel Seminary
B.A. from University of Minnesota—Duluth
I've preached some sermons
I've presented some stuff
I've written some other stuff
I've never published anything in a book before so I'm stoked
I also have some of the best mentors, friends, and counselors who have deeply shaped me

HERE'S WHAT THIS CONTRIBUTOR WOULD SAY ABOUT HERESELF:

Sara is committed to the work of becoming more human with others. She loves life and the people who are a part of the continued remaking of herself and the world about us. Life lived with friends, in the process of seeking to become more just and authentic than we were before—well, this is the stuff that brings her life and hope (as does laughter, frozen pizza with her spouse (Andy), Malbec, good food, and being outside). She's glad to be a part of this effort and is committed to a future of faith and theology that has space for people to breathe, to laugh, to be seen, and to live livable lives together (á la Butler). When she's not talking on the phone or FT with friends, hanging with Andy, or doing schoolwork, she occasionally blogs at sarawg.com or re-tweets things that strike her as important conversations at @sarawilhelmgarbs.

Beyoncé, Butler, and Caputo: Feminist Considerations of the Haunting.

Beyoncé's *Ghost/Haunted:* Explorations of the Spectral
December 13, 2013: It was end of my first term of doctoral studies. I was frantically writing final papers and awoke that morning to the news that Beyoncé had dropped her new album overnight without any publicity. Amazingly, it was kept secret until its digital release via iTunes, creating an instant clamor on the twitter-sphere amongst music critics and followers of Queen Bey. Beyoncé had done it again—disrupted the system, taken control of her music in an unprecedented way and, in the process, she broke sales records as the album reached platinum within a week. Marked by discourses of sexual empowerment and diverse musical influences, her self-titled release has been heralded by critics as, amongst other things, a "celebration of black womanhood" and an album filled with "subtle inversions."

But what interests me in view of this essay are the lyrics of her second track, *Haunted* (alternatively known as *Ghost/Haunted*), and the visual depiction of the second half of the song in her music video, *Haunted*. When I initially read Caputo's essay *Proclaiming the Year of Jubilee: Thoughts on a Spectral Life*, my mind recalled Beyoncé's music video which has, in a sense, haunted me since last winter. Why has it stayed with me, and why employ it as the central point of reflection in this essay? Well, not merely because of the word association of ghost/haunted that is shared between Knowles and Caputo, but because there is a spectral quality to the song and the essay that both represent, as Caputo writes: a "hauntology."

And truly, the album has haunted me: it presses just past the limits of what I grew up believing was possible for me in order to properly perform being the "good" white woman, even one who is a feminist. The video is a call to my 19-year-old self as I was awakening to being a white woman, resenting my skin and the ideology that is whiteness, knowing that my race, religion, education, and (perceived) class made me marked as one who would properly become the "good wife" whom men married. And in the nights of hatred of my own flesh as I loathed what my skin meant, I agonized over what to do with my skin, my body, and my passional existence. For although I didn't kiss anyone in my first 25 years of life due to the rigidity of the expectations of my faith community and family, I filled journals documenting obsession and tortured attraction; I desired the possibility of being held and of holding someone within my skin. I wanted a world where my body could become more than the terror of immodest dress or risk of immorality. And I've fought hard for years to find my way into having skin that counts—skin that makes me visible in this world. It is onto this scene that Beyoncé emerges, disrupting and challenging me once again to be all of my 33 years of a "grown woman" who admits that which I've always known: my sexuality and body disrupt and haunt me in ways that I can't quite articulate or control. Oh, what does it mean to let the ecstasy that is life in the body, to admit the haunting and know that I am undone already in ways that remind me that I am always being given over, defined, and am riven even as I am emerging as a self in the field of vision.

These notions of the erotic and life in the body resonate with the Jubilee of which Caputo speaks. Both are a haunting. Each has a spectral quality. Yes, we don't know what the haunting is, its anonymity always haunts, and it is that which "spooks and we are subject to it." For how does one capture the Jubilee? How does one narrate the self? (Perhaps) by admitting what ecstasy knows already—the promise of a future unknown and the experiences of selves that remain mysterious even to ourselves. It is the haunting of sex and the body that so terrified many Christian thinkers throughout history. They warn us: "beware of the body and sexuality for it puts one outside of rationality." Indeed, our bodies haunt us and the experiences of the erotic are beyond narration.

Haunted—the retelling of Beyoncé's Spectral Vision

3...2...1 of a motion picture intro reminiscent of theaters of days gone by. TV static transitions into a clear picture of a room covered in white sheets. It's closed up for the season. Whispers, moans, and laughter provide the soundtrack. Static, and then an eerie baby mobile song plays faintly. TVs are stacked together. An image of an eye emerges onto one screen. The camera pans to another room where mannequins are depicted at a 1950s family dinner.

The next room is a bedroom with ornate candelabras and chimes ringing in the background. X-ray images are flashed on another screen. Laughter and a scream. Next, a bedroom that has been converted to an infirmary with two beds, a wheelchair, an oxygen tank, and suitcases. Another room with a table for two. A fire ignites in the fireplace. Another image on the TV comes into focus...*Haunted.*

On December 18, 2013, Sesali Bowen published an essay on Feministing, entitled *Beyoncé Shows Us What We Really Fear in 'Haunted' Video.* Bowen invites readers to understand the scenes in Beyoncé's video as containing images of society's (sub)conscious fears, images (in her narration) such as: white women at the disposal of black men, empowered female sexuality, deviant sexuality, gender bending, suspicious black men, couples of vastly different ages, dying patients. These are scenes of things that are outside of that which we define as properly sexual, gendered, or human. As Judith Butler argues in Undoing Gender, these images are just beyond the norms and, as such, upset the "politics of truth." They are positioned "somewhere between the norm and its failure" and stand as critique of the norms which presses us to re-consider what we think we know and to find a "new legitimating lexicon" that allows for the possibility of the existence of those who already know themselves as possible.

"It's what we see...if I'm haunting you, you must be haunting me."

It's the way that the erotic and fantasy transgress the conceptions of the possible, the known, and that which we can even begin to see or understand. It's the haunting.

And as it relates to the gaze that disrupts and the lives that are viewed as fully human...I've always been confounded by human atrocities and small acts of dehumanization and violence. When I was younger I would cry when my best friends, who were siblings, would yell, "I hate you!" because hatred, to me, meant to deny the central truth to which I had committed myself: God loved everyone and had made everyone in God's image. Even more so, how could I make sense of genocides like the European colonization of the Americas, or Nazi Germany's eradication of Jews and other "undesirables," or any countless historical and present realities? So I spent junior high and early high school reading every book I could find on World War II because I needed make sense of how the Holocaust had come to be. Yet, if I am honest, I already know part of the answer for, as Martin Luther King reminds, from the moment of my waking I participate in small acts of erasure of the "humanness" of the people around the world upon whom my very existence depends.

It is the way that I find myself haunted by a spectral knowing that there is something to my inability to deny my connectivity to those who make my shoes and that my life is bound up in the living and the dead at all moments.

And this—what do I do with this?

Is this question, if anything, not to be the task of theology—to voice that which cannot be captured—the haunting that is the lives of the dead and living? It is the knowing that one is captured by when one touches the ground of Buchenwald or the soil of Chicago: the land itself haunts and speaks the stories of a people no longer living. It is the way that I haunt even myself.

How do I find a language to give witness to this, to give voice to the way that fantasy disrupts—just as Beyoncé's video depicts that which is just outside of the limits of being recognized as human?

The images cut to outside of the villa in a Mediterranean-type landscape with classical violin music playing in the background. A green car drives up to a villa. The door opens. A shoe emerges. She walks in with a swagger, carrying two of her bags with a fur draped over her shoulders. Though the doorway and the click of her heels echoes...she has arrived. Her coat falls to the floor. We see that all of this It is caught on security camera footage. Is this the haunting?

A butler meets her and lights the cigarette she has pulled from behind her ear. Exhale of smoke and faint singing in the background with whispers. Her lips and nails are red. She is sensual and sexual. The butler hands her a key with 94 on it. She stamps out her cigarette and moves up the stairs. She's dressed in menswear of sorts. Another layer of coat comes off. There are screams in the background. She walks down the hallway...click...click. Moans and whispers. She walks down the green carpet. Her face is on the TV and there are close-ups of her walking down the hallway. It flashes to a woman in black, then a naked feline with an old woman, then a man in a wheelchair. The music starts: "I know if I'm haunting you, you must be haunting me."

And this is that which I want to remember: that this haunting, that this which "spooks," is found in the midst of our bodied lives together. What does this mean for me, who grew up striving to be the perfect Christian, daughter, girl, and friend—who only in the past years has turned toward that which spooks...and is becoming human? It is the struggle to give an account in the midst of my humanity. And this spectrality has been the greatest gift of my life as I am wholly disturbed and wholly other, even to myself, in ways that I don't even know how to articulate or make sense of. And the eros of life gives me a language for a life that spooks: It is knowing the not knowing.

For how do I fully explain myself? How do I narrate the way that I love my spouse, Andy? Can I capture what the smell of his neck elicits in me? I will never be able to overcome or to capture this. It is his scent that wafts in and out of my memory and body. I close my eyes and tears form in the corners of them, for this is the spectrality of life, not that which I can bottle and fully capture, but that which has enveloped and consumes me—even as I am birthed in its wind and I find myself.

These ghosts haunt us even as we have built theologies to protect ourselves from such knowing. The spectral, the erotic, then is a theology that is found at the edges and beyond—that which isn't captured—it is a religion that is open to a future that is always never arriving and yet is present in every moment. It is the way that a song like "Secrets" by Mary Lambert resonates with me, because I know that it is not by telling our secrets that we exhaust them, but that by telling our stories, the ghosts come out and we are reminded that this haunting becomes an invitation to be human and to live lives that are worth living. And it is these lives precisely, the ones when we are haunted by our own selves, that we begin to find space for others to be human with us; our gaze becomes transformed when we are no longer afraid that we might see the ghosts but begin to know and see them as part of the spectral quality of life itself.

The courage to face this not "non-being" but that which we can't capture with being—that is the space between being and nothingness and is that which haunts...that which we can never quite overcome is that of which we must give an account though we can never fully narrate. How do we find words for this?

There are images of black men playing poker (looking like stereotypical gangsters) being served by a white, blond woman. Another room reveals a couple in the masks with animal furs and other oddities draped on them. Another features a Beetlejuice-looking couple. The beat emerges. A room with women dressed in sexy lingerie. An ambiguously gendered person in a tub with bubbles. The family from the 1950s. An ambiguously sexed person dances around in another room. Then black men with white paint on their faces peer out from a doorway.

Turn to Beyoncé in a bedroom with other women surrounding her in burlesque dance. "You want me...I walk down the hallway." This is juxtaposed with other images: the man in the bed/the mechanical bull/the woman with red nails and a head bandage/Queen Bey on the bed, reining in her evening finery. Other images persist: images of the erotic, the offensive, the outside of the norms or expected. She turns to leave and the fire is gone from the fireplace.

I've recently been revisiting my journals from when I knew everything about the life of faith. They are wrought with self-hatred as I narrate my inability to embody the call to which I believe I am responding. They are prayers to a God who I had captured though was pure being. They recount stories of violence as I evangelized my friend, Peter, as his Dad was dying of bone marrow cancer. These are the ghosts of my past, and they haunt me. And aren't we all haunted by ghosts? I want to join with Caputo as he says his prayer would be "for God to rid me of God, for God to send the God of Pure Being, Pure Light and Pure Truth packing. God give me purity, but not now, in fact, now that I think about it, not ever! I prefer impure thoughts."

In my version, existence would be weakened into insistence; Spirit into specter, the eternal into the momentary, omnipotence into the weak force of a call, necessity into the perhaps, infinity into the infinitival, divine providence into the risk of an unforeseeable future, perfection into the promise of the world, the all-good into the hope that it works, God's glory into the audacity to not exist, divine transcendence into a way to name the varying intensities which charge the plane of immanence with the anarchic energy of the to-come.

We are haunted by our lives in these bodies; we are undone by each other. Yet we have built lives, relationships, and theologies to inoculate us against remembering. But what if we remembered—if we greeted the ghosts that visit us? Might we not find our way into bodied life that knows its own precarity, and thereby opens to the promise that the erotic knows already?

With Love

Part 1: Ghost

And I've been drifting off of knowledge
Cat-calls on cat-walks, man these women getting solemn
I could sing a Psalm for a Solomon or Salamander
We took a flight at midnight and now my mind can't help but wander
How come?
Spoon-fed pluralized eyes to find the beaches in the forest
When I'm looking off the edge, I preach my gut it can't help ignore it
I'm climbing up the walls cause all the sh-- I hear is boring
All the sh-- I do is boring
All these record labels boring
I don't trust these record labels, I'm touring
All these people on the planet working 9 to 5 just to stay alive
The 9 to 5 just to stay alive, the 9 to 5 just to stay alive.
All the people on the planet working 9 to 5 just to stay alive
How come?

What goes up
Ghost around
Ghost around

What goes up
Ghost around
Ghost around

Soul not for sale
Prob'ly won't make no money off this, oh well
Reap what you sow
Perfection is so...umh

Part 2: Haunted

It's what you do
It's what you see
I know if I'm haunting you, you must be haunting me
It's where we go
It's where we'll be
I know if I'm on to you, I'm on to you
On to you, you must be on to me

My haunted lungs
Ghost in the sheets
I know if I'm haunting you
You must be haunting me
My wicked tongue, where will it be?
I know if I'm on to you, I'm on to you
On to you, I'm on to you
On to you, you must be on to me

You want me?
I walk down the hallway
You lucky?
The bedroom's the wrong way
Slap me, I'm pinned to the doorway
Kiss, bite, foreplay

My haunted lungs
Ghost in the sheets
I know if I'm haunting you
You must be haunting me
My wicked tongue, where will it be?
I know if I'm on to you, I'm on to you
On to you, I'm on to you
On to you, you must be on to me

It's what we see
I know if I'm haunting you, you must be haunting me
It's where we go
It's where we'll be
I know if I'm on to you, I'm on to you
On to you, I'm on to you
On to you, You must be on to me
You must be on to me
You must be on to me
You must be on to me, me, me, me, me, me

BARRY TAYLOR

cynical
english
bastard

THE FOLLOWING ARE THE MASKS BARRY TAYLOR HAS BEEN KNOWN TO WEAR IN THE PUBLIC SPHERE:

Musician, priest, teacher of theology and advertising, occasional writer of books and articles, sometimes conference speaker.

HERE'S WHAT THIS CONTRIBUTOR WOULD SAY ABOUT HIMSELF:

I live in Los Angeles, mocked by many as a vacuous celebrity-obsessed habitat for neurotics and narcissistic hedonists dressed up as deep and meaningful seekers, which is exactly why I love living there.

Sometimes I have been accused of over-thinking, I actually think that I have just begun to think, everything that has passed for thinking up until now is essentially foreplay.

I am haunted by a series of ghosts whose names I know well - melancholy being the chief among them, this is the wound that does not heal and is the lens through which I explore the world.

Oh and I don't eat fish and chips.

SOMETHING SPOOKY GOING ON: EVERY SEVENTH LINE

It's like 50 is a lucky number.
Very fancy! And you?
You have chosen a very strange profession.
the one big question I have is how to live with it
Karl Marx, one of the greatest of them
To critique is to exorcise.
but it is a very good way to draw a crowd.

comme s'était possible
nothing but a disguised or distorted form of y
who thought that Truth too was nothing other than an illusion
by means of very powerful Sacred Spooks and very Holy Ghosts
which we see in the opening line of the Communist Manifesto
Marx had a lucky number!
listen very closely to the cool dulcet tones

do not be ungrateful to the Enlightenment as the day wears on
admit that they are praying for courage
but the two sides share the same presuppositions
created and mixed with a dose of unreality
the other squints through its telescopes at the heavens
the one thing that just might be immortal is this debate itself
the bit of indigestible two worlds dualism religion has swallowed

that its time was out of joint,
that dualism deserves all the abuse
making itself unbelievable all by itself
do not believe this religion
big Strong Men of Reason and the Big Strong Men of Theology
that is what the figure of the specter provides
it has a special asymptotic annularity

Its subject matter is not ontology but hauntology
a secure base from which it launches missiles aimed at the heart of religion
engaging in a micrological exposé of the internal tensions
the aim is not to destroy religion but to "repeat" it
deconstruction behaves as if it has seen a ghost
believers will find no better formula for their beliefs than that
being, on our hypothesis is spooked.

and they have come back to see that these matters are redressed
that the death of Jesus did not save us
the past had the future on his disembodied mind
the living and the still to come
put it this way.
the first line is haunted by the second line
Plato was damning time with faint praise

the present is destabilized and discontent
hat will not destroy it but give it a future
for which we cannot prepare
disjoined by haunting specters taunting it from either side
the "moment" of decision
to deal with the spooks of undecidability
they shatter the settled and limited horizon of expectations

what does this specter expect of me?
it is destabilized by the irreal
to find a better case of spectral phenomena than religion
yet nothing more likely to leave us in the lurch time and again
a bit of undigested beef disturbing our sleep?
Is that the living God or something undead stalking me day and night?
God's purely penumbral presence

leaving us to wonder if there were real bodies beneath these black veils
these unsettling visitations
this is a serious case
I have somehow drifted unawares into dangerous and uncharted waters
but at the moment I do not even know what kind of doctor I should see
God is not an entity out there who answers to the name "God,"
pupils dilated

for one awash in tossing seas
there would be a kit which would contain a proof for my proposition
and everything dissolves into light and love
but not so thoroughly that we cannot still read the writing underneath
God is dead
to get back to Hegel's point
disturb the peace and violate the Sabbath laws with penumbral violations

it gets still worse
I am saying that God is not something present
the one who is haunting me
the reality of Being without turning Being into a being
"there is something spooky going on."
God does not exist, but that does not mean there is nothing to God
nor the hyper-being of mystical theology
in saying God does not exist

God is not a Pure Spirit ensconced in an immaterial realm
the name (of) "God" is temptation
I do not admit that I advocate an obsessive drive
I do not mean a dispassionate spiritual one
my defense will be that there is more than one madness
the spectral open-endedness of the "to-come" in the infinitival

if someone whose lucky number is 50 comes along
that would be the ham-fisted way the Men of Reason hear this saying
50 is not a matter of mathematics; it is a matter of hope
the force of the infinitival infinite is that of a broken, hyphenated force
it is always calling, insistently, unconditionally
a little rule of thumb
the whole world is spooked

to fill up what is lacking in its spectral body
they must be mad
my room full of spooks
the coming of what we cannot see coming
something insists
no longer in the accusative
God, I like to say, is not a projection but a projectile headed straight for my head

the least among us
the divine being shrinks down to an infinitesimally small point
on us
omnipotence into the weak force of a call
ask not what you can you expect from a specter but what specters expect of you
after all it cannot be easy to come back from the dead
specters expect to transform lives

the name (of) "God" is the name of call to which we are supposed to be the response
propositions inside our head picking out objects in the world outside our heads
and proclaim the year of the Jubilee
interpretation goes all the way down, into action
there is no such thing as an uninterpreted fact of the matter
languishing at the feet of Jesus
omnipotent superbeing in the sky

my main response to these questions is another question

It is the worst paganism
the year of the Jubilee is not the reward in the hereafter for sticking it out here below
God is not an infinite immaterial solution to finite material problems
who being eternal has a long memory
what more perfect perversion
the maximum of pain while being guaranteed the impossibility of death

that is why they called for a life without why
can the "it" which "spooks" be preached?
it is trying to sell the faithful
God is not a being who packs a punch
and it presses in upon us here and now
the spectrality of action
the coming of the Son of Man on the last day to separate the sheep from the goats

it's about Calvary, not the cavalry
the works of mercy are just that
and to make a lot of converts in the process
we pray in secret because praying
by the impossible everything begins
twist free of the constraints imposed by the religion on the outside
because her work is the Kingdom of God

and being humbly content with spectrality
under whatever name that is the audacity to hope in and for the coming of what we cannot see coming

JEREMY KENDALL

CONTRADICTED
RELUCTANT-
G I V E R
PRETENTIOUS

THE FOLLOWING ARE THE MASKS JEREMY KENDALL HAS BEEN KNOWN TO WEAR IN THE PUBLIC SPHERE:

Artist, Academic, Educator, Good person.

HERE'S WHAT THIS CONTRIBUTOR WOULD SAY ABOUT HIMSELF:

If I were to say anything about me, I would describe myself a man of contradiction. I have profound regrets and enormous triumphs coloring my human journey. The first word that makes sense to describe myself is "contradicted." I am both good and bad, and have had to embrace both to withstand the truth of myself. I paint for selfish reasons that ultimately produce something for others to experience, so perhaps another descriptor includes, "reluctant-giver." At times I believe I have a great story to tell with my paintings, but the process itself seems to be that which has any value. In my personal life I try and fail at getting my point across to others. My artistic work is a vain attempt of communication, which also commonly happens in my personal life. In the end of the conversation we both walk away with something we decided to understand from the event. We both walk away in a misunderstanding of what just actually happened, and I think that is a beautiful thing. This means that my final word I would use to describe myself is "pretentious."

A painting created in response, titled: "X Y" overleaf

CLAYTON CROCKETT

I N T E L L E C T U A L
HUSBAND
F A T H E R

THE FOLLOWING ARE THE MASKS CLAYTON CROCKETT HAS BEEN KNOWN TO WEAR IN THE PUBLIC SPHERE:

Professor and Director of Religious Studies at the University of Central Arkansas. Author or co-author of five books, mostly recently DeleuzeBeyondBadiou. Co-editor of the book series "Insurrections: Critical Studies in Religion, Politics, and Culture" for Columbia University Press.

HERE'S WHAT THIS CONTRIBUTOR WOULD SAY ABOUT HIMSELF:

I have lived in Conway, Arkansas, for eleven years and have a wife and two children. Arkansas is politically conservative, which I lament, but it has many natural parks and beautiful landscapes. In my work and life, I am interested in important ideas and how they fit together. Radical theology for me is a way of asking questions and a catalyst for thinking through other disciplinary theories rather than any sort of allegiance to a determinate faith tradition. My work is more explicitly theoretical rather than practical, but it is always affected by practical considerations. I am an intellectual and unfortunately not an activist; I seek ways to understand processes and situations so that actions can be efficacious, although it is easy for intellectualizing to become an end in itself.

For the past few years, in addition to working on French philosophers like Jacques Derrida, Jacques Lacan and Gilles Deleuze, I have been exploring ideas about energy from the perspectives of politics, economics, ecology, cosmology, philosophy and theology. Exploitation of stored energy reserves in the form of fossil fuels has generated our extraordinary civilization, but energy is becoming more expensive and our burning of oil, coal and gas is contributing to global warming. Energy is both fully material, completely immanent, and (I would argue) spiritual; it makes us what we are. The paradox is expressed in the first and second laws of thermodynamics: on the one hand energy is infinite and always conserved; on the other hand, energy in usable terms degrades as entropy. I am thinking and researching thermodynamics in terms of cosmology, ecology and politics, and investigating how that connects with issues of contemporary Continental philosophy and radical theology.

Ghosting Theology

Reading Caputo's text is both reassuring and haunting. His words and thoughts inhabit my being even as he insists upon their spectrality. Caputo for me names a person, a relationship—a friendship—and a faith, a faith that can only be performed but becomes an object of reflection. Caputo consolidates a certain form of theology, a postmodern or a radical theology, with which I identify.

I lost my faith at the end of high school, under the assault of biblical criticism and French existentialism. Belief in God became impossible, but my atheism was troubled. My "religion" has always been individualistic and intellectual, and this continued through an engagement with Zen Buddhism, postmodernism and a deeper engagement with philosophical theology. Inspired by Paul Tillich, but also wanting to radicalize his theology, I embrace a kind of theological thinking without any assurance or answers. This theology is deeply Protestant even as at crucial times during my life I have been confronted by an incredible Catholicism that has humbled me.

After encountering Nietzsche, Foucault, and Derrida in college, I wanted to pursue philosophical religious studies in graduate school because religion was the major that offered the greatest stimulation and inspiration during my undergraduate years at William and Mary. In some ways my pursuit of Continental philosophy in Religious Studies programs repeats in different discipline the way that students of postmodernism and deconstruction went into programs of Comparative Literature and literary theory in the 1970s and 1980s.

Theology in its more radical form offers an opening for a genuine and vital intellectual engagement at the same time as its more conventional forms threaten to close this down. Theology in the form of postmodern theology speaks in an academic language that is also engaged with very real intellectual and cultural phenomena, even if that requires a significant amount of translation to recognize. I ended up studying with Charles E. Winquist at Syracuse University, whose position Caputo came to occupy after Winquist's death. Theology for me has always been haunted and haunting, including being haunted by Winquist's presence, as well as his death.

Winquist participated in a movement of American postmodern theology that was influenced by Tillich and the death of God theology of the 1960s. The death of God remains significant, even if it is also, as Caputo asserts, insufficient. Postmodern theology in the 1980s and 1990s was a strange permutation of death of God theology, as it crossed this radical theology of Thomas J. J. Altizer, William Hamilton, Gabriel Vahanian, Richard Rubenstein and others, with poststructuralist and postmodern French philosophy, primarily deconstruction. As Carl Raschke puts it, "deconstruction is the death of God put into writing." For me, one way to think about the death of God is a twisting free from orthodoxy, and another is the insistence on the questionability of God. Here we free religion from God, at least from the traditional omni-God who exists, surveils and governs over all.

But, as Caputo says, that doesn't mean that we free ourselves from God completely. On the contrary, even if God does not exist, God insists. The insistence of God is the spectral afterlife of God, the undead divinity who does not cease to spook us, even as we in turn spook God. It turns around the "it," the specter of what Derrida calls differance, that irreducible differing/deferring that marks existence. In addition to his direct and personal influence on me, which is profound, Caputo also represents a locus of interconnection between two dead people, Charlie Winquist, as I've already mentioned, and Jacques Derrida. I met Winquist at a conference in Charlottesville, Virginia on "The Otherness of God." Caputo was a presenter at this same conference, and I got to meet and talk with Jack there. I met Derrida through Caputo, who brought him to Villanova multiple times, first for a roundtable discussion on religion and deconstruction, and then for conferences on Religion and Postmodernism. I saw, I spoke with, I interacted with Derrida on three separate occasions, and I have had many conversations about Derrida with Caputo. So Caputo mediates for me in large part my experience of Derrida, even if he does not exhaust it.

Although I met Caputo before I went to Syracuse, I didn't come to know Caputo until I was finishing my doctoral work, as Winquist was dying and then after his death. Caputo became friends with Winquist, and Caputo offered me much more hospitality and friendship than I felt I deserved. So I am haunted by the ghost of Winquist, my teacher and mentor, and I also think of Winquist when I think about and read Caputo. Humans and their thoughts, ideas and impressions fold upon and into one another as they form multifaceted layers of experience that are accessible in memory.

Derrida has said that deconstruction was about death, and I think that one can say the same of theology. Or if not death, than at least ghosts. I am haunted by Winquist, Derrida, Caputo, and also by Altizer, Tillich, Barth, Luther, Calvin, Aquinas, Augustine, Paul and Jesus. Or Christianity, which is a spectral form of Judaism, and remains haunted by it. For me theological thinking is about being gripped by an existential passion that does not make sense, but we try nonetheless, sometimes through prayers and tears, to make it work. But it never works. Winquist tried to write a theology "that does not disappoint." He means here a realistic and credible theology that does not force us to imagine a supernatural being who will answer all our prayers and fulfill all of our wishes. And this is a great goal, but any and all published theology necessarily disappoints. This disappointment continues to mark us and to haunt us in all of our thinking and living.

Jack's faith is a doing, and his ability to connect with people outside of the ivory tower of the academy is extraordinary. I am somewhat secure in my intellectualizing, but I am haunted by the notion of people like Caputo, Peter Rollins and others who put this theology into practice. At the same time, I am encouraged that some aspects of both radical theology and French philosophy can have appeal to people in their lives beyond the academy.

In the wake of the events of September 11, 2001, and the subsequent American invasions of Afghanistan and Iraq, my friend Jeff Robbins, who was also a student of Winquist and came to be friends with Caputo, put his finger on some of our problems with postmodern theology as we understood it: it was insufficiently political in its radicality. In a chapter called "Terror and the Postmodern Condition" that he wrote for a book I edited, *Religion and Violence in a Secular World*, Robbins explained that postmodern theology never took Marx seriously in the same way that it did Nietzsche and Freud. He claims that "while the interests of the radical and postmodern theologians were characteristically broad and far-ranging, moving seamlessly from philosophy and theology to literature, psychoanalytic theory, art, and architecture, the political was marked by its absence." The explicit absence of political theorizing for radical and postmodern theology meant that it was unable to adequately address situations like the post-9/11 world.

In his essay, Robbins calls for a "radical political theology" that "puts both the political and the theological order in question, whereas what passes as so-called radical theology uses its theological critique in service of a prevailing, even if unseen and unquestioned, order." Robbins raises the question of political theology, which has become more and more important for contemporary philosophy and theology. The contemporary discussion of political theology goes back to the early twentieth century German jurist and legal scholar Carl Schmitt, who in a famous sentence from his book *Political Theology* says, "sovereign is who decides on the exception." So then the question becomes, who or what is sovereign, and in the wake of the breakdown of secularism and the return of religion to political, philosophical and cultural discussions, how does the sovereignty of God relate to sovereign political power? Does the sovereignty of the monarch simply replicate the sovereignty of God, and then what happens when you shift to a political form of democracy, and the people are considered sovereign? If sovereignty is a theological term that analyzes the power to decide on exceptional cases, what does that mean for the so-called return to religion, and the implication of religion and politics in the world today?

In my more recent work, I have tried respond to Robbins' critique and to sketch out a radical political theology that would not be conservative in either political or theological terms. I have tried to engage with important political and physical realities in the world, including scarcity of natural resources as well as global warming. There is a sense in which capitalism is running up against real limits to growth, which leads to the concentration of wealth and intensification of inequality. Here politics opens up to an ecology.

It is interesting how pervasive apocalyptic scenarios have become in our imagination, not just religious apocalypses but also secular ones. According to Elizabeth Kolbert, we are experiencing the sixth great extinction event in the history of life on earth. The difference between this extinction and the previous five, however, is that human activity is the primary cause of this one. It's not just global warming, but also over-population, over-development, resource depletion, loss of ecological habitat, and increase of ocean salinity. All of these crises converge and amplify each other due to feedback loops. To live is to die, in individual and species terms.

We live on the edge of life, and death. Life and death are not simply opposites—there is a profound asymmetry here—and we are always haunted by death, by the dead, including our own. The dead are all around us; they continue to inhabit us, even as we become them. Who are we? We are they, the dead, who haunt and animate us, whether we know it or not. Death is the end of life, and we devise ways to try to avoid or evade that. God is one way, but it does not work; we are always disappointed in one way or another.

We want to talk about God, the name of God, to invoke the ultimate source of meaning and value, the foundational ground of everything that exists. But this source or ground does not simply exist. It insists, and it insists itself into everything we do, with social, political, ecological, linguistic and theological effects. What it is, is literally undecidable. Derrida says that "the undecidable remains caught, lodged, as a ghost at least, but an essential ghost, in every event of decision." The essential ghost of every decision dislocates our certainty, our determinacy, and our identity.

This ghost is located in a cloud, the cloud of unknowing or indeterminacy that hovers over everything we do and every decision we make. As Catherine Keller states in her book Cloud of the Impossible, all we really know and have is our relations, but she claims that "traces of God will continue to inflect our relation to that pressing excess that comes within us and before us—even when it goes silent and unnamed." To attempt to give voice to God amidst the cloud is also to acknowledge the intrinsic negativity in every effort of theological thinking and writing. Theology caught up in the cloud is a ghosting theology, weakening the forces of certainty, dogmatism, sovereignty and violence.

What can we do? For what can we hope? In his posthumously published interview, Martin Heidegger famously declared, "only a god can save us." If that's true, then we are screwed, because God will not and cannot save us. We cannot save ourselves, at least not in terms of how we normally understand the word salvation. Salvation, however, is related to salve, as in a soothing ointment. We cannot save ourselves, but we can at least salve each other.

Salving is performing what Jesus called the Kingdom of God. Jesus was likely much more radical than we would like to admit, even if our historical reconstructions are themselves indeterminate. Jesus says to forgive our debtors, not our trespasses, or sins. This is literally about debt, being in debt and being enslaved to debt. Jubilee is the name for the impossible work of abolishing debts every fifty years. It exists today as an impossible event, even if the ancient Israelites were able to carry it out to some extent in the past. As Caputo writes in his essay, "comforting the sick and dying already is the year of the Jubilee, the life of God in the world, the Kingdom of God, with or without God."

Ghosts spook, but they can comfort as well, especially compared to many other monsters, including ourselves. To experience someone who comforts amid our pervasive sickness and death is to experience a ghost, perhaps. And to enact the Kingdom of God, with or without God. Radical theology continues to attest to this spectral possibility, even if it lacks the strength to actualize it in the world. That is what you, readers, have to do.

DENISE CASEY

ARTIST

EDUCATOR

EXPLORER

THE FOLLOWING ARE THE MASKS DENISE CASEY HAS BEEN KNOWN TO WEAR IN THE PUBLIC SPHERE:

spoken word artist, poet, singer/songwriter, mindfulness teacher, educator, Program Director of Modern Mindfulness. Denise currently lives as a resident at the Center for Mindful Learning (CML) in Burlington, VT. CML is a modern monastery that offers residents an opportunity to fuse their aspirations for making a difference in the world with deep mindfulness training.

HERE'S WHAT THIS CONTRIBUTOR WOULD SAY ABOUT HERSELF:

I am a student first and a teacher second. I collect and tell stories. I am a mover. I think in pictures and pray in songs. I listen to trees and write out loud. I travel far distances to meet amazing teachers that aren't behind a pulpit, but sitting in the seat next to me. I am a sister, daughter, niece, granddaughter, friend and lover. I never knew I had brothers until one day a man called me "sister." Mindfulness is the hardest thing I do and yet I teach it. I am well-versed in eating disorders, addiction and hiding. I am learning to tell the truth. I am not afraid to tell the truth to large audiences. I am afraid to take naps. I laugh loudly, love being read to and reading out loud. I am consistently amazed by the power and beauty of human voices, including my own.

In January 2015, I will debut my first original performance, 26 Letters: From Silence to Song, a theatrical piece that uses song, dance and spoken word to express the healing power of stories in our bodies. I am working on recording a second album to be released later this year.

who are you, they say
who
do you think
you are
who are you to believe you can do this
to believe you can take this step
to step beyond God
step beyond the frame from which we so fervently live
who are you
to demand the insistence of holy hours
the insistence of the unseen
the unheard of
the unknown
who are you to shed these layers
to touch the base of your breath
to lie still in chaos
who are you to let go of believing in Me
to follow uncertainty so certainly
who are you to step into this
who are you
who are you
who
are
you

i don't know how to do this, i beg
they keep saying i can't, I beg
it's all i hear,
all i hear
it is
ALL
I
HEAR

i don't know this step,
this place
these faces,
this language
this body
i don't know how
please
please
please

this, you say
this call
this string of violently uncertain moments
this, you say
step into this
you say

but there is nothing here
nothing to hold
no affirmation of faith
no safety of knowing
no words to show my sanity
no direction to leave my trace or prove my path
there is nothing
nothing

i am scared here
i don't know who i am here
there is no voice here
even silence disappears here
there is nothing
here

-----

alone

i watch my body move for the first time
stranger to these limbs
curious of these movements
sound blurs like an ocean i cannot touch
the water swims me in
i am safe
i am here

-----

empty rooms have never felt so full.

BRIAN MCLAREN

Author

Speaker

Networker

THE FOLLOWING ARE THE MASKS BRIAN MCLAREN HAS BEEN KNOWN TO WEAR IN THE PUBLIC SPHERE:

Author, speaker, activist, former pastor, blogger.

HERE'S WHAT THIS CONTRIBUTOR WOULD SAY ABOUT HIMSELF:

Brian D. McLaren is an author, speaker, networker, and activist. His dozen-plus books include *A New Kind of Christianity*, *A Generous Orthodoxy*, *Naked Spirituality*, and *Why Did Jesus, Moses, the Buddha, and Mohammed Cross the Road?* Brian and his wife, Grace, live in Florida and have four adult children and four grandchildren. He is an avid wildlife and outdoors enthusiast. His newest book, *We Make the Road by Walking*, offers an overview of the Bible and a (re)introduction to Christian faith.

Will It Preach?

I love and am delighted by everything I have read by Jack Caputo. Even times when something he writes makes me wince, I'm soon smiling again because of his wicked wit, disarming honesty, and radiant lucidity.

But because I was a pastor in a local church for over half of my life, and because much of my work today has to do with supporting pastors in their monumental, impossible, maddening, and immensely important vocation, I can't stop with simply enjoying Jack's work. I have to ask myself, "How will Jack's spooky, haunted message preach in a typical local church?"

Whether we're talking about St. Peter's Roman Catholic uptown, First Apostolic Fire-Baptized Full-Gospel Pentecostal Holiness Church downtown, Mt. Zion United Methodist over in the suburbs, or Placid Valley Community Bible Church out in the exurbs, when I ask myself that question, one answer comes to mind.

It won't.

Preach, that is. In a typical local church, that is. Because most people—myself included, much of the time—don't want a spook or a haunting.

We want a genii with wish-granting power. Jack actually acknowledges this, in a backhanded way, when he implies that many people think of God as "an infinite immaterial solution to finite material problems." Jack has the audacity to deny that this is what God is.

Which is exactly why Jack's message won't preach. It is finite material problems that most concern most of us most of the time, and the bigger and more cosmic the solution, the better.

We want a genii who gets us out of trouble and its twin, responsibility, not a spook who leads us smack into both.

We want to be able to rub the magic lamp of prayer, and PRESTO! We have what we want.

We want to be able to say the magic words of the creed (or the "sinner's prayer") and PRESTO! We are among the elite, the righteous, the saved and sanctified.

We want to face a confusing question or knotted-up issue, apply a quote from St. Augustine, St. Thomas Aquinas, or St. C. S. of Lewis, and PRESTO! Problem solved, question answered, case closed.

We want to pray, "Our Grandfather/Grandmother in heaven, hallowed be your name. May we be spoiled rotten through your generous blessings. May our will be done on earth as yours is in heaven. Give us today our daily cotton candy and higher-than-expected return on investment. Keep our sins manageable and help those who find us annoying to stop being so judgmental and just get used to it. Lead us not into character formation or social action, and set us free from the pressure of having to worry about anything beyond our own sweet happiness. For ours is the comfort, the convenience, and the savings, amen."

We don't want an "it"—even if it is hallowed by quotation marks. We want a He, appropriately capitalized and fully masculinized, a Patriarchal Protector of Top-Down Power, because that is the only refuge we can imagine from the Things That Scare Us.

Near the top of the list of Things That Scare Us is certainly this: uncertainty.

And that is why we prefer "He speaks" to "it spooks."

Jack says, we do not simply believe or disbelieve specters. We do not know what to believe. We are too uneasy to just believe them but we are too unnerved to suspend our disbelief. These apparitions are not realities but they are not simply illusions.

And we just roll our eyes. We have bills to pay,

votes to cast, diap ers to change, emails to answer, and must-see shows to watch. We cannot afford the luxury of "not simply believing or simply disbelieving." We demand certainty, and if not certainty, clarity, and if not clarity, brevity. We prefer "a state of not knowing what to believe" to last no longer than one thirty-minute episode.

And that is why we prefer exorcism and explaining to inspiriting or haunting.

In other words, if you can't give us the Rev. Billy Graham or Mother Angelica, then give us the Rev. Bill Maher or Father Richard Dawkins. We'd rather be certain theists or atheists than uncertain, haunted, spooked (a/ana)theists.

And that is why we prefer a God who either exists or doesn't exist to a God who insists. The former is more like a condition we can define, adjust to, and be done with. The latter is more like a vocation that won't stop calling us, waking us up in the night, like some (un)damned ghost.

The "we" I have been using, of course, is rhetorical, referring to "most people in a typical church." There are exceptions. In my best moments, I am among those exceptions.

In fact, I've been wondering lately if there are more exceptions than the rule.

In my own work, I am surprised how many times people write to me and say, "I must be the only person at my church who ever questions anything."

Though no complex mathematical algorithms were involved, based on my email inbox, I estimate that ten percent of the people in a typical church think they're they only one. Or maybe it's twenty percent. Or maybe in some churches it's eighty?

I remember talking to a young ex-fundamentalist once. He had rejected faith with the same certainty and clarity with which he had once held it. He was smart, but smart within a kind of mental straightjacket. Analysis without imagination, you might say. I remember once asking him to put on a pair of sunglasses. Then I gave him my sunglasses and asked him to close one eye and rotate the lens from my glasses ninety degrees in front of the other eye. As he did so, sight out of that open eye went to complete darkness. When the light was double-polarized, nothing got through.

I think a lot of people feel that they have only two options: a) uncritical polarized belief or b) critical double-polarized unbelief. Either they see unseen things one prescribed way, or they see nothing unseen at all.

I think Jack's haunting project is an invitation to take off any and all sunglasses. Doing so creates a kind of temporary blindness: dazzling light that is so bright and unfamiliar that one tears up and closes one's eyes in a kind of pain reflex. But if one keeps blinking through the tears, one's eyes get used to the light and one finally sees everything.

No, of course, that's not true at all.

If you take off all sunglasses, you get a splitting headache and go promptly to a dark room to lie down. There you begin reflecting on the difference between wearing sunglasses and not wearing them, and then you begin to realize that there may be frequencies of light that remain as invisible without sunglasses as other frequencies were with sunglasses. And at that moment, you lose a certain kind of innocence. You graduate, not from the pleasant rose tint of sunglasses to the certain, clear light of day...but rather to the flinching awareness that all seeing is filtered in some way. This seems disillusioning...but it is actually dis-disillusioning. It leaves you with a haunting sense that what you see isn't all there is to see. Which is kind of spooky.

Which is why, even though I say Jack's work won't preach for most people in a typical church (a "typical church" being, the more I think about it, a harder and harder thing to find)...it is exactly what needs to be preached for a growing number of people in a growing number of churches. For this tribe, Jack's words make perfect sense:

I am haunted by this voice. "God does not exist; God insists." That is what I hear day and night, running through my mind like an annoying jingle I cannot turn off. I wake up with a start in the middle of the night, bolt upright in my bed, pupils dilated, looking all around. I could swear there was a voice in the room. I distinctly heard it say, "You know it but you will not say it. God does not exist. God insists."

If lots of people I meet were to hear this, and they would want to shout "Amen!" and testify, the way a Pentecostal does when she hears someone speak in tongues. "Yes, another one is filled with the Spirit!" she shouts. "Hallelujah! Another child has come into the fullness of the blessing!"

In recent years as a preacher, I have come to see a passage in Philippians 2 as increasingly central, revolutionary, paradigm-shifting and script-shifting. It is one of the texts I ponder and preach as often as I can. It is the passage Jack paraphrases like this, "God, although in the form of God, did not think existence something to be exploited, but emptied himself of existence, and took the form of insistence, humbling himself and being content with weakness, with the weak force of a call which calls upon us in the form of a slave (Phil 2:6-8). The call rises up from the bodies of ta me onta, the nuisances and bodies of the world (I Cor. 1:1-2), the wretched of the earth, the homeless, the displaced and deported, the least among us, the slum dogs who never become millionaires."

This, I am coming to believe, is the real new element in the "new testament." It is the catalyst that makes "new creation" possible—even inevitable: it is the audacious claim that God is not in fact "a super-hero, an existing, super-existing Superbeing, swollen in an excess of existence and phallic power, who ultimately—He bides his time and plays His cards smartly—squares all accounts and orders all the disorders that break out down here in our disjointed time."

Rather, God is imaged audaciously in a crucified man, declared a criminal and heretic, elevated for all to see in weakness, enthroned on a torture-cross, naked and bleeding, appearing foolish and defeated by "the powers that be," utterly non-retaliatory to the last breath.

Of course that audacious image is troubling. Of course that audacious claim is disconcerting. Of course it wakes one up in the middle of the night, sweating and trembling and hearing voices. The fact that the Christian religion proclaims it routinely every single Sunday and sings of it incessantly 24/7 via religious broadcasts and nobody seems in the least troubled or disconcerted by it is prime evidence that the Christian religion by and large hasn't found the treasure hidden in its own field or the unique pearl at the bottom of its own bulging jewelry box. (Which is why, as Jack says, the new atheists "are not nearly as good at discrediting religion as is religion itself.")

If we were to dare to preach, as Jack does, that "God is not an infinite immaterial solution to finite material problems," that would be a big disappointment to most, or at least a lot of, people in our churches. But what would happen if we followed it up, as Jack does, with this, "God is the problem of which we are expected to be the solution. God is not the 'answer' but the question to which we are to be the response. God is not a necessary being but a suggestive possibility, an almost impossible one, of which we are to be the actualization. God is a spirit, a specter, a call, a plea, an exhortation made to us to transform insistence into existence."

If this were the case, then preaching would be...a call to make the name of God come true; it should be preached without promising celestial cash rewards, eternal credits for temporal works, without threatening punishment, and without promising timely supernatural interventions to step in just in time when it has all become too much for us; it's about Calvary, not the cavalry.

Jack's words bring to mind a scene in the movie The Color Purple which, pardon the phrase, haunts me. A black woman, Sofia, who has been viciously brutalized by white racism, is in a store, tasked with buying products for her white boss's shopping list. But she is so worn down, so beaten down, so utterly drained that she can't complete her task. A neighbor, Miss Celie, herself no stranger to the consequences of racism and violent abuse, comes in and sees Sophia's mental paralysis. Celie quickly takes the list and fills the basket with the needed items. Years later at a family meal in better times, Sophia recalls that day: "I want to thank you, Miss Celie, fo everything you done for me. I 'members that day in the store with Miss Millie—I's feelin' real down. I's feelin' mighty bad. And when I seed you —I know'd there is a God. I know'd there is a God."

The scene is powerful enough, but what haunts me is this question: what if no help came? What if Celie decided to mind her own business? Would God, in that case, in that situation, not have been in existence? Or, to put it a bit more mildly, would the existence of God in that situation, if it were not manifested in the kindness of a neighbor, have been unknowable?

Jack in his essay proposes that this kind of existence for God—an existence that only matters and only is believable if it is instantiated or incarnated in and through us—is the kind that resurrects when the old Super-Being's Super-Existence dies.

Oddly, that resurrection would not be so spectral if our own manifestation of it were not so inconsistent. But then again, maybe if we preached the insistence of God with more vigor and passion, it would appear more commonly than it does. Maybe, in fact, it is already more common than we realize, if only we had eyes to see.

Jack talks about replacing the old billboards and bumper stickers that say, "Jesus saves" with new ones that say, "Save Jesus." But perhaps, if we were to preach what Jack preaches, we might bring people to the point where they realize that this is how Jesus actually saves...by delivering us from the vision of God as Super-Being who swoops in like the cavalry, and by revealing to us, in weakness and nakedness and unarmed audacity, a vision of a God who shows up at Calvary. In words borrowed from St. Teresa, God does not show up unless we show up "in God's name."

Christ has no body on earth but ours, no hands or feet on earth but ours. Ours are the voices through which God speaks to the world with kindness. Ours are the hands through which God works. Ours are the feet on which God moves. Ours are the voices through which God speaks to this world with kindness. Through our touch, our smile, our listening ear, embodied in us, God is now living here. So let us go now, filled with the Spirit, into the world, with kindness.

In this way, when we show up "in God's name," God exists and is present in the way that matters most. And in this way, "the sheer insistence of God, the call to make the name of God come true, is disclosed."

If God had a choice...to exist in the Super-Being, Super-Existence, Swollen Phallic Power sort of way, or to insist in the way of Christ crucified, and if God chose the latter, what would that choice mean?

If we had the choice...to think of God in the former way, or in the latter way...or not to think of God at all, what would our choice mean?

Might presenting these kinds of questions and these kinds of choices to people be the epitome of good preaching in today's strange moment?

Pay no attention to the Man behind the Curtain - 2

KYLE A ROBERTS

Seeker
Theologian
Daddy

THE FOLLOWING ARE THE MASKS KYLE A. ROBERTS HAS BEEN KNOWN TO WEAR IN THE PUBLIC SPHERE:

Kyle A. Roberts is Associate Professor of Public and Missional Theology at United Theological Seminary of the Twin Cities in New Brighton, Minnesota. Roberts is a Kierkegaard scholar, having published essays on Kierkegaard's use of the Bible and his influence on modern theology. He has also published essays on existentialism, Pietism, and the connection between eschatology and spirituality. His recent book is Emerging Prophet: Kierkegaard and the Postmodern People of God (2013); he is currently co-authoring a theological commentary on the gospel of Matthew. Roberts is also the Robert Guelich Lecturer in Theology at Colonial Church, Edina, MN.

HERE'S WHAT THIS CONTRIBUTOR WOULD SAY ABOUT HIMSELF:

Roberts was raised in conservative evangelical Christianity, as a "preacher's kid" and "preacher's grandkid" of Southern Baptist pastors. He was theologically trained in conservative evangelical contexts, too—though he found himself always pushing toward the edges. He discovered Kierkegaard as a theological mentor and found spiritual life in existentialist theology. Roberts taught at an evangelical seminary for nine years before switching recently to United Seminary, where he is working out what it means to be a post-evangelical, public theologian. Like everyone else in his demographic, Roberts loves dark coffee, dark beer, and fantasy football, and he (with his wife, Sara) can occasionally be spotted at Minnesota Timberwolves' games, hoping against hope, during the dead of winter. Roberts has two kids (Ella, 4, Luke, 2). Sara, his wife of seven years, was an elementary educator before taking on the thankless job of full-time parent.

From Haunting to Shaking

Caputo's God is a ghostly specter, a lovely phantom—a cryptic, unheard call.

Thousands of miles removed from the "strong God" of classical theology's substance metaphysics (onto-theology), Caputo's God is a radical intensification of Luther's theology of the cross, Kierkegaard's paradoxical incognito, Barth's divine hiddenness, and Bonhoeffer's God hanging on the cross. Caputo's ghostly God is a close cousin to Dorothy Sölle's suffering God—the One who has no hands but ours. In this spooky essay, Caputo offers up an edifying discourse, a theo-poetical pep talk for our journey into the abyss of whatever-is-coming-after-postmodernity. Personally, reading this essay felt like sitting by the campfire getting tutored in the secrets of life from a wild-eyed, postmodern Socrates who sees ghosts everywhere.

Caputo's specter now haunts me, too. It's a lovely haunting. Those words fit together: God's lovely haunting. This sounds almost biblical. Was not Abraham haunted by the Specter as he was minding his business in Ur? Was not Samuel haunted by the Specter as he was lying down in the temple, trying to sleep? Was not Isaiah haunted by the Specter—and his six-winged, ghostly seraphs? Was not Jesus haunted by the Specter, sweating blood in the Garden? Was not Paul haunted by the Specter, struck to the ground—blinded—as if he'd seen a Ghost?

But in fairness, Caputo's Specter is not exactly the biblical God who "speaks" to people, telling them what to do, where to go, or whom to put to the sword. Caputo's Specter does not elect some over others, or promise vengeance against one's enemies, or conspire to overwhelm the evils of creation with a final battle—the outcome of which has been decided from eternity. Even so, Caputo's lovely Ghost haunts—as many ghosts do—on behalf of justice.

We've got all this terrific suffering and injustice here. We've got deadly structural racism, beheadings in the name of the "Strong God" of religion, American drones hovering above quiet, Middle Eastern skies (hovering, like unlovely ghosts), young girls and boys snatched from schools and sold into slavery, and viruses of death killing off entire villages. Where is this strong God, we ask? Where is the watcher on the tower? We wonder why He seems to have abandoned the post. Or perhaps there never was such a Tower—or such a God.

We pray: "Oh Lord, please end the suffering." "God, please stop such-and-such and so-and-so." But so often, so very often, the answer is silence.

If God has left the tower—or if God never was in the tower—if, instead, God is the Specter, the Ghost, the lovely haunting spirit, then this persistent, terrible suffering makes a little more sense. All this suffering makes a little more sense, even if it is not sensible, if God is not in "control" over the events of history. If God is not the "strong God" of classical metaphysics, then the typical way believers think and talk about God's providence (providentia, to "look after") is a relic worth discarding.

Yet, Caputo is no atheist; certainly not in a way that Richard Dawkins or Christopher Hitchens are atheists. Caputo's God still haunts. The Specter is still active. A God who insists—who lovingly calls out in the name of truth, justice, and peace—who invites response and who calls forth action. That is, the Specter calls us, you and me, to act on behalf of the name of God. Much depends here on us. There is great freedom and responsibility, here—but is it too much?

Who is going to act? Who is ready to fill up what is lacking in the sufferings of Christ (Col. 1:24)? This text has, for some time, struck me as profoundly perplexing. I don't think I've ever heard anyone preach about it. As Caputo notes, it's counter-evidence to the strong God, for whom we passively wait to set the world right again. For Caputo, Christ, this Messianic figure who haunts, is waiting for us to be the ghost's flesh-in-the-world, to continue the sufferings begun in that great spooking called the incarnation.

I actually like that thought. But it does haunt me; scares me, even. I don't want to suffer on behalf of Christ for the church and the world. But is this our calling? Isn't this what it means to be for justice and against injustice?

What if, in fact, God is more like Derrida's ghost of justice than Anselm's being-than-which-none-greater-could-possibly-be-conceived,

Aquinas' first cause, or Calvin's Orchestrator of history? I am haunted, in a good way, by the prospects of joining up with the ghost of justice, to spook the world in the name of justice and in the spirit of Jubilee. I'm intrigued by Caputo's weak, spectral God. This God is like the nagging woman in Jesus's parable who persists in her insistence. That is a fresh interpretive angle: What if the woman symbolizes God? The Ghost of justice nags at us, pleading for us to act on behalf of justice in an unjust world. Do something! Anything! Or maybe God is the Ghost of Christmas and we are Scrooge; if we don't get the message and change our ways, what might become of the world?

But I just can't shake the idea that something is missing here. As he wraps up, Caputo says that "everything depends" on three things: (1) the Spectrality of God, which prompts us, and "which expects a transformation of our lives"; (2) the Audacity of God, which "empties God of God without remainder into the promise of the world, daring to leave existence to us"; and (3) us, and in particular our "audacity to think" and our "audacity to hope in and for the coming of what we cannot see coming…" It's this third contingency that most disturbs me—that is most dissonant with the hope that I have for us to eventually come to peace with ourselves. I can't imagine it happening, if our ultimate hope, in the end, depends on us.

When I take a good, hard, look at the world, it's hard for me to disagree too much with Caputo's radical restructuring of the concept of God from the hardened, objective classical (male) God of onto-theology into a God who suffers with and on behalf of the world. Recasting theology in light of the cross, kenosis (emptying), and suffering seems to be the right theological move to make in the midst of this Crisis we call history. His theo-poetic pep talk fits the empirical situation we face—even if our situation is really nothing new: The every-day dangers of the world, the grand-scale threats of contemporary life, the existential knowledge of our impending death (whether tomorrow or many years hence), and the great threat of non-being. In the face of all this, a triumphalist theology, a "theology of glory," is deeply misplaced. As Kierkegaard so emphatically insists in Practice in Christianity, we dare not skip over the cross to jump to the resurrection. Even though it's happened to Jesus, it hasn't yet for us. We live in Holy Saturday, between the cross and the resurrection. Caputo's God is the God on the cross, the suffering, weak God, the Specter who haunts. But when push comes to shove, can this God really help?

Kierkegaard is right: we dare not skip the cross to get to resurrection. But still, the resurrection stands at the end of history as our ultimate hope. What seems more than a little bit missing in Caputo's spectral "hauntology" is the resurrection. If Paul is in any way right, the basis of human hope lies in the resurrection—that event in which God gave Jesus a body that could digest fish and conquer the specter of death. In the incarnation the spectral, ghostly God became a living, fleshy, person—a single individual in time. In the resurrection, that living, fleshy person overcomes the power of time itself. The hope in the resurrection is the basis (Paul's "first-fruits") for the anticipation of the end of the horror—if not the end of the haunting. The resurrection signals the joining of heaven and earth, the city of God and the city of creation, the fleshing of ghosts with bodies and the filling of barren lands with enough produce for everyone to have enough.

Caputo rightly deconstructs our desire for power and critiques the projection of our ambitions onto God's "being" (as only he can put it:God "is not a projection but a projectile headed straight for my head"). But in what do we put our hope, ultimately? Is the Specter finally—tragically, perhaps—constrained by the frailties of our collective human efforts?

I have to admit that in this sense the Specter frightens me a bit too much for my comfort. It haunts me in a good way by critiquing my self-indulgence and chastising my complacence: What if—what if I am waiting for the God of justice to make everything right when God is actually waiting for me to get off my lazy ass and do something? And yet, when I go through the litany of evils, historical and current, they are too much to bear if Caputo's third condition is unconditional—that the righting of wrongs depends on our efforts.

In the end, for me, hope is not hopeful enough without the subjective conviction that an Eschaton is on its way and that, as Moltmann put it, God is coming. Is this coming of God, this anticipated arrival of a Kingdom, at odds with the Spectral reality, the Insistence, the perhaps, of Caputo's hauntology? Does a Moltmannian eschatological theology run aground on the banks of the strong God of classical metaphysics? Does it imply or necessitate that the frightening freedom of human agency may finally be revoked to make way for justice? It seems that in the answer to these questions we find the line between Caputo's Specter and the crucified God who is coming toward us, from up ahead, to set things straight. And yet, perhaps a theology of the cross in the sphere of Caputo's hauntology can allow for an anticipation of an Eschaton in which evils are put down, suffering is overcome by good, and justice wins out over injustice. Perhaps it is precisely through the weakness of God that the Kingdom will arrive. If so, I wish I could hear more about how the horror ends in this hauntology.

If the Spook that spooks is something like the hidden God of Luther, the divine incognito of Kierkegaard, the God-on-the-cross of Bonhoeffer, the suffering God of Sölle, and the coming God of Moltmann, then I find the God who haunts us to be a lovely Ghost. I embrace an overcoming of onto-theology insofar as it creates a space in the here and now for this spooky ghost of justice. Of course, none of this is up to me. Nor is it up to Caputo (as he surely would agree).

I am aware of the inner anxiety at work when I say that I want to know the basis, the ultimate ground, for hope. What is the narrative that we can tell each other that will offer us reason to believe in this Specter on the strength of the absurd? Why should Abraham believe that God would restore the son of the promise? Why should the father and mother who have lost their daughter to the forces of ideological violence believe they would see her again—if not in this life then in the next? Why should the oppressed believe that justice would finally be done?

Yes, the ghost of justice lurks and haunts. But when will the Specter end its quiet, lovely, weak haunting and bring its paradoxical strength to bear on the world? Caputo's God is fascinating and provocative; a corrective to the ideologies of power masked in the language of orthodoxy, classical theology and assured theodicy. But in the face of our world's sorrows and injustices, don't we need a God who is not, in the end, constrained by the contingencies of creation (namely, constrained by us) but a God whose futurity will eventually catch up with our history and whose hiddenness is ultimately undone by a Presence that no longer haunts, but shakes up the world?

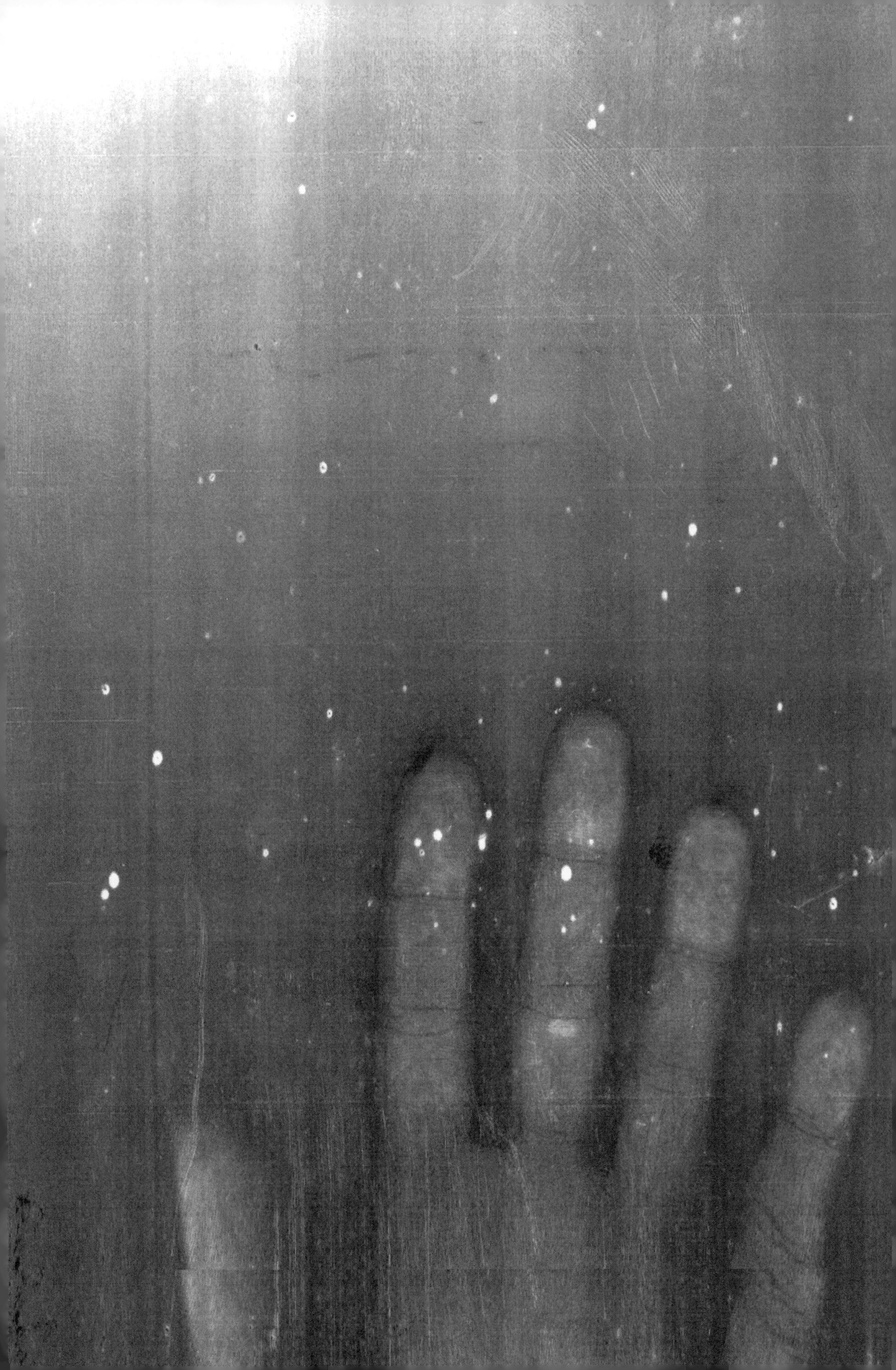

KELSEY SCHROEDER

ARTIST
DREAMER
CREATOR

THE FOLLOWING ARE THE MASKS KELSEY SCHROEDER HAS BEEN KNOWN TO WEAR IN THE PUBLIC SPHERE:

She is a graduate of Coe College in Cedar Rapids, Iowa with a degree in Fine Art Ceramics and French. Her work is featured in several galleries and includes a purchase by the Cedar Rapids Museum of Art for its permanent collection.

HERE'S WHAT THIS CONTRIBUTOR WOULD SAY ABOUT HERSELF:

I am an artist working out of my home, trying to create beauty in the world. I look to nature for inspiration for both my ceramic work and my painting, knowing that what I create is merely my musings on that which has already been made perfect. My hope is to eventually work full-time in my studio, but in the meantime I manage a bridal salon, which I also love. I currently live in Rapid City, SD, with my husband and look forward to the beginnings of our family at the start of the New Year.

Arrivants et Revenants

Inspired specifically by:

"So the present is exposed to the arrivants, to who or what is coming, as well as to revenants, those who are coming back. We live in messianic or spectral time, responsible to both the living and the dead, both the living and the still to come, to the whole community of saints. We live in the space between a memory and a promise."

ROSS PENNOCK

SONGWRITER

PERFORMATIVE

POET

WRITER

THE FOLLOWING ARE THE MASKS THAT ROSS PENNOCK (MILLER) HAS BEEN KNOWN TO WEAR IN THE PUBLIC SPHERE:

Hip-Hop & R&B recording artist and performer. Songwriter. Performative poetry writer and performer.

HERE'S WHAT THIS CONTRIBUTOR WOULD SAY ABOUT HIMSELF:

In the seventh grade I won a standardized writing contest by describing my fear of heights. Someone thought my thirteen-year-old self was entertaining, and I thought that was pretty rad. I don't remember what I wrote, but I remember deciding I would continue writing. Ten (or so) years later I'm still writing, but now more in the performative context. At the age of nineteen I discovered my passion for writing to a beat, and still songwrite now, at the ripe age of twenty-four. In the Spring of 2014 I released my debut full-length album independently entitled "Don't Stand Still." It's 14 tracks, 55 minutes, 4 music videos, 18 months of work and a tattoo to cap the experience. I intend to continue my journey of finding truth through words, in whatever rhythm inspires.

Eager Ears

Eager ears in times of weakness
Loose with words in times of strength

What's a life lived situational
Ode to principle, why the wait?

Paint a picture left so subjective
When the course of actions frame black and white

All the times that I've gained momentum
as the right direction turns out of sight

Race my mind until time is endless
All I'm open to calls relentless
Ease the pressure, I seek the pleasure
Repeat the measure 'til I get the message

Self discover my options limited
Make the most of it, case to case

Eager ears all too familiar
Guide these words in times of change

Wicked Lips

I acknowledge my piece in this chaos
I had you then pushed you away
You had me our distance in place
It was madness
You know in passing you knew too much
I know what happened, we hurt to touch
Earned the trust to burn it down
Like wicked lips just learned the sound
Of power over hopeful eyes
The sinking lows of Jaded times
I've seen your crazy open mine
To the idea I am from within
External world a sickly grin
That stabbed me deep and licked the blade
I forced it out kill the taste
Only death lives everlasting
Hope this breath fills every damn thing
That you think about
And trickles down all the ins and out
Of our imperfections
We love the answers but hate the questions
Our dust has settled this scripted ending
We played out my love

KATHARINE SARAH MOODY

T I R E D
A C A D E M I C
M O T H E R

T I R E D
A C A D E M I C
M O T H E R

T I R E D
A C A D E M I C
M O T H E R

T I R E D
A C A D E M I C
M O T H E R

T I R E D
A C A D E M I C
M O T H E R

T I R E D
A C A D E M I C
M O T H E R

THE FOLLOWING ARE THE MASKS THAT KATHARINE SARAH MOODY HAS BEEN KNOWN TO WEAR IN THE PUBLIC SPHERE:

An independent scholar working at the intersection of continental philosophy, radical theology and the empirical study of religion.

HERE'S WHAT THIS CONTRIBUTOR WOULD SAY ABOUT HERSELF:

Katharine has a PhD in Religious Studies from Lancaster University and is currently seeking funding to examine the political potential of religious practices that draw on radical theology and continental philosophy of religion. Her most recent post was Research Associate in the Department of Philosophy at the University of Liverpool, where she worked as part of the Philosophy and Religious Practices Research Network. She is the author of Radical Theology and Emerging Christianity: Deconstruction, Materialism and Religious Practices (Ashgate, forthcoming) and Post-Secular Theology and the Church: Truth, Tradition, Transformation (Wipf and Stock, forthcoming). She is also the co-editor (with Steven Shakespeare) of Intensities: Philosophy, Religion and the Affirmation of Life (Ashgate, 2012). She has been a presenter at Greenbelt Arts Festival (2012 and 2013) and is co-organiser (with Phil Snider) of the Subverting the Norm conference series, which brings philosophers, theologians and church practitioners together to explore the relationship between postmodern philosophies and church practices. Katharine lives with her husband Sim and their daughter Martha. She likes photography, Korean cinema, drumming, Winterreise, and Gillian Anderson.

Three responses

When I tell her I'm writing about ghosts, she tells me that after he died she cut The Reassurance out of a newspaper. She keeps it folded in his wallet in the drawer and says, 'because I had that dream'.

I never saw him dead, or after, fleshed out again. Instead, he was a spy, a spook on a secret mission. That was why she was learning Russian.

How like anyone to make themselves secure.

*   *   *

Life without Why

- 1 -

In the nineteenth century, Nietzsche observed that belief in the God of Christianity had become unbelievable. This was the century in which Feuerbach asserted that religion is the externalization, projection or objectification of humanity's most admirable qualities. His identification of anthropology as the secret of theology and his desire to transform lovers of God into lovers of humanity prepared the way for the materialist critique of religion as a form of false consciousness that alienates humanity from itself. For Marx, critique should therefore go further and address the material conditions and real distresses that require the consolations of religion as an illusory form of happiness. The criticism of the heavens – of theology and religion – should translate into the criticism of the earth – of law and politics. Religion replaces reality with ghosts; Criticism is exorcism.

This was also the century in which Freud linked his theory of dreams as the disguised fulfilment of suppressed wishes to a critique of religion as wish-fulfilment. The individual suffering the religious delusion escapes from the real world to a fantasy in which a better reality may be hallucinated instead. Religion is nothing more than a palliative. It relieves the symptoms of what Freud called our common unhappiness without curing this condition. Life is terminal and we find it necessary to employ certain consolatory cultural measures to endure it – principally, intoxication, enjoyment of art, sexual love, and religious belief. Religion is one of several auxiliary structures needed to support and strengthen the edifice of our existence. The world is unhomelike (James), the human condition is one of not-at-home-ness (Heidegger), and religion makes us feel at home in the unhomely (Freud). Religion gives us a ghost of a chance at life. The religious move is not that of recognising humanity's impotence in the face of the temporal and spatial vastness of the universe but that of insisting on humanity's importance, while the truly irreligious move is to hold to humanity's insignificance, to refuse to abdicate responsibility to a heavenly realm and to direct energy instead to the transformation of life on earth. It is to give up the ghost of religion.

- 2 -

Religion is nothing other than an illusion. Well, maybe. Perhaps, as Caputo likes to say. Peut-être. But maybe 'religion', s'ilyen a, is not just one thing. Maybe not just 'nothing more than…' Perhaps it is possible to think religion otherwise.

Deconstruction is a way of thinking about religion that is an exercise not in the exposure of illusion or the exorcism of ghosts but in the exhibition of what is going on in religion and the extension of a welcome: it sits down to listen for the spooks, to attend to the multiple, conflicting and still small voices of religion, if there is such a thing. It is a work of thought that offers hospitality to a haunting that is already happening in the historical religions.

Religions are unnerved by spectral phenomena that do not exist but that insist – the memory of undead revenants whose recall calls upon us to be responsible for their redemption and the promise of unanticipated arrivants whose advent asks for the reinvention of the horizons of hope and expectation with which we have grown accustomed and complacent. Our repertoire of religious narratives and images are part of the way in which this insistence finds a form of existence. And, as we learn to live in this spooky space between memory and promise, religions are themselves part of the way in which we respond to the call that is getting itself called in the ghostly figures of the past and of the future.

What is going on in religion? What is the 'it' that spooks it? Perhaps that was also Saint Augustine's question when he asked, what do I love when I love my God? What is it that I love when I love my God? What is the 'it' that I love that is going on in 'God'? What spooks 'God'?

It is not that there is a God that spooks – God does not exist; God insists. Nor that there are ghosts that haunt – ghosts do not exist; they insist. It is not that there are gods or ghosts that exist as entities but that what exists is beset by an unsettling insistence. This insistence, this 'it', disturbs names like 'God', to name just one divine name, and things like 'religion', if religion is just one thing.

Part of the uncomfortable uncanniness of an inexistent insistence is that it is impossible to identify who or what it is that spooks us or just what it is that this spectre expects of us. That makes us responsible for our response. There is nothing to ensure that everything will turn out well in the end. We are thrown back onto ourselves to assume responsibility for determining what is being called for and what is to be done in response. Hermeneutics goes all the way down, as Caputo also likes to say. And that is frightening. Because spectres expect the impossible. They do not expect us to follow a pre-determined programme of possibilities, but to do the impossible: to welcome the unwelcome, to love the unlovable, to hope against hope. To live life in response to spectres. To live a spectral life.

- 3 -

We feel ourselves to be immersed in the temporal infinity and spatial immensity of the universe, for the life of our planet or of our species has an eternal quality in relation to our own life span and we are so small, specks of stardust in the process of returning to stardust. But life is terminal. It is passing away. For Saint Paul, a present moment in life is passing away as a new time approaches. But for us it is life itself that is passing. (And life, ultimately, passed for Paul too, who taunted death, died and now lives on, surviving, as writers do, as a ghost.) The question of the time before the time of our cosmic death is the question of the meantime. And it is the question of life, for the time of the meantime is the time of life itself. How shall we live in the meantime-time between the Big Bang and our entropic dissipation?

For Derrida, learning to live is a matter of learning to live on. La vie est survie, he says. Life is survival. But survival is not about avoiding death or attaining life after death. Instead, survival is about life before death. It is living on, in the meantime, before death. It is an affirmation of life and an intensification of life: survival is the most intense life possible.

We are insignificant, unimportant, impotent and impermanent. But Caputo wonders whether such a nihilism of being-nothing is not without value. The transience of existence intensifies life. It is the mortality of life – in other words, life's impossibility – that is the very condition of its possibility. Life is im/possible. Our being-nothing-ness is a grace, but not quite a saving one, since this is a nihilism that confesses that we cannot be saved from death or kept safe from what Grace Jantzen calls the death-dealing structures of life. Life is life/death.

Learning to live would involve, Caputo suggests, not a flight from life, as in illusionary two-worlds theology, but learning to live 'as if not', as if we do not live, as if we who are living were dead or had not been born. Here we are, but we might not be here for much longer and we might just as easily never have been at all. It is all a chance of life that we have life and learning to live in the meantime-time before death should involve an appreciation of the time of life that has been given to us as a gift, a grace, by life. It should also involve recognising and reconciling ourselves to the way in which life is therefore lived for nothing.

Meister Eckhart said that life lives without a reason why, because it lives for itself. Life is not for anything. It is for nothing. Why does life live? Because it lives. And it lives for itself, not because of something other than or external to life itself. Life is for nothing, for no 'something else', but itself. It is for nothing else than more life – meaning not more life and no death, or more life in another world after death, but more life here and now, before death, and not just more life for me, but for others, which might mean giving my life for theirs.

If holding to our insignificance is an irreligious move, then religion in this account of life as being-(and being-for-)nothing must be a strange, irreligious religion. It must be a spectral 'religion' that spooks religion. It must be a religion that is for nothing but life, haunting religion as religion-for-something, religion as religion-for-something-else, transcending life, another life in another world. It must be a form of religion beyond illusion – realist and materialist rather than escapist. If palliative measures and auxiliary structures are necessary, then religion must console us but it must do so without a wishful flight from life. Such a religion would have to reconcile us to our being-nothing-ness and our being-for-nothing-ness. And it would do so by understanding itself to be but one of the ways we have to speak about that which spooks life, the memories and promises of life, the events of life and of more life that are the intensification of life.

* * *

She left church when her father died. She was seventeen. She went back when my father died. I was seven.

I heard the story of his death for the first time eight years later. When the lady that I saw at school because I hid in the toilets at lunchtime asked how he died, I said I didn't know; because we didn't want to see her tears, we didn't ask. And when they asked us, on the weekend away, to shout and scream at the world, at God, I couldn't do it.

We knelt, drawing, at picnic benches in the sun. Mowed grass and felt tip pens. Then we went around a corner with our pictures, pinned them to a wall and threw rocks at the objects of our anger. But I was not angry, I said.

* * *

Life without Us

- 1 -

In the nineteenth century, there was a fascination with folk legends, fairytales and the fantastic. This was the century in which superstition, spiritualism and supernaturalism – talk of spirits, séances and table-tappings – permeated Victorian society, and Victorian culture reflected both the folklore of the rural poor and urban underclasses and the 'salon lore' of the educated and elite classes. Spirit photography became novel amongst the latter, which used double exposure and other techniques and tricks to capture images of the dead amongst the living, most often their (paying) loved ones. Superstition and scepticism about ghosts, fairies and folk tales were often themselves represented in Victorian literature as divisions between high and popular culture, between class, education, race and religion. Under the influence of evolutionary theory, the Victorians projected their own psychological split between rational and magical thinking onto other cultures, and onto the lower orders of their own social and economic spheres – the poor, women, children, the mentally ill.

This was also a century of significant social and economic change. The move towards a principally industrial economy resulted in a shift in the perception of wealth, from the visible (gold and land, which constituted wealth) to the relatively invisible (paper money, which represented wealth). Financial success was itself created (and destroyed) in less tangible ways through the new economic activities of the Stock Exchange. Journalists and novelists writing about monetary matters therefore had to make visible the invisible. This concern is one shared by the ghost story, which is why ghosts can be read as economic entities. Marx's own use of Gothic language to express his critique of capitalism suggests the link between spectrality and economics. Under capitalism, the labour that produces commodities becomes spectral; while inanimate objects become alive with the life of the labour that produced them, subjectivity becomes alienated, disembodied, ghostly. Nineteenth-century ghost stories can be read as allegories exploring subjectivity and economics at a time when the negotiation of a new economic system required a re-negotiation of selfhood.

Andrew Smith suggests that the ghost story enables Dickens, for example, to identify and examine the ways in which subjectivity is formed within this new economy. When Marley's ghost drags along in death a chain of objects that were the products he forged in life, Dickens makes visible the invisible presence of labour within the process of commodity production. For Marx, the scepticism that arises from a change in the perception of such objects and the exposure of the occluded labour is the starting point for imagining socio-economic alternatives to capitalism. But, in A Christmas Carol (1843), while Scrooge certainly comes to see money differently, he merely becomes a better capitalist by returning his wealth to circulation through charitable giving. However, by 'The Signalman' (1866), Dickens has developed the ghost story as a political allegory in which we remain in the dark as to how to read or interpret the ghost. We do not know what the ghost means, what it is trying to say, or what it expects of us. Within the narrative, the answer to the question of what the ghost means is secondary to our ability to ask this question. Dickens uses the ghost story to engender the sort of attitude that might enable the kind of change in perception that is essential to alternative political thought and activity. Specters expect something. They expect something to change! Specters have high expectations; great expectations, Dickens might have said.

- 2 -

For Eugene Thacker, the genre of supernatural horror can be understood as an attempt to think the unthinkable, which is itself the horror of philosophy. What haunts horror is not death but life and our inability to think 'life'. A spectrum of spectral forms of life that live without life spooks this genre: the living dead, the undead, demonic possession of the living, and the ghosts of the deceased. As living contradictions – the zombie is an animated corpse, the vampire a decaying immortal, the demon a beastly spirit, and the phantasm makes material its immateriality by appearing as an apparition, affecting objects or manifesting itself through a medium – these figures expose the horror of the possibility of a form of life that is not that of the living.

Life-in-itself cannot be thought; any attempt to think it is only ever a thinking of life-for-us, the living, for it is us humans who undertake such a work of thought. As a way of thinking a form of life that exceeds the thought and the life of the living, horror exposes – and perhaps does so better than philosophy – the way in which life and the living are incommensurate. In horror, life is not precisely life-in-itself, since it is us, the living, who undertake works of horror, but life-without-us. It is a way of thinking about a form of life that is not our form of life. Horror is populated by things – The Monster, The Creature, The Thing, The Blob, the Unnameable and Unthinkable It – whose thingness is in question. There is, in horror, an 'it' that lives a form of life that is not that of living things. Life is more than that-by-which-the-living-is-living.

Why does life live? Because it lives. Why is there life? Because there is.

It lives. It Lives! There is

life.

But this 'it' and this 'there is' are impersonal forms, as in 'it rains'. As in it spooks, esspukt, and there is something spooky going on. It is not that there is something, an it – life – that is or that is there, spooking us. At the very moment I can say, this is what is spooking me, the spook disappears and is gone forever. If 'God, perhaps', then so too 'Life, perhaps'. It spooks, but life is not 'it' either. Rather, the 'there is' and the 'it' of life are conceptual horrors, haunting thought. Life disturbs the thought of life, our ability to think 'life'. We, the living, are spooked by a spectral form of life that is not that of living things or of human beings. This form of life does not exist; but perhaps it insists – as the spectral life of the dead and of the still to come that haunts the life of the living with a call to live in messianic or spectral time, responsible to both the living and the dead, both the living and the still to come.

- 3 -

Theology has historically been a work of thought about what Thacker would call the world-for-us. We give the world meaning, even when we construct it as a world without meaning; the world is a world for us either way: it is a world-with-meaning-for-us or a world-without-meaning-for-us. The supernatural horror genre enables us to think about the world-without-us, without reducing the world-in-itself to the world-for-us. Horror makes possible a work of thought about a form of life-without-us and life-without-being. As an enquiry into non-life and non-being, it is a way of thinking about that which is non-existent – non-anthropomorphic and even misanthropic life-without-us.

Does radical theology think life-as-if-we-did-not-live and life-without-why in such a way as to make possible a work of thought in which the world is its own meaning and in which life is not reduced to life-for-us? Life is not for us. It is for nothing but itself. And more life does not necessarily mean more life for us. Does radical theology make possible a style of thinking not only about a God who does not exist but about a form of spectral life that lives without us?

*   *   *

I was angry and not angry, and I knew it then and didn't know it then. And definitely could not say it, not to them and certainly not to her.

And I know it now and I don't know it now. And I still can't say it. She reads everything I write, so I hide behind others who say it and don't have to face my ghosts.

Because how could I ever rewrite The Reassurance? The Comforting and Consoling as The Unsettling and Unnerving? The Heartening as The Haunting?

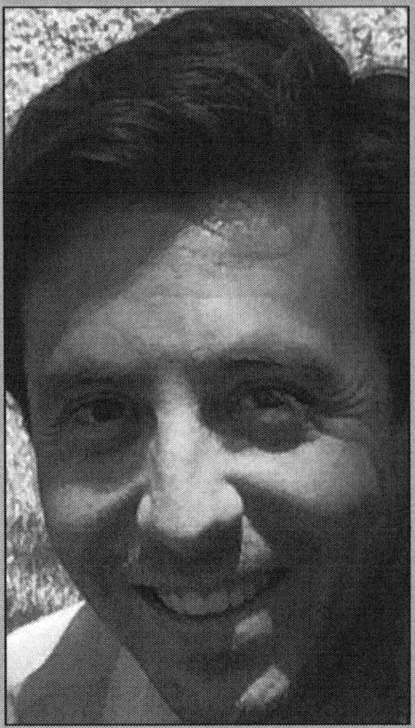

MIKE HERNANDEZ

Father

Nomad

Cartographer

THE FOLLOWING ARE THE MASKS GREGORY MICHAEL HERNANDEZ HAS BEEN KNOWN TO WEAR IN THE PUBLIC SPHERE:

Gregory Michael Hernandez goes by his middle name, shortened to "Mike". He is a visual artist living in Los Angeles, CA. Primarily working in painting, sculpture, photography, and site-specific installation, his projects can be viewed online at www.exilechild.com. The art of GMH is in numerous private collections, and is in the permanent collection of the Museum of Contemporary Art (MOCA), Los Angeles.

HERE'S WHAT THIS CONTRIBUTOR WOULD SAY ABOUT HIMSELF:

With much love and respect for my wife, I have grown to consider fatherhood the only pure relationships I will ever have. I chose my wife, and I could un-choose her, but my children feel like they were torn out of my rib cage. The relationship must be slightly one-sided however, because I don't feel duty-bound to my parents in the same way I feel bound to my children. My children will eventually drift off to their own life, but if I have one identity in this world, I am a father.

Exile Child is a working pseudonym that I chose fifteen years ago after traveling through Israel, the West Bank and Gaza. Exile Child is meant to describe someone who was born into a state of uprootedness. Never having personally set foot on the homeland, their identity is mediated to them. I began my quest into exile as a conceptual project in my early twenties. Then I deconstructed my faith, went through a divorce, and didn't speak to my extended family for two years. Exile became real and painful for me.

Now I wander and make a home. Through my landscape-based work I mark time, activate empty places, revisit haunts, and create systems for producing more work. I do these things under the umbrella term Mapping Perspective, which I use to describe my attempts to represent and translate the view from within outward, for myself and others. I think one key to reducing hostility in the world is the ability to see through somebody else's eyes, and stand on their ground.

Violence and the Sacred #1, Kill the Dead

81" x 37", acrylic paint on concrete doorframe, 2013-2014.

Art as metaphor? Too contrived. Art as vessel? Too porous to float. Art as provocation? Too weak to punch. Art as prophetic? Time will tell. All I know for sure is art as relic: something happened and art is the proof. Also, art as residue: why is this spot sticky or rubbed smooth? Also, art as a regenerating mechanism: something keeps getting produced and we can't pinpoint why or how. Also: art as a series of representations that keep compounding and refracting, layer upon layer, enchanting us further from the point of conception. Which is most interesting: the origin or the journey away?

There are ghosts alongside the freeways in Los Angeles. They form along the cracks between slabs or slide down the concrete faces, underneath overpasses and bridges. It doesn't often rain in L.A. but when it does, the ghosts are nourished. They appear as apparitions, arms outstretched, or perhaps they are just moldy fungal colonies. They silently breathe and eat the dust and exhaust. They are blind, but they absorb the vibrations of rolling weight and noise. I captured their photographic portrait from the opposite side of the urban river, and reproduced the printed images in paint on a concrete doorframe. I framed the painting and showed it in a gallery. Nobody bought it. I dragged the 200-pound representation into the desert wilderness. I made it stand there; naked and out of context, and I threw stones at it. I took its picture, dug its grave, pushed it in, buried it, and walked away. The real ghost is still underneath a bridge alongside the freeway, breathing and changing form. My painted image of the image is dead, and lies in an unmarked grave.

Kill the dead. Bury the future. Give birth to the past. Keep dividing in half for eternity. -GMH

CAMERON FREEMAN

p h a i l r o a s o d p h o e Passion x

p h a i l r o a s o d p h o e Passion r

THE FOLLOWING ARE THE MASKS CAMERON FREEMAN HAS BEEN KNOWN TO WEAR IN THE PUBLIC SPHERE:

Cameron Freeman completed his PhD in Philosophy from the Flinders University of South Australia (2007) and currently teaches at the University of South Australia in the School of Psychology, Social Work and Social Policy and the recently assembled Global Center for Advanced Studies within the Institute of Critical Theology.

As an inter-disciplinary researcher, Cameron has a wide range of research interests that focus on the intersection of continental philosophy and radical theology, and including New Testament and historical Jesus studies, the philosophy of religion, psychoanalysis, Eastern philosophy and the sciences of emergent complexity.

Cameron previously has worked in the United States as a content editor for Integral Life (Boulder/Denver) and in 2011 received funding to complete the Jesus Database Project (with John Dominic Crossan) as a researcher atthe Centre for Public and Contextual Theology, at Charles Sturt University. He has also been a PhD supervisor in the school of psychology at the University of Adelaide.

Cameron published his first book "Post-Metaphysics and the Paradoxical Teachings of Jesus" (Peter Lang, 2010) which one reviewer called "the most forward thinking work of theology in the 21st century" (Dierkes 2011) and is currently completing a new manuscriptoncritical-historical Jesus scholarship and radical theology, while applying for funding to continue research on the interface of science and religion.

HERE'S WHAT THIS CONTRIBUTOR WOULD SAY ABOUT HIMSELF:

Why so much eagerness to believe that you have a soul? Afraid of the emptiness within...? In this dreadful awakening to a groundless abyss, I secure for myself a phantoms chance of protection from It's monstrous anonymity with the blissful intoxication of an alcohol-fuelled stupor that yet again promises a fleeting fortification against the chaotic vulnerability of the It spooks, while the unreasonable delight that is sure to fade by the morning only masks the faceless abyss that inhabits this fractured soul But inheroic self-torment, my routine paraphernalia of suffering and escape invokes the burning question of what's at stake. So while this sleeping shadow gives no rest, I suffer in silence with the return of the repressed, and in manic derangement I live on the edge of the impossible decision Do I welcome this uninvited menace in out of the cold or again send It back to the groundless abyss from which it came? Does a random act of violence ever become a new form of kindness? While constantly overwhelmed and agitated and impulsive drive to minimize the threat of nothingness, I take pride in this my secret affliction, where I can see beneath surface and admit to myself the madness that saturates all my attempts at living a meaningful life. Have I gone totally insane in simply by pretending to have my shit together? Am I wasting my life with pseudo-solutions, the impossible pursuit of imaginary perfection and the art of consumer living? Or even worse, are my antagonistic tirades against the banality of wealth and power merely an effort to disguise my shame and humiliation about not having all the goods? But then again, what if all this questioning and self-doubt is not really a brutally honest response to this anonymous call that spooks me day and night, but a cowardly shirking of my responsibility to act now and change my life? Or who knows, maybe the truly crazy thing is that I'm not so crazy after all!

The haunting memory of Yeshua: The spectral call of an unknown God

A specter haunts Christianity, the specter of a charismatic 1st century Jew named Yeshua. Within this name simmers the dangerous memory of an itinerant Nazarene rabbiwho cameto us as one unknown, as one that we didn't see coming, like a thief in the night… And as we can now see looking back, in his brief but meteoric career he was as a teacher, a healer, and a trouble-maker for the established order of his day, as he walked the dusty roads of Galilee in a religious backwater of the Roman Empire - and set off a disturbing, wildly unpredictable chain of events…

The task to be undertaken here, then, is to see if we can let the fire that still burns within the name of this flesh and blood historical Yeshua begin to unsettle and to disturb the doctrinal formations of the Church which was founded in his name. For sometimes the only way to save a faith tradition is to violate it, and so here we shall let the spectral memory of this Yeshua haunt or spook the theological dogmas of a religious institution that has now all but exhausted its own innermost possibilities. That is, here we will re-activate the dangerous memory of this Yeshua and attempt to burn through the mythic supernaturalism of the Church and its increasingly incredulous faith confessions and rituals, by exposing the Christian tradition to the specter of the uncertain, ambiguous, indeterminate and strangely paradoxical event(s) that first called it into being…

While the specific focus here is on the historical flesh and blood Yeshua, there is also a moment of madness in our response to his provocative question to all who come after him:"Who do you say that I am?"For the somewhat unnerving case to be set out here is that the dangerous memory of this 1st century Jew intensifies and interrupts our existence with the haunting spectre of a call in which the "divine" and the "demonic" are inextricably intertwined. In other words, the reconstruction of the historical figure of Yeshua that is being introduced here, summons us with an anonymous call in which the promise of God and a menacing Monster mutually interpenetrate each other, without any final or proper resolution...

However, this haunting spectre, and the dangerous memory of this 1st century Jewish rabbi is to be welcomed. For in what follows, it will also be argued that as soon as we attempt to silence the spook or eliminate the un-decidable spectre of this Yeshua and his proclamation of the kingdom of God - by collapsing the irresolvable tension between God and a Monster into one of our favourite divine names, by way of all too familiar battle lines, then we prevent the event, i.e. we foreclose on the dangerous memory of Yeshua, eradicate the instant of faith - and ruin everything...

Josephus' Fragment

For many people today the scandalous memory of Yeshua as he walked the dusty roads of Galilee nearly two thousand years ago is almost completely lost in the fog of history. As a result, it has become increasingly plausible for modern skeptics, secular atheists and postmodern conspiracy theorists alike, to not simply deny the traditional Christian claims regarding the divinity of Christ, but to assert that this 1st century Nazarene rabbi never existed in the first place. According to theproponents of this view, Christianity is nothing more than an ancient myth wholly invented by the early Church communities, an elaborate fantasy-construction almost completely stolen from the pagan religions prior to it, and then propped up by centuries of theological propaganda.

However there is one precious piece of historical evidence for the actual flesh and blood existence of Yeshua, a textual fragment from outside the received New Testament canon that not only testifies to the historical existence of this 1st century charismatic Jew, but also details some strikingly specific features that disclose what this Yeshua was like as a flesh and blood historical figure. Josephus (c. 37 - c. 100), a Jewish historian for the Roman Empire and a vehement non-believer, in a much discussed passage called the Testimonium Flavianum, writes:

"About this time came Yeshua, a wise man, (if indeed it is appropriate to call him a man). For he was a performer of paradoxical feats (paradoxônergônpoiêtês) a teacher of people who accept the unusual with pleasure, and he won over many of the Jews and also many Greeks..."

While virtually all historians agree that this text has been tampered with by later Christian writers and apologists,a significant majority of scholars also accept the authenticity of this key sentence: "...a performer of paradoxical feats, a teacher of people who accept the unusual with pleasure." Now, if we may grant the historical authenticity of just this one fragment of Josephus' non-Christian testimony, then we find that Yeshua was a 1st century Jewish rabbi (teacher) who spoke in "paradoxônergônpoiêtês", i.e. Yeshua was a paradoxical poet.

The word paradox (paradoxôn), literally means "against (para) orthodoxy (doxa)"; and against orthodoxy basically means "heresy". From this rare vantage point external to both the theological embellishments of the first gospel authors and the political agendas of the early Christian communities, the historical Yeshua therefore looks be a heretical Jewish poet, one who spoke in shocking or mind-bending paradoxes, while attracting unconventional followers who joyfully received his unusual, counter-intuitive teachings.

Significantly, the "paradoxical poetics" of Yeshua, first evidenced here in a tiny fragment of Josephus' rare historical testimony, is also the key theme to be unpacked in the historical reconstruction of Yeshua that follows, where a poetics of paradox (paradoxônergônpoiêtês) lies dormant in the New Testament gospels, hidden in plain sight, as the haunting, spectral call that constitutes of Yeshua's central proclamation of the kingdom of God.

Yeshua and the Poetics of Paradox

"From the outside it may sound quietly or even stridently insane. One must risk entrance before one can experience its validity."

The basic presupposition of critical-historical scholarship on the figure of Yeshua over the last few hundred years is that the world-shattering impact of this 1st century Jew's brief public career was soon domesticated by the early Christian communities, who found the radical challenge of his life and teachings almost impossible to live with.The central task of historical reconstruction, then, is to dig beneath themythic and supernatural encrustations that were built up around Yeshua and then ossified in the developing streams of early Church traditions (e.g. the Virgin Birth, the 'only begotten' son of God, substitutionary atonement, the pre-existing Logos, the Second Coming, etc.) in order to re-activate the event that these traditions harbor, the dangerous memory of this Galilean sage prior to his subsequent inscription within the New Testament canon.

So contrary to much modern day skepticism about the historical reliability of the Christian gospels, the central claim here is that if we simply "suspend" the Church-sanctioned theologies and moral allegories that have only obfuscated the authentic teachings and earliest memory of the historical Yeshua, then we encounter the haunting memory of "poetic paradox" at the very heart of almost all of those parables that have been handed down to us in the gospel record.

Just as Josephus testified in the 1st century - with a fragment from outside the received tradition, there is a paradoxical poetics(paradoxônergônpoiêtês), or what we might also call a spectral ambiguity, within the deep structure of the vast majority of those parables that were first remembered, and then retold and finally written down for us in the synoptic gospels. And moreover, the significant claim here is that Yeshua's characteristic signature - or original voiceprint, is embedded within the narrative core of his most memorable parables.

So what would the parables of Yeshua look like if we extracted from them all subsequent Christian interpretation over the past two millennia, and let the event that simmers away within his proclamation of the Kingdom be unleashed in its first, disturbing, immediacy?

First of all, a poetics of radical paradox(the teaching strategy first attested to by Josephus), constitutes the deep structure of Yeshua's most universally recognizable parable, theGood Samaritan: for just as the agents of neighbourly love, i.e. the devout Pharisee & Levite priest, are exposed as morally and religiously bankrupt; the morally and religiously bankrupt, i.e. the half-caste Samaritan, is an agent of neighbourly love.

We again recognize the paradoxical shock of Yeshua's parables in the Prodigal Son, where the explosive event that simmers beneath the standard moral-allegorical interpretation of the Church traditions, erupts and breaks apart orthodox doctrinal formations: for where the younger wayward son, who is lost in rebellious exile from home, is saved with the father's homecoming feast, the older dutiful son, who is saved in righteous obedience to his father's home, is lost in rebellious exile from the homecoming feast.

With a paradoxical poetics of bi-polar reversals that slips through the grasp of our inherited structures of meaning-making, the parables of this itinerant Nazarene rupture the built-in assumptions and distinctions that constitute our established ways of seeing the world (saved/lost, dutiful/rebellious, etc.), as everyday expectations and are turned on their head in ways that are almost always shocking, offensive or atypical.

The explosive event buried beneath the conventional (moral-allegorical) interpretation of the parables is also discharged in the paradoxical poetics of the Vineyard Workers: for just as the privileged status of those who started work at day break is the source of their envy and their sense of injustice; the envy and injustice of those who started work just before sundown, is the occasion for their privileged status, (when both groups receive equal pay from the vineyard owner).

We can also begin to see how a spectral un-decidability informs the narrative structure of Yeshua's language-events. For the shattering reversals of these paradoxical parables also cut across and de-stabilize the entrenched distinction that is habitually made between insiders and outsiders (or the righteous and the sinners), in the Pharisee and Tax Collector: the self-righteous Pharisee, who is saved in as a Temple insider - is lost, just as the sinful Tax Collector, who is lost as a Temple outsider - is saved.

We can begin to see here how a spectral ambiguitythat refuses to let our standard binary oppositions settle into place is built into the structural dynamics of these parables. We can imagine that it's almost as if Yeshua's audience don't quite know what these parables really mean - they just know they don't like it. In the following parable of the Two Sons: the acceptance of the first son is a refusal to work in the field, and the refusal of the second son is an acceptance to go work in the field.

When it comes to the more pressing question here of how we are to live a spectral life, it is important to notice here that the simultaneous invitation/challenge of Yeshua's spectral call involves a certain degree of comfort in living with irresolvable paradox. We also encounter the irresolvable tension of Yeshua's paradoxical poetics in the Friend at Midnight, where: the refusal of a friend becomes the acceptance of stranger, while the persistence of a stranger is the faithfulness of a friend;and again In the Shrewd Manager, where: a shrewd business manager has condemned his employer as a fraud, as this fraud is praised by his employer as a shrewd business manager. And once again in the Unjust Judge we see: the refusal to back down of a fearless judge is a merciful delivery of justice, just as the merciful pleas of the widow for justice are a fearless refusal to back down.

These radical paradoxes can never be properly resolved in accordance with our conventional demands for objective certainty, we can only surrender to them, while accepting that this un-decidable, spectral ambiguity will always be there, and that these paradoxes are always decentering us, always putting us into question, while exposing us to the disruptive novelty of the event that is harbored in Yeshua's radical call for the coming of God's kingdom.

The parables are thoroughly spooked. And those who welcome this haunting call will also find themselves inwardly disturbed by Yeshua's strange paradoxes, which disrupt our quest for cognitive certainty with an 'aporetic anxiety' that interrupts our pre-given horizons of expectation. However, it is precisely this built-in un-decidability in the parables that sets up the necessary conditions for the decision of faith, where faith is born in the midst of ambiguity and contradiction, and takes place in a moment of madness that involves risk and uncertainty in the face of a seemingly impossible situation.

So rather than providing a pre-packaged set of moral maxims and ethical rules, or a program of procedures for admission into the Kingdom, these language-events disorient their hearer with a paradoxical turn in the expected storyline at its deepest level, in giving voice to the haunting spectre of "doubt against all security". That is, the paradoxical poetics of Yeshua's short stories put language under pressure and push us to the edge-of-chaos, where we encounter the limits of meaning and signification.

At the heart of Yeshua's Kingdom teachings we encounter a spectral call that questions, subverts and disturbs our taken for granted assumptions about reality. By inviting their hearer's to relinquish their quest for either a secure, stable meaning or some hoped for final reconciliation, the parables of Jesus (as poetic paradoxes), thereby enact a rupture that opens up a gap in our meaning-making systems. That is, the parables shatter the basic co-ordinates of our dominant cultural narratives or world-space, but not simply as a transitional moment or phase leading us to a new or higher dawn. Instead, we are exposed to a fundamental antagonism at the heart of things, without any proper resolution, which is itself a direct expression of the very meaning of the Kingdom. This means that we are called to embrace life in a world without stable, secure grounds or ultimate guarantees, in a permanent eschatological challenge that never settles into a stable or settled structure. And in this sense, as Altizer contends, the parables of this iconoclastic Jewish rabbi embody a deeper internal discord than the teachings of any other religious founder or tradition.

Simply put, the kingdom of God is a world with a void of meaning at its core. Or as Crossan states, "he who finds the meaning loses it, and he who loses the meaning finds it..."The basic message here, then, is that when we are busy saving our lives then we are in deep danger, and only if we are living dangerously do we have a chance of saving ourselves. By consistently deploying such radical paradoxes to de-typify the self-evident façade of the commonly accepted world, the parables of Yeshua also remind us that sometimes we have to violate our cherished traditions in order to save them, just as those who want to preserve their tired and worn out traditions usually end up destroying them…

And while we cannot cover the entire body of Yeshua's poetic paradoxes here (see note), it is also worth briefly pointing out that virtually all of the parables that have been handed down to us are populated by "immoral heroes" - rebellious sons, idle vineyard workers, corrupt managers, disaffected widows, strangers in the dead of the night, tax collectors, half-caste Samaritans, a list to which we could nowadays include: alcoholics, illegal immigrants, Muslims, whistle blowers, atheists, bulimics, drug addicts, false prophets, prostitutes, gays and lesbians, transvestites and terrorists...

Here we have demonstrated that a language of shocking paradox informs the very texture of Yeshua's central Kingdom message, it is now possible to release the event, to re-activate the dangerous memory of this 1st century Nazarene Jew as he lived and taught, before his haunting memory was spoiled by the later inscription of Yeshua into the Christian tradition proper. The simple but significant point here, then, is that the parables of Yeshua are so distinctive in their underlying structure, and so memorable in their paradoxical shock, that it is now clear that the earliest memory of Yeshua has indeed survived the historical process of oral and written transmission in the 1st century, with the original signature of this itinerant Nazarene Jew's historical voice-print still intact.

The Messianic Secret

We now turn to the gospel of Mark, the earliest and the most cryptic of the four gospels, and one of the most enigmatic themes in Mark's text, what's called the Messianic secret. The term 'Messianic secret' refers to a much repeated motif in Mark in which Yeshua continually refuses the temptation to provide others with knowledge of his identity. And briefly, the case to be made here is that the Messianic secret provides an unnerving, spectral insight into the historical Yeshua and his own self-understanding. For just as the un-decidability and ambiguity at the heart of the Yeshua' paradoxical poetics discloses the event that is contained in his preaching of the Kingdom, the haunting spectre of the Messianic secret in Mark—which also interrupts expectations and de-stabilizes fixed identities, uncovers a disturbing awareness into what is sheltered within the name of Yeshua, an unsettling insight that is also almost completely lost in the haze of history.

The figure of Yeshua is spooked in the Markan narrative, a text which haunts its reader from the outset with a shadowy, cloak and dagger feel, where

Yeshua comes to us as a solitary, restless and misunderstood stranger.From the beginning of his public ministry until his death on the Cross, his self-identity remains an impenetrable, anonymous and penumbral phenomenon. He silences those that call him the Messiah, he deliberately obscures his Kingdom message, and he gives instructions to those he heals not to make his healing-miracles public,and all the while his true nature is continually shrouded in the specter ofan elusive secrecy.

From the outset, the very first to proclaim that Yeshua is the 'son of God' were the demon possessed, and Yeshua immediately commands these tormented souls to be silent, "Whenever the evil spirits saw him, they fell down before him and cried out, 'You are the Son of God'. But he gave them strict orders not to tell who he was." In a strange paradox that spooks and haunts the earliest memory of the historical Yeshua, the first Christological statement in the historical development of Christianity therefore comes from the disturbing voice of those possessed by Satan. And rather than confirming their claims, this obscure Nazarene immediately tells them to be silent and then moves on to another town before local townsfolk can attempt to turn him into a prophet to be worshiped, a decision that evoked vociferous public debate about the identity of this singularly enigmatic figure.

A further intimation of the Messianic secret can again be witnessed in Yeshua's use of parables as his preferred teaching method. Most people think that Yeshua spoke in parables to make it easier for people to understand his message about the Kingdom. However, in this strange passage from Mark (seen also in Matthew), he comes out in the open and says that he does not expect everyone to make sense of what he is saying to them.

When he was alone, the Twelve and the others around him asked him about the parables. Yeshua told them, "The Secret of the Kingdom of God has been given to you. But to those on the outside everything is said in parables, so that, 'They may be ever seeing but never perceiving, and ever hearing but never understanding; otherwise they might turn and be forgiven!'"

In this passage, Yeshua claims that his public practice of speaking in parables was strategy intended to spook his audience, by deliberately obstructing their hearer's attempts to attach a stable meaning to his teachings. The "secrets of the Kingdom" have therefore been given to those who are troubled and disorientated by Yeshua's paradoxical poetics. It is those who are thrown off center, those who "know that they do not know" and therefore aghast with expectation that are in on the secret, while those who "cannot see that they cannot see", those who are prone to either say "I've got it" - or to shrug their shoulders in indifference, that remain unchanged by his Kingdom message. And so, in precisely the same way that Yeshua refuses to disclose his own identity or self-understanding, while telling anyone who claims that he is the Messiah to basically "shut up", his parables also resist any common sense understanding by defying his audience's background expectations, and resisting the hearers attempts to reach the firm ground of cognitive certainty.

Later in the Markan text, as Yeshua's earthly mission moves towards its last week in Jerusalem, he takes his three closest disciples away from the encroaching crowds and asks them the question that cuts the heart of the secret that surrounds his self-understanding: “Who do you say that I am?” In the early Markan account of this dialogue, as soon as Peter confesses “you are the Christ”, Yeshua rebukes him, basically telling him that he has it dead wrong - and then commands him to remain silent, just as he did earlierwith the demon possessed who made similar messianic claims about him. In other words, in the early bedrock of the Gospel traditions Yeshua did not ask his followers to believe he was the Messiah (or Christ) and when they did make this claim he opposed them directly and commanded them to remain silent.

Immediately after insisting on his disciple’s silence regarding who they think he is, in another jarring announcement, Yeshua then explains to his inner circle of male disciples that he is about to go to Jerusalem to suffer and die. As soon as the unbelieving Peter attempts to deter him from his inevitable death, he receives another severe rebuke from Yeshua who now says “Get behind me Satan!”, and he says this to the one who just called him ‘the Christ’!

A Spectral Messiah?

Neither a member of the Jewish religious hierarchy, nor a revolutionary zealot calling for violent insurrection, neither an otherworldly ascetic like John the Baptist, nor a learned reformer of public morality like the Pharisees, Yeshua is an elusive and spectral figure who always slips away from our neat and tidy categories and continually resists our attempts to possess or seize control of him. And so in view of this spectral anonymity, the burning question to be asked here, then, is: what if the Messianic secret in Mark originated in the life-situation of Yeshua himself, and is in essence both historically authentic and more faithful to Yeshua’s own self-understanding than the later, the post-Easter inventions of his followers? In other words, we can here propose the following: the Messianic secret stems from a haunting, but very real early memory of the historical Yeshua, and reminds us that - just like any other flesh and blood human being who responds to the spectre of an unheard call, this Yeshua was a Secret not just to others, but also to himself!

If we can grant that this elusive Nazarene was himself spooked by an anonymous, indeterminate or spectral call, would this not also enable us to see, perhaps for the first time,exactly why he consistently refused the securities and certainties of fixed identities and proper names? And in this sense, are we not better off simply suspending these all too familiar divine names (such as ‘Christ’, ‘Son of God’ and ‘Logos made flesh’), which almost all contemporary scholars agree to be post-Easter inventions of Yeshua’s followers that were then projected back onto his public ministry?

That is, Yeshua expressed his central Kingdom message through the spectral un-decidabiity of poetic paradox in calling us to relinquish our compulsive grip on those inherited absolutes of habit, custom and law and embrace the spectral ambiguity of a world with no firm or unshakable ground. In the same way then, perhaps Yeshua refused to be identified with any Messianic claims because these divine names and titles only obstruct the very message he was trying to embody and enact? We therefore remain faithful to Yeshua by suspending the stability and security of those divine names that have been built up around him, for these predetermined titles only silence the spook, and foreclose on the anonymous spectral call, thereby preventingthe dangerous and dizzying risk/promise of the event that simmers within the haunting memory of this itinerant Nazarene and the coming of his un-kingly Kingdom. In other words, when it comes to the question of Yeshua's self-understanding, the big difference, it seems to me, is whether we can respond to the spectral call of an unknown Messiah, without being scared?

The Death of a god-forsaken God

The radical dawn of a spectral life is born right here at the Crucifixion - at this point of bleakness and abandonment where our highest aspirations are shattered before the impossible passion of a god-forsaken God. It is precisely here, where innocent victims of the powers that be faces the impossibility of an escape from his unbearable suffering, and is thrown mercilessly into the meaningless abyss... it is here where we arespooked to the core by the sheer contingency of life, haunted by a spectral un-decidability that goes all the way down, and directly exposed to the senseless nightmare of a world that neither cares or knows that we are here... It is right here, that the secret seeds of a spectral life are sown.

At three o'clock Yeshua cried out with a loud voice, "Eloi, Eloi, lemasabachthani?" which means, "My God, my God, why have you forsaken me?"

Previously in Mark's narrative only the demon possessed "cried out in a loud voice", indicating that in his final moments Yeshua also suffered from demon possession, dying in an extreme state of tormenting madness. Overwhelmed with the shocking failure of his life's mission and suffering to the point of manic derangement, the shocking irony here is that Yeshua ends his life with the same desperate cry of those that he once commanded to be silent for claiming that he was the Son of God…Also called the 'howl of dereliction', what we see here is a visceral response from the depths of human suffering that something is horribly wrong with the world, a tormented cry of utter abandonment, as Yeshua, in his final moments, becomes a god-forsaken atheist and dies with the demonic howl of a madman possessed….

And in a final disturbing turn, it was the Roman centurion at the foot of the Cross (probably the very same guard that had hammered the nails into Yeshua's tortured flesh), who first confessed that "truly this man was the son of God". Throughout his entire public career it was only the diabolical figures of the demon possessed and Yeshua's Roman executioner who ever claimed he was the son of God. From beginning to end Yeshua's messianic identity was spooked, shrouded in a dark ring of spectral ambiguity, where the divine and the demonic are inextricably intertwined within the haunting memory of an unknown call...

The Resurrection: a Case of Mistaken Identity

With a spectral quality not dis-similar to the paradoxical poetics of Yeshua's parables, the resurrection stories in the gospels are abrupt, ambiguous, unsettling and vivid. The specter of the resurrection appearances is also most obvious in the strange but consistent pattern of "mistaken identity" in the resurrection stories: the risen Yeshua is not at first recognized, and then as soon as he is identified in his resurrection body, he again slips away or disappears from view.

We begin see this basic pattern in the short ending of Mark. The three women first apprehend the reality of Yeshua's resurrection by coming upon an empty tomb and noticing he is not there... And then after the women experience a brief angelic vision the story abruptly ends: "They said nothing to anybody because they were afraid". We are left speech-less, there is a spectral un-decidability in the earliest accounts of the resurrection, where the initial sense that Yeshua has been raised from the dead is intertwined with an absence or incompleteness, and where paradoxically, the first Easter announcement takes on the form of a terrified silence of three women in flight from an empty burial site.

Then, on the road to Emmaus in Luke's gospel, Yeshua walks with two of his shattered followers as they mourn his brutal execution. They do not recognize him. This strange traveler then explains who the Messiah really was with a secret reading of the Jewish Scripture. Following this, as he joins them in breaking bread over table fellowship, they instantly recognize this itinerant stranger as the resurrected Yeshua, the promise of a new birth, and just as suddenly disappears from view.

And then again, when a forlorn group of disciples come back empty handed from an all-night fishing trip they do not see that the stranger waiting on the shoreline is Yeshua. The anonymous bystander then tells them to cast their nets out to sea once more, they become suddenly full of fish, and the disciples immediately recognized that this man is indeed their executed Nazarene leader. Then, in a return his previous anonymity, while sharing a meal together, no one dares to ask him who he really is...

As a fragile and ever-elusive spook that continually interrupts our expectations and then slips away again, the post-Easter resurrection appearances are impossible to grasp and constantly vulnerable misperception. In their earliest expression, the resurrection appearances provide us with a "fluctuating, uncertain, undecidable,para-being of a specter, which leaves everything to us, which calls upon us to respond", as they haunt us by keeping open the boundary between life and death, presence and absence, body and soul, proclamation and silence, and then slip away again just as we think we finally have a handle on it all.

The Spectral Call of an Unknown God

Yeshua comes to us as one unknown. He arrives on the scene as an unfathomable spectre, as an outlandish intrusion into our safe and settled ways, as one who slips through the cracks in our predictable common sense world in a shocking display of scandalous proportions. Yeshua is simply not the Messiah that we want or expect... Nonetheless, overcome by an unsettling ambiguity and exposed to the instability and transformability of our lives, we are to live with his enigmatic question "who do you say that I am?" without the security of proper names, so that our response to his spectral call is entirely self-grounding, where we embrace the utter contingency of our own being, having relinquished the futile quest of having it confirmed from the outside.

We are on the receiving end of an address, a simultaneous invitation/challenge, and this unknown, spectral Yeshua demands our response. This means, as Jack Caputo puts it: that Yeshua (i.e. Jesus) doesn't save us - we are to save Yeshua, which means that we are responsible for making the event, the paradoxical madness of the Kingdom, happen in the world. The name (of) "Yeshua" is the name of a call to which we are the response, which means that Yeshua is not the "answer" to a question but a question to which we are the answer, and we are to answer this question with our very lives...

A spectral life is marked by paradox, by an unknowable, un-decidable, unanswerable question that continually spooks our illusions of security and keeps the future open by resisting the temptation to keep things safe and settled with easy answers that are again within our grasp. In a spectral life, there is no safe space. We are exposed to the trembling in things, we live in a world that is spooked all the way down, and it is precisely this lack of secure and stable grounds that is the very condition of possibility of faith, hope and love...

It's only the demon possessed cry out that Yeshua is the son of God, just as this crucified Yeshua cries out like one demon possessed. In other words, our standard oppositions are not reducible to one or the other, for as soon as we collapse the undecidable tension between any of our favourite twosomes, then we prevent the event that is harboured in his name. In other words, just as we saw with the poetic paradoxes of Yeshua, when we resolve the paradox into a stable identity and make everything turn on a clear-cut distinction between God and a Monster, or the Divine and the Demonic, then we ruin everything. No one has the master key to let others in or out of the Kingdom. For the moment we disambiguate the saint and the heretic, the messiah and the false prophet, the sacred and the obscene, we cover over the event still simmering within the name of Yeshua, and that is the foreclosure of faith, the end of hope and an obstacle in the way of love!

And isn't this precisely what Yeshua was trying to get us to see all along, in his paradoxical parables, his refusal to disclose his true identity by way of a proper name, in the crucifixion of a god-less God, and in the elusive, fragile,undecidable specter of his resurrection? We are called to live with an unanswerable question, and it's a question that we cannot escape. In our response to the dangerous memory of this charismatic Jew, are we responding to the voice of God or a diabolical Madman? For when the boundaries between Christ and Satan collapse, and when there is no way of telling a terrorist from a freedom fighter, a democratically elected leader from a fanatical tyrant, a civilized and peace-loving nation from the cultural decadence of consumer zombies, an illegal bombing from a just war, then we are in a spectral space, and confronted with a void of meaning that eludes all our programs of mastery...

Do we have faith in our deepest moments of doubt, or doubt in our deepest moments of faith? Is our passion for life now without any deeper meaning or is our passion for meaning now without any deeper life? Is it our love of power that leads us to fear how vulnerable we are, or the power of vulnerability that leads us to fear how lovable we are? Are our secret lovers really our greatest enemies or are our secret enemies really our greatest lovers? Are we exposed to the depths of despair when we embrace an inexhaustible hope or are we exposed to an inexhaustible hope when we embrace the depths of despair?

To live a spectral life means we are to live with paradox. It means to respond to an event in which these two opposing poles cease to contradict one another but join together, inextricably intertwined, to form an altogether new horizon, an altogether different order of truth, in a devastating but obstinate refusal to disambiguate the unspeakable trauma of existence from the irrevocable promise of justice and mercy...

Untitled

Micah Purnell

JOHN HARDT

A LETTER TO MYSELF ON THE OCCURRENCE OF SIGNING FOR A STUDENT LOAN.

To Whom It May Concern,

Do you remember me? We haven't met. But we know one another very well. We have been through it, and we will continue to live it. Again. And again. It will never leave. It will never arrive. That piece of paper you are about to sign? It doesn't do what you think it's supposed to do.

I know you have no reason to believe me. I could give you all the back story. But you still wouldn't believe me. And if I told you about the next two decades, you wouldn't believe it either. Because right now you believe the lie. And the lie looks good. The lie is safe. The lie is what we have always been told and what we will continue to be told.

This, plus this, equals that. Work hard. Get good grades. Go to college. Get a good job. Follow the rules. Just look at it. It's all there.

But why am I bothering? Because we are bothering. Now and still. And ever. "You can't put a price on a good education."You hear it, so I've heard it. Bullshit. We will see the price tag once a month. Every mother fucking time we log on to that mother fucking website. We will feel it all month. Every month. You can't fathom that kind of money because it's not real. Not yet. Not ever.

What's a website? Ya, you'll see that too. But you're getting ahead of yourself.

As we do.

See, the thing is, we will still believe. That "if I just..."feeling never goes away. And it only makes it worse. It's good for a daydream now and again. I know that you know what I am talking about. It's no different than those hours playing in the woods behind the house. Dreaming of being anywhere but where we were.

Are.

Will be.

Imagining a different life.

Which is okay, when you're a kid. Except it sets us up for all kinds of pain. All kinds.

For starters, women are gonna trip you up. Not intentionally. And I'm not talking about the magic power these mysterious shapes have over our ill equipped notions of romanticism. We have no one to blame but our own conviction that the right one will make us happy. There is a reason romantics are hopeless.

No one makes you happy.

Well, actually, a dog will make you happy. Because a dog gets it. And when you have to decide between things and money and food and bills. He'll understand.

The smaller portions. The time away. He feels it. And he'll still love you. And it helps.

A bit.

Mostly, though, we are responsible for our own happiness. Mostly. And we will work on that one. Now and still. And ever.
But that piece of paper? It's not it. All the things it promises will never happen. All of the things we were told it promised will never happen. All of the things we have imagined it will do will never happen. Do you get it?

Okay, let's bring it closer to home.

Our dad told us we had to go to college. It was the best way to "get ahead." Ahead of what, we should have asked.

We never ask.

And now we always ask.

But we listened. We believed. We followed. We chased our father's dream. An American Dream to be sure. But what you don't know is that he gets lost. He's already lost. He's still lost. Which may be why he's selling the lie. Misery loves company. I don't know. He chases trains and sunsets. We chase lies. Because getting lost is all we can do. It's a numbing form of the daydream. It fits into an expectation that makes it okay to be away from the reality of the situation. Because no one can really see it. Just us.

A little closer?

We love Christmas. Christmas will be the worst. All those warm, fuzzy feelings. Always hoping for Christmas morning. Trying to recreate an idea that doesn't exist. Maybe never existed. Maybe always exists.

Year after year.

That's the trouble with nostalgia. It's always there. So, avoid it. Whenever possible. It creeps in and weakens our immunity to the lie. Nostalgia for us walks a fine line with guilt. And when it crosses, we're fucked. And our heart and mind check out. We're lost.

Closer still?

The art. Our art. And that expectation that our art will rescue us. Because I know that you know you will "make it."Everyone tells us. Everyone loves what we do. Or so we believe. And it comes so damn easy. Easy with a lingering expectation. And it is in the art we can stay lost. It frees us from regret. From guilt. From reality. From past and present. And future. But if it's going to work.

Stop. You must live into the art of the moment.

Do you see it? Yes, we do.

Sign now and you will forever be chasing the expectations of both yourself and another. Walk away and a great adventure awaits. Or perhaps it doesn't. Maybe it's just another version of our same self. But we will never know. Whenever we try to do something we will always be haunted by whatever we think we have left behind. And we are restless by the spectre of what is to come. Or so I've heard.

Have I convinced you yet? Of course, not. Still, run. Run far and fast. Being is unhinged by time. And all we have is this moment.

Most Sincerely,

You

ERIN NICHOLE

mystic monkette

monstrous

THE FOLLOWING ARE THE MASKS THAT ERIN NICHOLE HAS BEEN KNOWN TO WEAR IN THE PUBLIC SPHERE:

Campus pastor, conference planner, collaborative performer, circle practicer, container preparer.

HERE'S WHAT THIS CONTRIBUTOR WOULD SAY ABOUT HERSELF:

The current experience I have of life feels deeply dense and beautifully bright. It seems I continue to find that the more I learn of life, love, and humanity — the more there is to learn.

Often when we share the meaning we're making it feels like trying to describe the indescribable...I suppose that may be part of why I believe in attempting to listen past the words and in encountering what we might if we create places for what's being conveyed in the spaces between.

The Space between a Memory and a Promise

"I identify myself in language, but only by losing myself in it like an object."

~Jacques Lacan

I have read and re-read (and then re-read again) Jack's chapter. And I am of the opinion that it's genuinely good stuff—it inspires and invites and dares and declares.

That having been said, it has proven less than simple for me to evoke a written response (and sadly I am not particularly artistically endowed). Best as I can tell, this great exertion has had more to do with the "written" part than it has the "response" part.

Maybe it's because of the insufficiency of language…or the way that each time I allow a word to attempt to contain a meaning, the two remind me of how a child lathered in liquid soap glides ever so quickly across the surface of a wet slip-in-slide on a bright summer day—there's contact made (to be sure), but it's often not a lasting connection.

Maybe it's because of the seemingly impractical task of concrete communication taking place… or the way that you and I may or may not (likely) share a comparable life experience or for that matter a similar locution with the words we choose that would lend itself towards our mutual understanding.

Or maybe it's because of the "spookiness" of the topic at hand…or the way that encountering specters can encourage silence—and the unsaying of words.
Yet no matter the soil where this struggle sprung seed, words are after all what (a wish?) we wield.

So…
How to proclaim the year of Jubilee even though it never comes?...How to lead a spectral life?...How to be the ones the dead ones were waiting for…How to know without knowledge and to dance without music…How to bear witness to a call…How to make our lives into a work of truth…How to save Jesus…How to live lives of dangerous and daring hope?...

How to live in the space between a memory and a promise?

Jack's questions (or other semantically similar versions of them) have kept me company through the years. They've both haunted and hallowed the halls of the Christianity I continue to expand within. For me, they are questions of

BE-ing,

and of LIFE-ing,

and of EXPRESS-ing.

BE-ing

to exist, to become present in the now

There is a quote by Thomas Merton which (minus the "he's") goes something like this: "Every moment and every event in every person's life plants something in their soul." I suspect the truth in this quote will continue to echo its way out and back into the threads which weave together what I might call my soul. And in an effort to share some of what has been planted there I submit to you that somewhere along the way in this "faith journey" I had everything fall to pieces….my beliefs began to bleed beyond the boundaries a bit, and my capacity for contradiction couldn't keep pace (I do not posit this to be a unique phenomenon). When the so-called smoke cleared, the new story I tried on was one which acknowledged my stupidity for having committed so much to something so silly as a God come to earth to save us from hell. This "new story outfit" was one which was filled with suspicion and scoffing and an ever increasing existential undertow. It had long, dark sleeves to help me feel truly seceded, and I found that the pants were a little bit snug as a result of my no longer concealed (though probably still ridiculously rejected) internal embarrassment. It had holes in the socks to acknowledge instability and impermanence, and of course the collar was popped (up!) to remind me of my freshly discovered lack of a need of belief in a deity. I wore this new story outfit every day—and explored the mixing and matching of many accessories—for about half a year.

Then something unexpected happened.

The short of it is that on my kitchen counter I encountered a real live Spook. Perhaps even the same-yet-entirely-different Spook which has been spooking me for as long as I can remember…just as Jack proposes, "God" seems to me as the most undead of all. It's difficult to describe, but what I can tell you is I instantly shed that particular new story outfit and some curious faith was planted within me that day… of the spectral, penumbral, and hauntological variety. In the death and the releasing of God-as-I-imagined, there was born a tiny window of possibility for God-as-outside-my-imagination.

And thus ushered in my introduction to meditation, to monasticism; to breathing, and to the question of BE-ing.

I'm guessing you will not be shocked to learn that I have found this God-as-outside-my-imagination to be so much more than I ever permitted God-as-I-imagined to be. It turns out all these boxes and labels into which we often place ourselves and others (including the big Other) aren't actually able to contain what they advertise. Go figure.

But what does this all have to do with existing or BE-ing? Great question! Did you ever play Chinese jump-rope as a child? It's alright if you didn't. I briefly googled it a moment ago to make sure I was "correct" in my remembering of the specific chant which accompanies the jumping so that I could proceed in making the comparison I had in mind; however—to my chagrin—I discovered there were apparently MANY different chants used for this game and I even failed to find the precise one I remember. Regardless, I bring it up because these days, post God-as-I-imagined, I can (for the first time ever –maybe?) sometimes observe myself existing similarly to what I remember chanting and enacting with the circular elastic string for Chinese jump-rope:

inside,

outside,

side-by-

side,

on,

in,

out.

Stay with me here and I'll see if I can manage to pull this together for you. A big piece of this has to do with encouraging intentional consciousness of the stories we tell ourselves about ourselves, and also of the current presuppositions we hold and why we hold them. In other words I am suggesting that the question of BE-ing has much to do with lessening the cognitive dissonance we maintain between what we "say" and what we "do". I've said it before, but I'm more curious with how we exist than with what we say we believe. And with the way I remember Chinese jump-rope—what you are saying MATCHES what you are doing (in relationship to the rope).

Who would have guessed the seemingly frivolous games of our youth might prove to be decent metaphors down the road?

LIFE-ing

being manifested by growth...the power of adaptation to environment through changes originating internally

I like to think of the question of "LIFE-ing" as "BE-ing" manifested by growth. Wendell Berry once wrote **"Be like the fox who makes more tracks than necessary, some in the wrong direction..."** One might say that in my ever-unfolding spiral of growth, I have taken my fair share (and then some) of "wrong" direction trails. How else to learn, but by doing? –I believe Aristotle spoke to this using the Greek word praxis. One of the current experiments of praxis I am engaged in involves where I live; where I practice this thing called life.

I live in a building we call Shelter50…it's the name of a place where innovation, imagination, & interrogation merge. It is a place of hospitality which invites people to explore the ways we manifest in the world and to investigate the ways our beliefs function in our lives. It is a space which hosts a wide variety of experiences aimed at bringing people together in meaningful & transformative ways. Shelter50 derives its name from the song *Shelter* by Jars of Clay in which the main chorus extols, "In the shelter of each other, we will live." The "50" (haunted as it is in its ever-coming-never-arriving nature) is connected to the Jewish concept of Jubilee and to the Christian notion of Pentecost. Each of these events centered on equality, justice, and new life possibilities for the communities…with an apparent recognition of our interconnectivity. Shelter50 is a space which seeks to be colonized by none, and to be open to diverse expressions and imaginative undertakings (www.shelter50.com).

As you might imagine, it can often be a fairly happening place. And as with many such undertakings, there are accounts of the failed attempts which have forged a way forward… which have propped open a door for the impossible. These walls are etched with stories of rhythm, rebellion, and reverberation…and they are painted with hope.

One of Shelter50's rhythms—nearest and dearest to me—is a (new) monastic one: daily prayer/meditation in the morning, the midday, and the evening. It's complicated to depict in words what is seemingly—continuously—becoming… from such a rhythm. So then part of what Life-ing looks like (for me) is participating in this Rhythm. And I find that this Rhythm whispers of Jack's questions, and is relentless in Its call.

I was in France almost four years ago, set to spend a week at the monastery in Taize. It could be said that I carried some residual skepticism of the authenticity of large Christian gatherings, and at that very first evening prayer service, I tore apart every reading and every song with my perceived ability to accurately BS detect. I went to bed that night feeling frustrated and annoyed I had even come on the trip. I woke up to the bells ringing, and as soon as my feet entered the same chapel - this time for morning prayer- an understanding washed over me. These monks were simply living their lives and inviting others to join in if they so desired. It had nothing to do with the numbers or with putting on a good show. It had everything to do with hospitality and with carrying the burdens of others. I wept the entire day…this Rhythm emerged.

I was in Rome two New Years Eves ago, with over 40,000 young adults. The event had us traipsing all over the city- visiting fountains and holy sites, "meeting" the (no longer) pope from about 200 feet away, and witnessing the impressive beauty of each ancient Basilica. I traveled all that way from South Dakota with a group of friends who were working together to plan a similar (though MUCH smaller) event at Redshirt Table on the Pine Ridge Reservation near my house. And one of my travel companions had been asked to bring along her incredibly beautiful jingle-dress in order to perform a traditional Lakota jingle dance for some of those who gathered for the event, along with any passer-bys. In the end it took place within a Basilica that had originally been a pagan temple but that had been conquered and colonized by the Christians—stripping it of its former magnificence (and of course heresy) and labeling it "good". Sounds incredibly familiar to what took place in the Black Hills ("Paha Sapa") with the non-native Christians and the native folks who lived there first—the not so distant relatives of the native folks who were my travel companions in Rome. And the irony slash momentous significance of my friend (Quinetta, born and raised in a post-colonized reservation) dancing her heart out to the drum in her jingle dress in the middle of a post-colonized Basilica did not miss me. I let the beat of the drum and the jingles of Quinetta's dress carry my awe and tear-filled eyes up to rest on a stunning stain-glass window…this Rhythm emerged.

I was in Ireland for a Pete Rollins event last year, at a breathtaking place called the Giants Causeway. The light and shadows of the day shone on the surrounding hills as I sat on one of the infamous basalt rock columns. It was early afternoon and rather conveniently the perfect backdrop for a midday meditation. I slipped my feet into the water, simultaneously spotting a medium-sized rock with its upper half dry - destined in that silence to be held by (and to hold) me…and as each wave touched the shore where we were sitting -announcing itself-powerfully, gently…this Rhythm emerged.

I was in the Shelter50 courtyard last week, enjoying the warmth of the sunshine of some unseasonably nice weather this fall and winter. I had painted one of the courtyard walls a burnt orange and was now on phase two of our Wall of Wailing and Wake project -endeavoring to hang up strips of chicken wire that would soon hold ribbons and paper prayers (not unlike the wailing wall in Jerusalem) from those in the Rapid City community as well as from those who pass through our space. I observed myself becoming emotional—acknowledging how ill-equipped our culture seems to be when it comes to walking through and wading in our grief, dying, and loss…and concurrently allowing my own burdens (along with those I hold with others) to wash over me as I worked. And in the midst of those moments, the train whistle sounded (as a very brief caveat, the train whistle has through the years become a tool of awakening and a marking of the Holy for me… almost as if I am a singing bowl and the train sounding is the wooden mallet with which I am "gonged" and immediately centered)…this Rhythm emerged.

I would be lying if I said this Rhythm doesn't transform—doesn't insist and infiltrate and disrupt—me from the inside out. So what if, as these different experiences convey, It is all around us?

What might it mean if It is within us?
ALL of us?

Albert Einstein spoke of something he called spooky action at a distance. Even without having any previous knowledge at the time of the ins and outs of quantum entanglement (or for that matter the EPR paradox), the very first time I heard those words: spooky action at a distance my heart definitively skipped a beat. Call me crazy. Label me what you will. But when I get quiet...when I am still enough to SEE... something within "me" recognizes and responds to something within "you". Our separateness seems hazy and

deep
cries out
to deep.

As many of my Lakota Sioux Nation neighbours articulate: Mitakuye Oyasin (we are all related & connected). What might our lives look like if we—the two-legged and the four-legged and the finned and the winged and the rooted—all accepted this indescribable-bounded-up-ness that we share?

Often this acceptance looks like anything but the overly romanticized, idealistic way I may be describing it. Instead I would suggest—as Einstein surely did—that this "spooky-ness" is layered in a haunted unsettling.

And It leaves us undone.

For being unheard, this call is persistent is it not? (that...OR I am merely persistent in my "meaning-making/projecting onto" each of the Rhythm scenarios, etc.- which presently I feel okay with acknowledging as a distinct potentiality).

In any case, when placed in its context the Wendell Berry quote I brought up earlier ends with these 2 words: "Practice resurrection." I can't help but admit—it is to this end I am "LIFE-ing":wrong paths taken, Rhythms regularly recognized, and all other experiments with the unknowable included—and it is with each plummet from a perceived place of permanency; with each rupture in the real; with each unrequited, unimagined, and unfamiliar understanding…that possibility is beckoned near.

I can't help but agree with Jack that 50 is not a matter of mathematics; it is a matter of hope—and a clearly far-fetched hope at that.

Nonetheless, this Rhythm continues to emerge… to show up in increasingly unanticipated ways. Which again reminds me of Jack in that, There's nothing riskier than having commerce with the unknown, the unexpected, the unforeseen, with calling for the coming of what we cannot see coming.
But even Jack recognizes that "risky" is what we must dare to be:______ aude (not sure of the Latin for that one!). After all, God is not the "answer" but the question to which we are to be the response.

EXPRESS-ing

to show up, manifest, reveal, to exude or emit

Consequently, this question of EXPRESS-ing is one of incarnation for me. I resonate deeply with Jack's words of "letting the event that stirs within the name of God happen, letting God's insistence acquire mundane existence." What would it mean for "God" to get out of the way of God ever being embodied, or EXPRESSED, in us and through us?
Well my friends, I submit to you that EXPRESS-ing might taste an awful lot like the froth atop a perfect London Fog, might sound an awful lot like the band The Weepies, might feel an awful lot like wet paint on your fingertips, and might look an awful lot like a blank piece of paper… motioning to you. What does any of this mean? Hard to tell. But what I am abstractly working to do here is convey, albeit unconventionally, that divinity is a human work…and I happen to think it is hinted at everywhere we look—from warm yummy drinks to great music; from allowing ourselves to be child-like to our innate ability to create.

Thich Nhat Hanh is recorded to have said the following, "Every thought you produce, anything you say, any action you do, it bears your signature." I might add that it also bears God's signature. Subsequently, not to over pressure us and yet simultaneously not to let us off the hook… what exactly is IT that we're doing here? Here, in a macro-level sense (meaning on this planet) and in a micro-level sense (meaning with one another and with ourselves in our daily lives)? I must admit at times it feels like we're in a repetitive "Groundhog Day" film, or that we got shipwrecked and then utterly drugged and distracted on the Lotus Eaters island (of Greek mythology and Homer's Odyssey)—both of which speak candidly to the fairly nonsensical ways we can be inclined to manifest. What I find myself interested in is experiments in the shaking of things up…in the different ways of snapping out of this lulled expression of Christianity so many of us continue to participate in and heck, maybe even revealing God a bit along the way. I'm immersed in the experiment of emanating a spectral life... and I think a lot of others are, too.

And so, if as Jack concludes, "Hope is the air, the ambiance, the element of a spectral life"…then as we attempt (with an ever increasing propensity) to BE, to LIVE, and to EXPRESS—together—in this space between a memory and a promise …

let us breathe deeply of this air.

"So the present is exposed to the arrivants, to who or what is coming, as well as to revenants, those are coming back. We live in messianic or spectral time, responsible to both the living and the dead, both the living and the still to come, to the whole community of saints. We live in the space between a memory and a promise".

~ *John D Caputo*

YES, BUT ABSENCE
IS THE HIGHEST FORM
OF PRESENCE.

AARON MURPHY

PROVOCATUER

EXISTENTIALIST

PHILOSOPHER

THE FOLLOWING ARE THE MASKS AARON MURPHY HAS BEEN KNOWN TO WEAR IN THE PUBLIC SPHERE:

Uncle, Son, Brother, Aspiring Academic, Advocate, Introvert.

HERE'S WHAT THIS CONTRIBUTOR WOULD SAY ABOUT HIMSELF:

One of the things my autism makes me is overly-sincere. My biography, therefore is also a confession.

I have always loved philosophy. Over ten years ago, I sat in a philosophy classroom. Every night I would read pages from our philosophy text for fun. Then, all of a sudden, while reading about Jean-Paul Sartre, I had profound feelings of anxiety. It was like I was floating weightlessly in space with no one to stop me. What if Sartre was right? What if we're all alone? What if nobody is "out there" to help us? I began asking people to give me answers that didn't exist so that I could have some sense of certainty. In order to relieve myself of the crippling weight of the anxiety I felt I threw away the philosophy book that I loved so much, and became a fundamentalist. The rigid way of thinking that it offered gave me a feeling of relief the same way as a man who is afraid of floating away might get relief from being locked in a jail cell. Ultimately, it was the sheer weightlessness, the very lightness, and groundlessness of being that made me anxious. As an undergrad in a Christian college, where Christianity was very much a performance necessary for acceptance, my questions turned into a full blown anxiety disorder.

I was afraid of death, and to tell you the truth, in many ways still am, but you know what? It's okay. So are you. So are all of us, and I'm here to tell you it's okay. We are all marked by a mutual wound: we are aware of our own existence, yet do not know what the future holds for us. I have learned that this wound is also a gift.

The Things That Haunt Me

There are things that haunt me. I am not superstitious. After all, I am child of the Enlightenment, and am grateful to my intellectual forefathers for teaching me the importance of rational inquiry. They dispelled much of the superstitions that held our ancestors at bay. Yet, their project came with a great cost. The thrust of the western world has been towards becoming detached observers, who in the words of Isaac Asimov, "see all the world as if it were in a balloon." While the scientific way of looking at things is useful, it's hegemony seeks to reduce all phenomena into problems that can be solved through observation alone. Little do they know that they are too situated in a place. As our position changes our perspectives and ways of thinking rise to another with each one.

Such a way of thinking undermines the idea of the self as an essential substance. As I go from place to place throughout my day the gestalt that I am constructed from shifts. The ego can be thought of as those perspectives, stories, and symbols that I identify with that I make into a coherent whole from separate sources like a collage while the others are pushed out towards the periphery of our awareness.

We all have things that we would like to believe about ourselves by identifying those practices and cognitive patterns as our own, while at the same time others go unnoticed or ignored by us all together. Many times these patterns erupt into our conscious undermining the ego-construct we have made to identify with ourselves with fragments of unconscious material that has not been integrated into our identity.

This is why, in honor of Jacques Derrida, I say that I can rightfully pass as a Christian. Even though that is the identity that I have constructed there are other stories in me. They function much like Abigail, the pre-cognitive in the movie Minority Report who has another story about the overall plot.

1. I Am Haunted by My Unconscious.

I therefore recite a little prayer to God to open me up to the things that I would rather not believe about myself:

Peel me open like a tangerine
Lay me open like a book
Blow through me like a violent breeze,
so I can see what falls out when I'm shook

Freud, being the man of reason he was, broke open the human psyche to reveal a cellar deep within each of us filled with unintegrated psychic material. We refer poetically to this repressed material that we would not like to admit to as our demons. I therefore pray my prayer as an exorcism, a way of bringing that which I would not like to admit to into the light of consciousness.

I always approach the unconscious with the awe of a scientist looking through a telescope into the vastness of outer space, the anxiety of a man standing on the edge of The Grand Canyon, and the disgust of a rookie plumber in a clogged sewer. It is both a quagmire of filth and a deep spring of potential for personal development. The strangest thing is there isn't anything down in there that I didn't already know. I never pictured the unconscious as having rigid boundaries. Instead, it has gradients with carrying shades of white that transition through shades of gray to pitch black.

Every gesture, every little slip of the tongue or double take reveals in me something that I would rather not like to know about myself. Lacan would probably agree with me that these things are ways of revealing my true intentions against those of my ego image. The more and more this happens to me the more and more I have to approach myself with an air of mystery. I am constantly having to defer any final self definition. As soon as I say "I am" another layer is uncovered. While the unconscious haunts me, constantly undermining my rational self-definition due to past experiences, there is also an openness to what is to come, to the unseen.

As much as I would like to believe that I believe all the time, there are carrying shades of doubt and belief within me, each of which I have a differing level of awareness of. God serves as a midwife, who through a maiuetic uncovering of my unconscious helps my doubts surface so that I can then confess them to God. So in a sense I need God to help me discover that I already have doubts about God. When doubts rise to the surface, therefore, it should be seen as a gift-a holy act.

2. I Am Haunted by Poetry.

Alain Badiou contends that ontology is mathematics. Math just is. A always equals A. Just accept the facts, move on.

Poetry however, is hauntology. We can't let go of our favorite verses. They stay with us long after we read them. They emerge from the sea of language, submerge again, only to resurface once again, with a whole new meaning. This is because, unlike math, poetry, prose, narratives need us to read them. They never speak for themselves. They are dead without us.

The ghosts of language, the ghosts of the past entombed in their mausoleums of paper and ink need us to speak them. They call out for us for life...and yet they elude us, for they are shifting entities that keep on taking on new shapes. Language, unlike math slides around. Not just on the page, but inside us. As our situation changes and culture, the meaning of those words change. Poetic and narrative language has, after all, a double action. It reveals what is and erases what it is talking about in the same action. Nothing in language just is. Language is hauntology. It clarifies only through obscurity. It tells you the answer only by leaving you with more questions than you originally had in the first place.

The ghosts of The Bible. The ghosts of the book reach out and touch us begging for life, and as they do so we reach down into them. As we stare at each other like awkward teenagers, a horizon forms. This is what a Paul Ricuoeur called a hermeneutic horizon. We touch them, they touch us, worlds collide, and an interpretation is formed the same way a zygote is formed in a mother's womb (and you thought hermeneutics couldn't be sexy).

This process is ongoing. When we take words into ourselves they linger. They hold on to us with their dead hands! Every time we take those words out and look at them their meaning shifts. They are like a puzzle box with infinite layers. No termination point seems to be in sight, because meaning is always deferred, like a movie that won't seem to end, or a light beam being bounced off an infinite number of mirrors. Like ghosts, words never die, yet are always dead without us. We are possessed by them, born into them. They change as we do like amorphous blobs of ectoplasmic meaning.

While language needs us to speak it, it is also our mother. She structures our consciousness with her utterances, writing us as we write her. Stories of who and what we should be linger within us as we linger in the sea of language. We are haunted by stories, haunted by the marks of their letters. We are marked by their marks, written by their marks. The ones we were told when we were children of who we should be, who we are, and even what we like. They never dissolve or leave us, and we are thrown into them, as well as a language at large with no choosing of our own.

3. I Am Haunted by the Future

Phenomenologically speaking, I experience the present as an opening where the sum of all my past experience meet the possibilities of what is to come. Time is much like an oculus, the open domed roofs in Roman architecture. In a very real sense these roofs are unfinished the opening presents a promise/threat. There is no guarantee of what might come through it. Sunshine or rain must both be expected, and yet even the threat of catastrophe is a blessing, for it proves that there is an opening, and that means something other than endless repetition of the past. The future allows for the hope of change. Even disaster testifies to the fact that existence is more than just endless repetition of what has already been.

Human beings are unique in that we are aware through the gift-curse of self consciousness of this opening known as the future, and therefore of the incompleteness of time and of being itself. In order to seek a sense of closure we are able to imagine what our future might be like. The act of imagination is in fact, the birth of an object before it even arrives. Imagine for instance, a surprise party. In the absence of the party's actual honoree, the guests still speak of the person of honor even in their absence. It is the honoree's party, and yet while waiting for the person to arrive they still speak of them as if they were already there. By speaking of this person in their absence, it is "as if" they are there with the party guests. This is what Derrida would call an arrivant- the presence of something that has not fully arrived yet.

If we could imagine a couple who are trying conceive a child we might have found the example par-excellence of the arrivant. Even though the child is not yet there in body, his parents pick a name for him, imagine his future, make a space for him in the house with a crib, and talk about him as if he already had full-fledged being, giving him a whispy quasi-presence. The parents are not delusional. They know the child is not there yet. Through their actions they have begun to give birth to this child who is not even an embryo yet present through their naming him and speaking about what he might be like. The child himself has not yet arrived on the scene, but in a very real way he is partially present, if for no other reason than the fact that he has a meaningful signification in language. We cannot say that if one of his two prospective parents found out they were infertile they would be happy, would they? They would in a very real way be mourning the death of the child that they never had. The child that was never able to fully arrive into his own existence.

The Kingdom of God is also an arrivant. It is an activity of imagining and creating a world to come that is not here yet. At the same time, what gives birth to it is the acting out of it in partiality. This is why the Kingdom of God must be incarnate. It cannot exist without some kind of materiality by being embodied in some kind of act, or a deed. This is why Christianity is a materialistic religion. When I speak of materialism I am not speaking of excessive spending or hoarding. Materialism in the sense I am using means that the stuff-ness of the world matters. The Kingdom of God makes the profane sacred through the action that is embodied in it.

In order to do something as simples as love, something material must be exchanged, whether it be a physical gift, a kind word, or simple affection. All of these are instances of The Kingdom of God in material acts. The tendency by religious people from the physical world and concentrate solely on their inner life is actually borrowed from Plato, and was considered a heresy in the early church. It's followers sought escape from the earthiness of Christ's teaching. This is why many of the gnostic gospels re-worked the incarnation so that Jesus was a pure spirit being who was above the corruptibility of any form of material.

The truth of orthodox Christianity makes a claim that is more radical. The incarnation makes the human flesh holy by making it the site of God's presence in time. Eternity is not separate from temporality, but is embodied in it. Being like Christ then, is an existential project that all who follow him must do with their very being through the way they live in the world, in which we become eternity embodied in time through our deeds.

The Christian claim that eternity is inscribed in Christ also changes the way we must look at the human subject. Often times the self is referred to as some in-born essence, however it is more accurate to say that human beings are a set of relations between the eternal and the temporal. In terms of creating the Kingdom of God here-and-now this makes things problematic because eternity is disproportional to temporality. When we say that Christ was sinless, it is because he lived within the tension, and felt the disproportion while maintaining a perfect ontological balance. Sin is the misalignment that comes from not being able to hold ourselves together in perfect unity like Christ did. The original concept of sin for the Jews reflects this idea, as it did not mean some sort of original sin, but a "missing of the mark."

The Kingdom of God symbolizes being devoted to a cause so just, or another person that we are willing to give ourselves away piece by piece to them or it. At first the claim that we must have a cause to live and die for might sound a little bleak until that is, we realize to be fully human means to have such a cause, which is what Kierkegaard meant when he mentions "the power that establishes it," in The Sickness Unto Death. If we were to use a rational economy for such a cause it wouldn't make any sense due to the very absolute demand assigned to it. It is enough to say that you only want to feed a rational quantity of children, because in doing so, you are saying that it is totally acceptable for some children to die, nor can you set a fixed number of hours to devote to a romantic partner the way a professor devotes a fixed number of hours to being in his office on campus. The infinite demand exceeds our finitude.

While having a desire that exceeds our finitude might seem fruitless, it actually is the very thing that grounds our being. They establish in us a desire that can never be filled, which in turn causes us to create and mobilize ourselves to change the world, because we know that we are now marked by a lack that goes so deep that it can never be filled. At the end of Schindler's List, which is about Joseph Schindler (a businessman who lied and manipulated Nazi officials to save Jews from being killed in Auschwitz), is seen contemplating how much more money he could have given to save even more inmates from death. The Jews he saved give him a ring that is marked with a Talmudic quote: "Whoever saves one life saves the entire world." The thing is, for Schindler, every life he saves is that one life. He is haunted by the infinite desire to save everyone, because of their irreducible singularity. It is the singularity of the other that makes the Kingdom of God more than just an abstraction that stands as an other-worldly afterlife. By making every other totally other, we encounter Christ in every person we meet, not as some type of phantasm that haunts us from outside the world, but a mysterious presence that haunts us from within the heart of their very being. Eternity and the Kingdom of a God itself haunts us through the flesh of every other who we truly meet as a thou, or to put it more succinctly, every other that we meet as a thou, shows us the face of God.

This is not a form of idol worship, it is instead what Levinas was getting at when he talks about the other. When we approach God, we are deflected from God towards the other where we see God in the other. Such a structure is not reducible to simply the other person, since there must be an intentionality on God's behalf that directs me toward seeing God in the face of the other. To better understand how we are haunted by the other, imagine a young man who meets a young woman at a cafe. The first time he sees her he essentially lives an entire lifetime with her. He just doesn't see who she is now, but sees an entire future with her. Their first date, their wedding, their children, even the hardships that they will face. Even though he has just met her, and he doesn't know if she will answer his response even for a first date he has seen forever with her. Incarnate time is the ability to see eternity embodied in the present. The other haunts us as an inverted oculus. Finite on the outside, yet opening within to a world of endless depth.

SARAH KING

Unfinished

Reaching

Daughter

THE FOLLOWINGTHE MASKS SARAH KING HAS BEEN KNOWN TO WEAR:

Mother, wife, multi-tasking homemaker, neighbor, friend.

HERE'S WHAT THIS CONTRIBUTOR WOULD SAY ABOUT HERSELF:

I'm a mostly un-credentialed stay-at-home mom whose introversion tells me I've no business contributing to such things as this, but all the same find myself being stretched and finding the courage to (sometimes) put myself out there anyway. These baby-steps feel significant.

UNTIL TOMORROW

God's will. My will. Wilting.
Willing. Will-do, God-willing.
At some point I lost track of how to gauge all this.

S t i l l
I feel satisfied with the empty spaces. There is reasonableness to these holes filled with Who and What. The uncertainty is an uncomfortable comfort that I can blame and fall into and love and understand.

A n d y e t
I continually revisit What I know is good. Who I feel is good. I'm unsure of where I fit in that scope, but always there is gratitude for the North Stars and the grace of time and process.

A l w a y s
I can almost feel the greatness. I poke my fingers at It with hesitation and walk a well-worn path around It's edges, even in the darkest times. All the relevant irrelevance, so beautiful in it's meaning, adds up and up.

It's easy to stand safely in audience looking outward to somewhere I am not. Yet.

JONNY MCEWEN

troubled reformed instigator

THESE ARE THE MASKS JONNY MCEWEN HAS BEEN KNOWN TO WEAR IN THE PUBLIC SPHERE:

Dubh(http://dubh.bandcamp.com)

HERE'S WHAT THIS CONTRIBUTOR WOULD SAY ABOUT HIMSELF:

I am an artist with a background in painting (abstract landscapey drippy stuff). I recently completed a Masters in Fine Arts (distinction), where I have been working with video and computer code (though still sort of painting). I also create electronic music (deep, gentle glitchy, ambient stuff).

I was one of the founder members of the Ikon collective, and have somehow survived. Part of my work has involved engaging as an artist and facilitator with Northern Ireland's troubled past, developing new ways of working, facilitating conversations, encouraging creativity and scribbling.

Still from a video of an american soap opera,
recorded at 2am in the Hemmingway Hotel, Havanna.

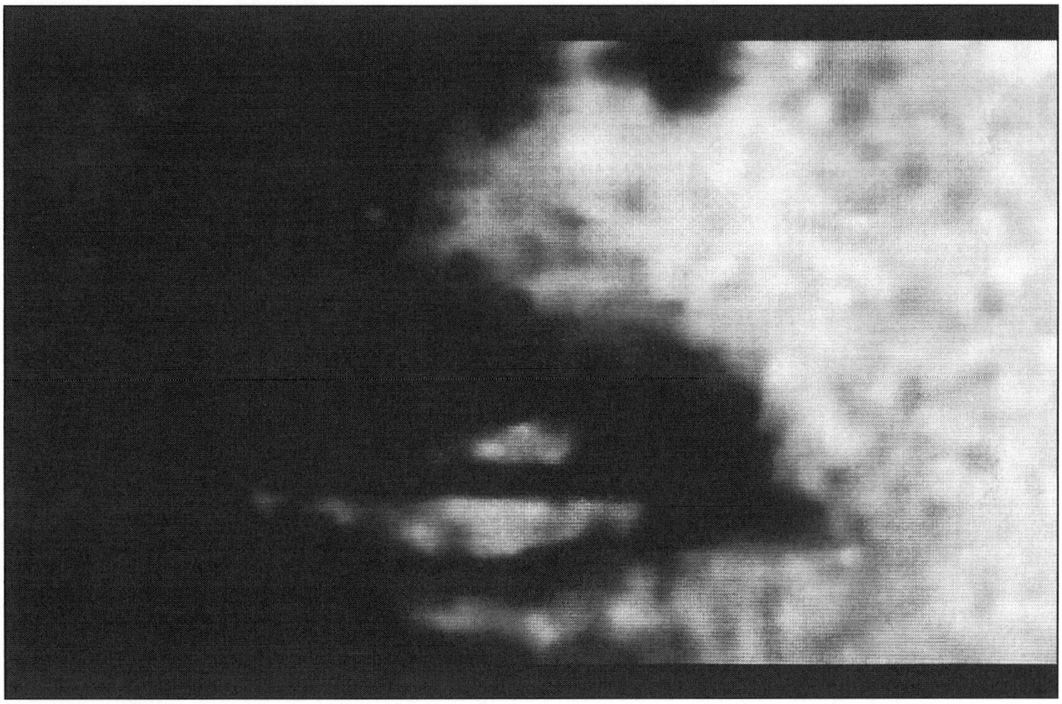

KEEGAN OSINSKI

LIBRARIAN MALCONTENT IMPOSTER

THE FOLLOWING ARE THE MASKS KEEGAN OSINSKI HAS BEEN KNOWN TO WEAR IN THE PUBLIC SPHERE:

Librarian,
student,
pseudo-academic,
lover,
fighter,
and graceful
hell-raiser.

HERE'S WHAT THIS CONTRIBUTOR WOULD SAY ABOUT HERSELF:

Keegan has her BA in Philosophy & Theology and her MLIS and spends her days with books and/or people who read and write them. Her interests include sacramental and postmodern theology and facilitating knowledge-sharing between scholars and clergy in new and creative ways. She likes plain cake donuts and the sound of paper cups dropped gently on a hard surface.

Haunted Houses, Spooky Rituals, and Practicing Perhaps

Walking into church is like walking into a haunted house.

It's a voluntary encounter with an expected unexpected.

You know the house is haunted. Or at least that's what you've heard. Its reputation precedes it. The murmurs and rumors are as unique and numerous as the town's residents. Each has his or her own testimony.

"I felt a cool breeze."

"I heard footsteps."

"It's all bullshit."

So you know what you're getting into when you show up, but also you don't.

Even the pros, the veterans, the ghost hunters who've coordinated stakeouts regularly for years get a bristle of gooseflesh upon entry—what will happen this time?

Joining in the liturgies of the church is a way of entering the house and facing the possibilities there. That is, as we engage in the performance of preaching and hearing the Gospel, of repeating well-worn collects and creeds, of administering and receiving the sacraments of baptism and Eucharist, we expose ourselves to the possibilities of the spectral non-presence of a non-existent, insisting God.

Liturgy—particularly that of the Eucharist—is the playing-out of the risk of hoping for Jubilee. The risk of hoping that perhaps now we will see the year of the Lord's favor, perhaps now we will see God's kingdom come (while recognizing also that perhaps we will not). Practicing this risk, this hope, in the liturgies teaches us lessons that extend to our politics, our relationships, and beyond. The process of opening ourselves to the unknown, of really facing risk, takes practice. It's never not hard, but in practicing it we can become brave.

Participating in the liturgy is a way of practicing perhaps. In the liturgy we learn to expect the prospect of the Jubilee. We learn Derrida's unconditional hospitality, a hospitality open to perhaps—perhaps friend, perhaps foe—which entails a certain surprise, a certain unexpectedness of the guest. But, again, it is an expected unexpected. You are still expecting (hoping, looking for) the arrival of the guest. And to be truly hospitable, you must be prepared to greet the unexpected guest, whoever or whatever they may be. You must set the table for this unexpected one, and be prepared to eat and drink with whomever may appear. By returning and repeating, we make a habit of setting the table, of being ready for an event that may or may not happen, that may be joyful or tragic. The point is that we show up. This hospitality can be an attitude or an outlook, able to be practiced anywhere, but we are bodies, inhabiting space, welcoming a God whose body we constitute, whose insistence we make extant in our bodies, as one body, through the body we receive at the altar. Caputo says that "the disembodied spectrality of the call must be incarnated in the world of flesh and blood," and the flesh and blood of bread and wine in the Eucharistic liturgy embodies this response. Perhaps the ritual is not a requirement, not the exclusive Way, but it is a way—a unique avenue of meeting (maybe) this insisting God, of looking forward and practicing the perhaps of Jubilee.

Caputo says that "preaching should be a call to make the name of God come true," and further, "the name (of) 'God' is the name of a call to which we are supposed to be the response," and "the call is heard only in the response." The response to preaching, in a typical liturgy, is to gather at the table for Eucharist—consuming the body and blood of Christ and becoming the body of Christ as the church. This spooky ritual, where the presence of Christ is substantiated by his absence, where the bodies of the gathered become one body through a shared meal, is a response to that unheard call. The call that says "Taste and see," "Eat this, all of you," "Do this in remembrance of me."

God is this call, God is this response—the response is God's body, broken and poured out, the bread and wine consumed, also by God's body, God's people. The call is only embodied in the response—and the response is the flesh and blood. The flesh and blood of people gathering, the flesh and blood of bread and wine. The sacrament is a response to this call—an "I hear you," a "Here am I." We simply show up, perhaps cynical, skeptical, perhaps frightened, perplexed. We come to the table, hold out our hands, receive what is given to us. Kierkegaard says that "if you do not hear [Christ's] voice, then you go in vain to Holy Communion." He's very clear that the Eucharistic liturgy is a response to a unique call from God-in-Christ. It's something that inexplicably draws people to participate But often this call is actually unheard—an insisting intuition, not in the whirlwind, in the earthquake or in the fire. It is the in the response that we ultimately may experience the call. So it is not vanity to respond to the unheard call. It is faith.

This call that haunts is, perhaps, a "desire beyond desire," which may be "sparked by the eventive energy" of the insisting God.The call does not demand an ethic or an orthodoxy, providing schemata. But it insists, commanding the shape, though not the sequence, of our response. Caputo quotes Derrida's saying that "Emancipation is a promise not a program." This insistence does not make demands, and yet somehow a response is required, if not by the caller than by something within the hearer. Caputo says that radical theology points out the maybe-about-to-happen event within that which is happening. That which is happening is liturgy, but there is something else haunting every service.

The absence is an integral piece of the haunting. In the scariest horror movies, you never actually see the monster, and it's the absence of the presence that has the potency. Caputo uses the parable of the sheep and the goats in Matthew 25 to illustrate this seeing without seeing. Those on the right fed and visited and clothed the Son of Man, and yet they ask "Lord, when did we see you?" They were only able to do these things because they did not see. Caputo says that "everything in the story depends upon the invisibility of God, the inexistence of God, the spectrality of God." This is also true in considering Eucharist. Take another example: When Jesus meets the disciples on the road to Emmaus and explains the Scriptures to them, it is only possible because they do not recognize him. When he breaks bread with them—shares the sacrament—he vanishes. The moment in which we've come to expect the presence of Christ is met with his absence. Like a ghost, he disappears. The real meeting with meaning occurs in its inexistence—the revelation of absence, the negative theophany.

The experience of this specter, the unidentifiable longing for we-know-not-what, may not arise ex nihilo, but may be encountered and developed through a formation of Christian identity via the liturgy—the practicing of perhaps. In the liturgy of Eucharist we cry "Viens!" to the impossible. We welcome the (im)possibility of the absent presence of an insisting God, of a crucified Christ, who has promised—impossibly so!—that the elements we receive are indeed his body, and that he is there with us, in us, as us, as we consume this bread and wine.

Truly, the Eucharist is the spooky ritual of a creepy cult. "He who eats my flesh and drinks my blood has eternal life," Jesus said. "My flesh is true food, and my blood is true drink" (John 6:54-55). And even when the horror and awkwardness of cannibalism is explained away by a facile symbolism, the fact remains: Jesus told his disciples: This is my body. This is my blood. And we return to it every week. Martin Luther rejected both the answer of simple signification and the metaphysical confabulation of transubstantiation, opting instead to lean into the spookiness, retain and revel in the mystery. This is the body of Christ. The body of Christ happens here. We know not how, but we know it calls to us from within the ritual. The spectrality of God incarnated in flesh and blood. When we receive the body, when we become the body, we bear witness to that call.

It's not magic, though. The spirit cannot be contained or predicted. No priest-medium can summon forth this ghost on command. The ritual itself does not cause the event. And the event—as its capricious nature dictates—may not even happen. May not ever happen. There may just be an open window or a creaky floorboard. You may leave a skeptic. But there will always be the question: What if you try again?

The repetition, the re-entry, re-expresses old ghosts and reveals new ones, who add their infinitely differing facets to the ever-nuancing call, to which we must continue to respond but may never fully answer.

Walter Benjamin says that "every moment is a door through which the Messiah could enter." This is why we must return, repeat, re-check each door. The spooky things, the real things, become apparent in the repetition. Initially, everything is foreign, everything may be startling. But to return again and again to the liturgy until it becomes familiar reveals the difference in the same. Repetition of the same liturgies brings out the differences in each manifestation. Even seemingly identical services are never truly identical. There is différance in the ritual.

Repetition of the ritual is what opens you up to the possibility of the impossible. The ritual repeatedly exposes you to what might happen—is it the fiftieth year now? Now? What about now? You never know, and so you must keep trying. And it is a repetition that is fraught with risk, for you may always hope but you may never know. Nothing is certain, even when so much is expected.

The cliché is that the definition of insanity is doing the same thing over and over and expecting different results. And that's kind of what we do in the liturgy. We might say it belongs in Kierkegaard's category of "higher madness," which he calls "the most concrete of all categories, the fullest, since it is closest to life and does not have its truth in a beyond, the supraterrestrial, but in a subterranean below." This is a concrete madness that manifests in bodies—bodies who return to a building and receive bread and wine and chew it and swallow it and then come back next week, believing this bodily ritual is the response that fleshes out the insistent call.

It's some crazy combination of despair and hope and insanity and promise that keeps you coming back. And for some people, the despair is too much—they've been let down too many times. For some, the insanity is too futile—How long, Lord? And that's understandable. The foolishness of the spooky ritual, the silliness of returning to the haunted house after so many fruitless visits is apparent. But still, always that question. What if? A kind of madness, certainly.

This is why we need not demolish the haunted house. The specters may follow you home anyway. They may be encountered in a closet or under a bed, but you can almost always count on their concentrated non-presence in the haunted house. Returning there reaffirms your commitment to hearing the call, to engaging the specters rather than fleeing.

While they may find you and haunt you anywhere, it takes a certain kind of courage to face them on their home turf.

The specter of the insisting God calls silently to us in myriad places and forms. Yet in the haunted houses of churches and cathedrals it hides in plain sight. Church may be exactly where you would expect to find God. But when the veil is torn, you find you are standing in an empty room, and yet you may still hear whispers, still feel a chill. Here in this room, with others who have been drawn to this spooky place, you may come to embody the response to that unheard call in the liturgies and sacraments.

So as you hear the benediction and go in peace—or pieces—you take with you this habit-forming practice of perhaps, which will continue to spook you into looking forward, into preparing a table, into asking What if? Perhaps all is for naught, but perhaps it is not, perhaps we are, as always, just on the cusp of Jubilee.

Pay no attention to the Man behind the Curtain - 3

AMY HIGGINS

Inquisitor

Independent Learner

THE FOLLOWING ARE THE MASKS AMY HIGGINS HAS BEEN KNOWN TO WEAR IN THE PUBLIC SPHERE:

Amy is addicted to learning and has collected random academic degrees to support the habit including a Bachelor in Biology, a Master in Marriage and Family Therapy, and a Master in Public Affairs. She has worn unrelated masks in varied working environments including that of teacher, counselor, legislative aide, auditor, and analyst in the hopes that one day she will figure out what she wants to be when she grows up. She has also been an ardent believer/disbeliever, leader/detractor, and conformist/heretic in multiple Christian circles but as of late prefers the more intimate environment of a [no name] community and exploring themes of philosophy and radical theology in her spare time.

HERE'S WHAT THIS CONTRIBUTOR WOULD SAY ABOUT HERSELF:

I am a collector of experiences. Things I love: Fall, the smell of rain, my big comfy chair, snow-covered mountains, Texas bluebonnets, road trips, sea breezes, playing with my nephews, crape myrtles, deep conversation, star-filled skies, wistful lyrics, fireplaces, cinnamon, the sound of rushing water, sacred moments, fiery sunsets, and furry critters (not rodents).I do not believe in the myth of the runner's high. I crave variety.I have a low threshold for nonsense. This is not evident from my life career choices. I am close to my family and have many friends I consider to be family. I am a left-brained analytical, problem-solver type, extremely jealous of those with creative talent - the arts make me alive and I am a passionate observer. I am a Dallas Cowboys fan in good times and bad, for better or for worse.I have no poker face. My brain leaks out of my eyes. quite inconvenient.Most valued quality in others: authenticity. One of my few life regrets is that I never studied abroad, so to make up for it, I travel every chance I get, to see as much of our world as possible. What makes me most angry: injustice. To relax, I go out on my back patio where I can see some of the Texas stars through the light pollution and sit back in my anti-gravity lawn chair. I despise playing video games, unless it is with my nephews, then I love it. It is physically impossible for me to read only one book at a time.I am greatly annoyed at answers that are too simplistic. Greatly annoyed is probably understating my reaction.I am an introverted actress playing an extrovert. Future life goals: live ardently and make more mistakes.

Haunted Community

Being spooked

I am overwhelmed with anxiety. Addressing the question of spectral living fills me with apprehension. Indeed, my fingers hover over the keyboard, paralyzed, unable to type, and my breathing is labored. Perhaps this is a fitting response? After all, anxiety is an appropriate physiological response to seeing a ghost or encountering a specter, is it not? My angst is proof that I have been spooked and I recognize well one of the specters Jack describes: God-as-specter. That ghost in particular has done a number on me. I am not a gracefully haunted person, if there is such a thing. It spooks applies to many different kinds of people – the devout, the irreligious, and the skeptic. I am writing as one whose previous assumptions were shaken to the core when my matter-of-fact-God became God-as-specter that torments me persistently with this silent call.

After all, anxiety is an appropriate physiological response to seeing a ghost or encountering a specter, is it not?

My unease testifies to Jack's thesis that "it" spooks. Perhaps "it" is even spookier to those of us who previously thought we had everything settled with an arrogance of certainty. Some of us had God figured out quite well, thank you very much! We knew his voice, how to contact him, how to please him, how to anger him, and what words to say to convince him to act on our behalf. We could explain it all to you in five easy steps. Or conversely, perhaps we were certain that faith in God is a psychological crutch, a concoction of boorish people who have no knowledge of basic physics, math, or biology.

We had it all figured out.... that is until we got spooked by "it," and, once spooked, everything changed. Suddenly, our tried and trusted methods of coping with life's anxieties no longer work. We couldn't assuage the spooky voice with our go-to Bible verse or meditative prayer. The music no longer soothed. The scientific formulas do not add up. The hypotheses fail. How do other people cope? People who never had my Answers. How do they deal with stress, anxiety, sick loved ones, broken dreams, love lost, death, and our own precarious place in the universe? What do they know that I don't? Perhaps I am not the right person to write about the spectral life. I am doomed from both sides of the fideism/scientism battle that Jack describes. I have relied on religious Answers for most of my life and my first foray into higher learning was in science – Biology to be exact. The scientific method is ingrained so deeply in me that I am scarcely conscious of it when I begin to problem-solve. I want to attack this essay with the formulas I see in religious, academic, and scientific circles. I want to provide a systematic path forward for living spectrally in a clear way that leads to a happy life, healthy communities, and overall positive functioning in the world as a....haunted person?

S i g h .

I see the faces of the spooked souls I have encountered (and my own face staring back at me in the mirror) and realize.... no, this isn't going to be pretty.

So I will start there - where the spectral life originates - with a spooked, haunted soul. Have you seen a person who is truly spooked by something? She (or he) has the anxiety-ridden, hollow-eyed look of someone who has been locked in a bomb shelter for years stepping tentatively out into the world, jumping nervously at every loud sound, frightened of her (his) own shadow. Spooked people wander about aimlessly with blood-shot eyes from sleepless nights of wrestling with ghosts, constantly peering over their shoulders looking for something of which they know not what.

Like the protagonist in our favorite stories, the haunting that leaves a spooked soul in shambles often happens when she (he) is isolated, alone, and more likely to disbelieve the experience. Ebenezer Scrooge does what any rational person would do when confronted with the gruesome sight of his undead colleague – he explained the specter away to suppress his terror "for the spectre's voice disturbed the very marrow in his bones." Perhaps if Marley had visited earlier, when Scrooge was with Bob Cratchit, someone else would have been present to confirm the experience, to assure Scrooge that he had not lost his mental faculties. When spooked people have exhausted all options available under the names of theism and science and can no longer deny the spectral encounter, isolation is somewhat inevitable. Haunted people are difficult to be around. They do not see the world the same way anymore and have a hard time following its unspoken rules. They ask difficult questions that evade easy answers and frustrate the listener. Sooner or later, it is often easier for the spooked person to withdraw her (his) questions and continue to wrestle alone.

Creating God

I must further inspect the evidence of my hauntedness, my anxiety. Anxiety is defined as:

"an abnormal and overwhelming sense of apprehension and fear often marked by physiological signs (as sweating, tension, and increased pulse), by doubt concerning the reality and nature of the threat, and by self-doubt about one's capacity to cope with it."

This is central to the anxiety – I do not know the reality and nature of the threat of "it" that spooks me. The "it" that Jack describes is anonymous. It is undefined. Null set. It has no name.

To suppress anxiety, we silence God-as-specter, rob him of his anonymity, delimit his existence, and give him a name. Whatever calls out under the name of God is often defined, controlled, and managed by the powers-that-be who determine the character of God, what or whom God loves and hates, and the rules to follow in order to placate him. Naming what spooks us provides a comforting illusion of manageability and control. And if there is anything that we desperately want to control, it is the concept of an omniscient going about blessing some and cursing others – blasting out power on an unsuspecting populace. That is entirely too spooky.

Naming a thing not only provides the mirage of control, it also seals ownership on what is created as illustrated in the creation story, when God created and named Adam.

Then God said, "Let us make mankind in our image, in our likeness, so that they may rule over the fish in the sea and the birds in the sky, over the livestock and all the wild animals, and over all the creatures that move along the ground." So God created mankind in his own image, in the image of God he created them; male and female he created them."

God created mankind to rule, and mankind returns the favor. By delineating the boundaries of God – naming what he wants, how he works, his home on high, and even his enemies - we create "God." Through creeds, rituals, traditions, and hermeneutics, religion creates a God that mimics the people ruled by him. Observing the striking similarities between a culture and its God is disturbing to me.

Vengeful people have a vengeful God.
Misogynistic people have a misogynistic God.
Compassionate people have a compassionate God.
Conservative people have a conservative God.
Liberal people have a liberal God.
Apathetic people have an apathetic God.

Is it possible to separate the person from their God? When we delimit God and steal his anonymity, we write a twisted account of the creation story.

Have we not, in effect, said,

"Let us make God in our own image, in our likeness, so that he may rule over us?"

But a God that is a specter cannot be named and cannot be controlled. When we cannot make out exactly what is calling us, or the specifics of the call itself, we stay agitated. We cannot contain it. We cannot name it. Maybe it is good that God wasn't keen on sharing his name with anyone:

"Moses said to God,

"Suppose I go to the Israelites and say to them, 'The God of your fathers has sent me to you,' and they ask me, 'What

> is his name?' Then what shall I tell them?" God said to Moses, "I AM WHO I AM. This is what you are to say to the Israelites: 'I AM has sent me to you.'""

I always found this passage odd. Why would God be so squirrelly about his name of all things? I think it may make more sense to me now.

We are all authors of our own stories and we name our outcomes in ways that suit us. We write narratives that explain who we are, what role others play, and even who God is or is not. We pile our expectations upon God so high that it is impossible to separate God from them. Letting God maintain his anonymity requires valor. We can no longer say we are "simply" following God when what we believe or what we do in the name of God is questioned. With a spectral call, there is no one to blame, no one responsible but us. This is both liberating and frightening all at the same time. Personally, I find it more than spooky – terrifying to the bone – to question my concept of a God that is out there somewhere protecting me with an overall plan that somehow, someway will transform the bleakest of outcomes into something beautiful for me. Surrendering that makes me feel alone in the world. Encountering a specter can make us lonely, and none more so than an un-nameable, unmanageable, uncontrollable God-as-specter. Who can I tell after all? I am doubting my own sanity here. I certainly do not need someone else questioning it also.

Haunted Communities

While this kind of loneliness cannot be cured, I have found some respite by participating in what I am calling haunted communities. Recently, I have found venues for meeting other spooked people at short-term events and through multiple online forums. In these settings, I have observed pervasive themes of isolation. The relief that comes from meeting others spooked by the same specter makes haunted people willing to travel great distances just to be in the same room as others with similarly spooky tales, or to stay up late to talk online with spooked people on the other side of the planet. Encountering another person who knows the sound of the unheard call is beneficial – someone is present to reassure me that this whole experience is not just a figment of my imagination or some sort of personal neurosis. I am not just being disturbed by undigested beef, as Scrooge hypothesized. Finding a haunted community – whether in person or virtually - can mitigate the sense of isolation that being spooked can cause.

Some spooked people, like myself, cannot flourish in traditional religious communities.

Some spooked people, like myself, cannot flourish in traditional religious communities. I have often heard religious institutions self-describe as a hospital for the soul. In my experience, this is an apt metaphor. Hospitals are quite sanitized. Everyone inside – nurses, patients, and visitors alike - follow the orders of the doctor-in-charge. Hospitals are a risk-averse environment – exceedingly precautionary, concerned about any kind of contaminant penetrating the highly controlled internal environment and infecting those inside. Nurses and doctors wear masks and gloves to protect and separate them from the sick; though ironically, a hospital is a likely place to contract a stubborn infection resistant to treatment. Hospitals are bright with those irritating florescent lights which are tough on bloodshot, sleepless eyes. The sounds of beeping and whirring machines fill each room to signal even the slightest change in the patient's condition to caretakers.

Spooked people may be more at home in a haunted house than a hospital. Haunted houses are the opposite of sanitized - full of decay and rot. Dried blood is visible and disconnected bones litter rancid rooms. They are crawling with cobwebs, snakes, spiders, and rats. In haunted houses we don't find the blinding light needed for surgery, but drafty darkness. The only visible light is faint moonlight, which seeps through the cracks of rotting walls and ceilings, granting a small peek into the next room of horrors. The sounds of hooting owls, slamming doors, smashing objects, and inhuman wails startle the visitor without warning or pattern. Whenever a haunted house appears in a story, we know that something ominous is about to happen or something heinous already happened. The music doesn't soar with victory as it does in religious institutions; instead, the music that accompanies spooks and the spooked is filled with dissonant minor chords and nonlinear sounds that leave us apprehensive. We know without words that something spooky is in the works.

To live a spectral life is to accept a messy life and the very messy, haunted communities in haunted houses. What do you suppose will happen when spooked, lonely, anxious people come together? No, this isn't going to be pretty at all. We cannot expect those who have encountered the undead to function any better than those who acknowledge only the living, can we? We are talking about specters after all. This won't be serene. It won't be clean, everyone will not always be pleasant that's for sure. Haunted people may have negative emotionsto express– fear, anxiety, anger, loneliness, depression. There may be wailing, moaning, and gasping in fear.

So many spooked people remain isolated in their own corners of the world, which makes me grateful for the small, haunted community that I have the privilege of seeing every week. We go by the "name" of [noname]. We are not experts on living well as haunted people. We do not have a long list of successes to discuss. The individuals that make up [no name] live very different lives. Our family and relationship statuses, methods of making a living, and even our spiritual (un)beliefs are different. Some of us read the Bible regularly, occasionally attend traditional church services, and self-describe as having a personal relationship with God. Others have almost a biblical aversion and would not be caught dead (ahem) in a church building. How do you name a group of people who do not have the same beliefs and do not worship a God with well-defined boundaries and unshakeable creeds? How do you name a group who cannot put forth a defining statement or articulate with a single voice why it is we even come together? We are called many names by others but we can own no name for ourselves, for there is no name that would encompass us all without leaving one of us out.

[Noname] does not have everything figured out – well, at least we don't anymore. Most of us thought we did at one time.We were once leaders in our previous religious circles. We believed in the God created for us, and the one we created ourselves. We believed it with no holds barred until we could no longer suppress the haunting voice of what was left out in the well-defined, well-controlled, and well-named God.We became haunted people, difficult to be around. We asked questions that made others uneasy. Somehow, over the years, we became more comfortable with the spectral undecideability that Jack describes. Comfortable is probably not the right word. But we know the undecideability. We learned it the hard way. Honestly, we often think there must be a better way than this.

We have not mastered how to live in response to the unheard call, but we know what that call is like– the tortured whispers from faceless specters. It is fragmented, disorganized, uncertain, and often incoherent. When attempting to answer the call, I often do not know whether I am responding to it or fighting against it. My community is trying to live with the undecideability that Jack describes instead of controlling, suppressing, delimiting, and naming it. We are hoping for the courage to let God maintain his anonymity and live without certainty.

Hosting spooked people takes a strong stomach. The voice of apprehension, pain, restlessness, and hope deferred can be daunting to those that hear it.

Haunted Hospitality

A haunted house is undergoing de-construction – it is rotting, becoming un-pieced together, deteriorating. Jack has stated that deconstruction offers ghosts hospitality. Spooked souls residing in haunted houses become more accustomed to the presence of ghosts and comfortable to the point that they can show ghosts hospitality by becoming more attuned to the ghostly whisper. Perhaps hospitality to ghosts begins by being hospitable to those who see ghosts – to those who agonize at the spectral call that challenges the religious, scientific, and academic institutions that once made us feel safe by providing a proper name for everything. When I discovered that God is not confined to what I created him to be, I needed time to lament and transition into a space where God is free to insist without the chains of my expectations upon him. Hosting spooked people takes a strong stomach. The voice of apprehension, pain, restlessness, and hope deferred can be daunting to those that hear it. My community is anything but sanitized when it comes to this:

"God is a sadistic bastard."
"God could have saved my baby and didn't. God was supposed to be protecting my baby, but he let him die by negligence."
"God is just another man who has rejected me."

How does a haunted community respond to the hauntedness of its members? If such a community can continue to "be" with each other through painful statements that cut through to the heart then perhaps, this is a way to be hospitable to ghosts.

Great comfort comes from connecting with those who have seen the same specters in haunted communities, but this does not mean that haunted communities will run smoothly. The interpretation of spectral events is unlikely to be the same among individual spooked people. In haunted communities, we can demonstrate hospitality by exhibiting tolerance for haunted hermeneutics – this is how [no name] exists without unified beliefs. We understand that everything is interpreted, and nothing more so than an unheard call. We value the singular experiences had by the members of our community and we respect unique interpretations of the spectral call.

As we experience the spectral life and listen to various interpretations of the unheard call, questions will arise. Jack discusses the courage to ask any question, which I believe is crucial to haunted hospitality.

Yes, any question. Not just the safe ones. Not just the ones that I am comfortable fielding. Not just the ones that do not cause me to question my own assumptions. Not just the ones that do not arouse my own fears and anxieties. Any question.

We have created an environment where any question is acceptable.

My community does that. We have created an environment where any question is acceptable. However, this does not mean that all questions have answers. In [noname] we do not have Answers though we may sometimes have answers. Haunted communities must resist the temptation to provide clichés and easy answers to mitigate hauntedness. Easy answers will not help those who have been spooked. Can you imagine providing an over-simplified solution to a terrified Ebenezer Scrooge? No, it was the very fact that Scrooge was haunted that he began to engage his fellow-man, his own humanness, and care for those around him.

Ebenezer Scrooge was transformed - and he was transformed precisely because of his encounter with ghosts, not in spite of them. Jack said that specters expect a life of transformation. I wonder if transformation is really possible in isolation – locked away in a room alone. Indeed, Scrooge was not changed until he left his bedchambers and went out on the streets of London and encountered his fellow-man. I believe that relationship with others is a critical ingredient for transformation – and this is why it disturbs me that many spooked people are isolated from a community that could aid this transformation. As strange as haunted communities may appear to more traditional groups, I believe they are desperately needed to provide the encouragement needed by spooked people to respond to the unheard call and show hospitality to specters.

Haunted hospitality requires courage. By definition, haunted people are risk-takers – answering a call that is unheard opens us up to all kinds of risk. If living spectrally means, as Jack has said, that we need the hardiness to say yes to the coming of what we cannot see coming, a different kind of courage is called for. How can you say yes when you are not sure who is calling, what is being said, or what it means for your future? This is a very courageous yes.

According to Jack, "The only witness to the call is the response; the rest is spectral, invisible, ghostly. To the rest of the world those who are moved by God look like dancers where no one else can hear the music." Haunted hospitality enables dancing. [no name] dances, but our dance is not a flowing waltz or a graceful ballet. Our dancing is more like flamenco dancing. I saw flamenco dancing in Spain and it is one of the most moving artistic expressions I have ever witnessed. Flamenco involves voice and guitar and a passionate dance with sweeping arm movements-not to mention loud foot stomping, and hand clapping. Flamenco is known for its intense display of emotion. The singing that accompanies this dance is like guttural moaning. I could not understand the words because I do not speak the language, but I recognized every one, I felt every one. Flamenco is most definitely haunted and the expression and passion of the dancing can seem almost violent and angry. It is one of the most beautiful things I have ever seen. Sometimes the dancing in my community is painful to watch, but every once in awhile, someone makes a move that takes my breath away.

Haunted hospitality provides the courage to be present with each other without trying to repair each other.

Engaging in haunted hospitality in haunted communities can be difficult, uncomfortable, and often ugly. Why wouldn't it be? As I have mentioned haunted people are often anxious, isolated, disappointed, lonely, and restless. But they are also incredibly courageous and beautiful. Haunted hospitality provides the courage to be present with each other without trying to repair each other. It allows us to come together—not around belief or mission, but around love, companionship, and maybe even survival. Haunted hospitality can mitigate the isolation that follows a visitation from a specter, and it can provide the environs for transformation.

Interfering for Good

Ebenezer Scrooge made a pertinent observation of the spectral world during Marley's visit:

"The air was filled with phantoms, wandering hither and thither in restless haste, and moaning as they went. Every one of them wore chains like Marley's Ghost; some few (they might be guilty governments) were linked together; none were free. Many had been personally known to Scrooge in their lives. He had been quite familiar with one old ghost, in a white waistcoat, with a monstrous iron safe attached to its ankle, who cried piteously at being unable to assist a wretched woman with an infant, whom it saw below upon a door-step. The misery with them all was clearly, that they sought to interfere, for good, in human matters, and had lost the power forever." (emphasis mine)

Scrooge observed that the specters' chief misery was not the chains weighing them down, but the inability to act on behalf of the living. This pinpoints the source of hope for haunted communities, and why as Jack says, we can dare to hope. Like our friend, Ebenezer, we still have the power to interfere for good (or evil) in human matters – and our hauntedness enables us to see this opportunity. For me, that is the driving force for moving forward –to acknowledge and embrace our ability to affect what happens in the world and to see it for the gift that it is, while we are able. If there is such a thing as a goal in haunted communities, that may be it: To interfere for good in human matters.

Haunted communities may not be able to organize around shared beliefs, but they can organize around the hope that comes from the ability to affect outcomes. I see this in my community - the individuals who are part of [no name] have individual passions that reflect their own spectral experiences. One hears the unheard call from Africa and has taken steps to gather medical supplies to interfere in the lives of the impoverished and sick there – and our community supports such efforts. We also support another member who works with women in crisis pregnancy. [no name] does not have an organized program of good works, we do not contribute monthly to any one cause, we do not tithe to a group fund; we simply support each other in whatever ways we can to interfere for good.

Is it possible to organize around love instead of belief?

Leading a spectral life is not about denying or embracing religion but, as Jack said, about re-reading and re-inventing religion. In spectral living, much of the gospel is preserved and may resemble life in some religious communities – works of love, mercy, and compassion - not to store up treasures in heaven but because we do not want to squander the ability to interfere for good. The motivation for action is different. Jack makes a big accusation in his piece – making God a divine accountant is the worst form of paganism. I cannot help but agree– if we act for a heavenly payoff in the sky, what are we really doing but turning works of mercy into capitalism: Wise investments for a long retirement?

Instead, response to the unheard call is love for no reason, love what you do not understand, love the people who understand it differently, and love the humanity we see in each other.

> *John had it right. "No one has ever seen God; but if we love one another, God lives in us and his love is made complete in us."*

I cannot figure out what holds my community together unless it is just that. Somehow, in our ugliest moments, in our wretched pain, we fell in love with each other. Is it possible to organize around love instead of belief? That is our little experiment. The mystics embrace life without why, [no name] is trying feebly and imperfectly to love without why. We attempt to love the messy in each other perhaps in the hope that we can accept the messy in ourselves. We continue to wrestle with a way of being in the world, post-being-spooked.

Jack challenges us to dare to hope.

I agree.

I would add: Dare to love.

Dare to love the unlovable,

the confusing,

the messy,

the frustrating,

and the haunted.

By the impossible everything begins by Denise Casey

let's tie our tongues into nonsensical sounds!
rave in silent syllables
let contradicting shapes crash against each other
until all we have
are tiny prisms
refracting fragments into colors
we cannot confuse with consciousness

then,
let us dance a square
into a line
into a circle
into a breath

then,
let us bend our thoughts so far they become the wind
bend the wind so far it becomes a cry
bend a tear so far it becomes the river
the water
that feeds us
cleans us
and remembers us
into life

MICHAEL

WHIMSICAL GYPSY

ENNEAGRAM 5/4

GUNGOR

THE FOLLOWING ARE THE MASKS MICHAEL GUNGOR HAS BEEN KNOWN TO WEAR IN THE PUBLIC SPHERE:

Musician, composer, author

HERE'S WHAT THIS CONTRIBUTOR WOULD SAY ABOUT HIMSELF:

I live in Los Angeles with my wife Lisa and two daughters, Amelie and Lucette. I spend most of my days making music and not quite enough of my evenings demonstrating the hypocrisy of my confessed love of non-violence by killing many, many people on my Playstation 4.

Once upon a time

there was a musician who was plagued by the possibility that music did not actually exist. Every morning when he approached his piano, the pent up anxiety quickly found its way back to his stomach, and the whole fight began once again.

Why should I waste my time at this piano if all I am doing by playing is spreading the illusion that such a thing as music really exists--as though there were actually some sort of platonic form of reality that could break into the human realm of perception through the vibrating strings of a Yamaha upright piano? What is that piano after all but meaningless and empty space tinged with chaotic relationships of conflicting energy? What is music then but just more emptiness and violence and entropy? What is it but a grand illusion that preys upon feeble human minds in offering unfulfillable promises of Beauty and Meaning?

Many would consider questions like these to be silly indulgences afforded only by privilege, but these were the kind of questions that clenched at his mind and clogged his heart every morning as he tried to play. And every morning, he found himself fighting these doubts with a fierce but somehow slightly less believable apologetic for the meaning and beauty of music.

After all, music is objectively beautiful is it not?

It is made of mathematical relationships that seem to have real empirical weight. If those mathematical relationships were not "real", then nothing about the universe as we experience it is "real." And if nothing is real, then perhaps the meaning of real ought to be redefined anyway, and the original question loses its own weight. So rather than play his piano, the musician found himself spending more and more time and energy wrestling with such ideas. Some days the internal fight caused pacing and agitation, other days it caused over eating or the bed ridden laziness that can accompany existential depression.

The musician sometimes received emails from people who praised his work and told him stories of how his music influenced their lives: stories of emotional healing and opened hearts. The musician experienced a disturbing ambivalence when he'd come across these stories. He was both inspired and embarrassed by them.

He felt like both a healer and a trickster--a vendor of musical placebos, a purveyor of both good and evil, truth and falsehood, if such distinctions had any meaning.

He was happy that these people seemed to be made happy by his music, but he felt it to be a shallow and cheap trick. What sort of fragile happiness could it be after all--that which came and went dependent on the random vibrations of the Chaos? He combined frequencies in a way that tricked the mind into thinking that the ear was hearing something real; something that existed and gave the universe an illusion of grandeur, beauty and order. Was he nothing but a snake oil salesman manipulating people's emotions and ultimately championing the egocentric violence and narcissistic falsehoods that these poor souls based their lives on?

As strong as his nihilism barraged him however, he had other things to worry about. His rent, for instance. If he wanted to live the life he wanted, he needed money, and if wanted money, he had to work. And he wasn't very skilled at anything except music--at crafting these sonorous parlor tricks that made people feel like they should pay him for their emotional experience. He was sort of like a whore or a crack dealer, really. Offering good feelings to whoever regardless (or at least not fully aware of) all the long term consequences of such mind-fucking. But a man has to eat.

So every morning, he tried to make his music. And every morning the music was interrupted by the questions. And it wasn't long before the music started to change. To some people's ears, the music was becoming more theoretical and mathematical and less emotional or heartfelt. After the poetry and mysticism of music had been deconstructed, all that was left was empty words, mathematical relationships and some staff paper. As the musician's perspective had evolved from the naive romanticism of his youth to a more calculated and reductionist modernism, so did his music. He had begun to experiment with novel tunings and extremely dissonant tone rows. He experimented with time and tempo in new and unique ways. After all, if time was simply an illusion, why should everyone in the band feel the need play to the same tempo? After a few years of this sort of composing though, the musician began to lose interest in the novel. After all, although he no longer felt like a manipulator of emotions, he still was engaged in a field that was largely meaningless to him. Why did it really matter in the scheme of things whether a string vibrated 440 times in a second as opposed to 430 or 450 or whether or not he came up with a completely new and novel tone row sequence? It didn't.

So, once again, the musician found himself in the grip of nihilistic depression. As the color had faded from the world, the soul had faded from his music. He had lost the desire to compose.

Still, the musician had to eat, so one morning, after seeing that there was literally no more food left in his kitchen cupboards, he begrudgingly came back to the piano once again.

Screw the intellectual idealism. He was going to write a hit and pay some bills. But as he placed his fingers upon the keys, he had no idea what to play. As he racked his brain for some sort of tempo, key or melody, he was simply unable to hear anything. The music was gone. Nothing remained but emptiness. A dizzyingly silent vacuum of nothingness. He closed the piano, held his head in his hands, and began to cry. His heart had finally broken and the tears contained within spilled out onto the stained wood of the piano. With deep guttural sobs, his soul purged some sort of poison that had been there far too long. Then, suddenly he had a revelation and the tears stopped. He knew it in a moment, and in that moment the world changed. Music was finished for him. He didn't believe in it anymore. He would no longer try. He would have to find a different career. He had wasted so much of his life at this piano. Thousands of hours for a meaningless illusion. But there was no use in wasting any more of it. It was time to stop. As the tears came to an end, so did the angst. So the musician who had given his whole life to music finally stopped believing in music. He stood up from the piano, wiped his eyes and decided to go for a walk.

And that's what the musician did every day for the next few weeks. He stopped thinking about music. Instead, he took walks. He spent time with his family. He got a part time job at a local bookstore. He started living his life again.

The strangest thing about it was that he would often be heard in parks or at work unconsciously humming these little melodies.

Melodies that were surprisingly complex and beautiful in the ears of those who found themselves eavesdropping. Then one night, as the musician was walking up the stairs to go to bed, he noticed the upright Yamaha piano gathering dust in the corner, but for some reason it looked different to him now than it always used to. Before, it had become a responsibility, a chore, a source of fear and guilt. Now it was just an interesting possibility. Without really thinking much about it, he began to accompany the melody in his head.

It was months later, after the debut of his newest piano concerto that a reporter asked the musician about his philosophy of composition. The musician laughed and said, "I don't actually consider myself a musical composer anymore. I have no ability to understand or philosophize about music, but I do love what happens when I sit at that empty space full of conflicting energy called a piano."

CATHERINE KELLER

theologian
friend
earthling

THESE ARE THE MASKS THAT CATHERINE KELLER HAS BEEN KNOWN TO WEAR IN THE PUBLIC SPHERE:

Catherine Keller is Professor of Constructive Theology in the Theological School and Graduate Division of Religion of Drew University, where she teaches multiple populations and aspirations. She steers the Transdisciplinary Theological Colloquium at Drew annually, from which spring co-edited volumes such as Ecospirit, Apophatic Bodies, Polydoxy, Divinanimality. Her monographs include.... [fill in as many as you like) And most recently, The Cloud of the Impossible: Negative Theology and Planetary Entanglement.

HERE'S WHAT THIS CONTRIBUTOR WOULD SAY ABOUT HERSELF:

The actual life? It got off to a chaotic start, not without adventures, traumas, gifts. I am grateful for the teachers, the seminary communities, the stabilizations that pulled my life together. I empty it into my teaching and writing and worrying about the life of the world, but replenish me through-a hit of friendship near or far, yoga class, making squash soup, a cozy evening with Jason or a murder mystery, some Bach, hearing from former students...

Dear Jack:

I am hoping that by writing this response to your essay, which compresses in itself the vast theology of The Insistence of God, in the genre of a letter, I will avoid writing a book. It is difficult to think with you without expanding, exploding into the multiplicity of riffs and replies, excited agreement and worried difference that your work provokes. And now more than ever. Indeed your own genre invites it, with its voice-and so singularly vocal a voice it is, vocare, calling -of passionate appeal and punchy polemic. On the one hand you undo the bully-tactics of thought, all top-down "omni-macho" language, Word; on the other you are summoning "troops on the ground" for your inexistent but insistent God. (Any king is weak without His troops, one might retort, a bit snarkily; oh but come, this is no sovereign mobilization, this is urgent cosmic dependence, one says back; perhaps, says another.)(What, am I now going to tuck the possible book, the one I will not write, the one that will spook every sentence, into parentheses?) (No, I promise not to, I may resort to a list of questions instead, and for any point of mine that seems underdeveloped and in need of cites and notes exceeding this epistle, please just buy my Cloud of the Impossible.)

What I want to say above all is this: you, John D. Caputo, reach right into the wretched heart of Christianity with your daunting and haunting "perhaps." You reach right into the bloody mess of it, of us, with your insistence "that God is not something present, a pure, perfect and complete presence, presiding over all, an omni-being who out-knows, out-wits, and generally overwhelms His (sic) creatures." You penetrate the hard-core doctrine of the pater omnipotens that keeps most of us cringing, except for those guys in robes or suits who speak knowingly of and for Him. From the onset of your contemplation of the "weakness" and then the "insistence"-no whimpy weakness, no mere lack or absence, that weakness, after all that of Paul's "weakness of God"--you nail the problem of power, which is in my book a way of unnailing His poor son. With a prose that feels no weaker than does a Pauline epistle, but that fortunately lacks all magesterial authority, you rip off the mask of all-controlling power, exposing there a God, a haunting, haunted Perhaps, who needs us. Who needs our meaty bodies, "to come to its aid." You reveal an infinity-nothing enclosed and self-sufficient, but infinite in the root sense of unfinished, incomplete-to conjugate its infinitive. Let me shout hallelujah! Or if that is too Protestant, uncouth, unwhite here, make that a "oui, oui!"

Of course your point if I reveal the full sentence is this: "When I venture to say that God does not exist, I am saying that God is not something present, a pure, perfect and complete presence, presiding over all..." etc. So if God does not meet the standards of classical orthodoxy, God cannot exist? This is where I fall into a bit of confusion-my hallelujah breaks. And that might be the best thing for a hallelujah, if we croon it ala Leonard Cohen. But really I have to admit that I am still a bit hooked on a logic that runs in an apparently opposite direction: if I would venture to say that God exists, I am saying that the omnipotent, complete God does not. Perhaps the boisterous bug of feminist theology bit me too early: I wasn't about to let Him define God for me. Make that 'we': we were not going to yield God to the Big Guy in the Sky doling out Pie (that someone else baked). "Neither am I," I hear you saying, that is the point: it is just His existence that is at stake. Those decades of feminist intensity may just be demonstrating the insistence of something harbored in the name of God. A name we were always uncomfortable with, undoing and redoing with pronouns (S/he/it!) and substitutions. Right. And besides, feminist theology was not worried about the question of divine existence as such so much as what kind of human existence it fosters: the concrete embodiments of theology in our collective existence. Yes, yes, that embodiment, that actualization, is also your objective. (Hallelujah, brother.)

So then let me more formally express my resistance to the theology of insistence denuded of existence. It is because I encountered a theology according to which that deus omnipotens does NOT exist, that I continued to think God just might exist. It was a theology that teaches that God the controlling and intervening one does not exist. Indeed it offers a whole litany of non-existences: the all-foreseeing omniscience, the unmoved Mover, the changeless eternity, the moralist judge, the masculine superpower. These are the attributes of a tragically entrenched idol of power. [cf C/G]. "The Church gave unto God the attributes which belonged exclusively to Caesar." That is a line of A. N. Whitehead in 1927, and I am speaking of course of process theology. I wandered onto other discourses-as process theology encourages one to do-and because among them was the attractive alternative of Derrida and his people, I might have abandoned process theology. As after all-a cosmology. Metaphysical. Ontological. Out of style, out of pace.

But I couldn't do theology, I found, let alone teach it, without the process arguments. It kept cutting through the theodicy problem suffered by almost every sensitive student I have taught: they have been tormented (a strong form of haunting) by the question of how God could permit or directly will such sorrows, such horrors, such holocausts. How can they believe in a God who . And over and over I witness the burst of luminescence as they realize-that God does not exist. What might exist, what might be worthy of the name of God--and I admit my language has always been more elusive, more perhapsy, than that of many process theologians-would operate not through coercion but through persuasion. Not through the imposition of a will but through what Whitehead called "the Eros of the universe." There is not a Big something that Exists and imposes its will upon all the little existences it has made. For process theology all along the act of existence is actualization in and as actual creatures, humans and all the others. The divine input is the lure to a possibility that may otherwise remain impossible. But it doesn't, it can't, do the actualizing. That is our job. As I teach my students.

I think for you (Jack) if I were a truly "radical theologian," I would have gone on while I had their wide-eyed attention and announce that not only does the classical God not exist. No God exists. Tada! Then of course go on to clarify that this is not atheism That the problem is with the metaphysics of "to exist "

Problem is I am speaking here of my seminary students, who feel (insistently) called to some form of ministry. Problem is they are not mostly white and male philosophy students but wildly and cross culturally diverse folk; some of them, for instance, are Black inner city survivors whose Pentecostal or Baptist faith has indeed saved their lives. I am not interested in any theology that cannot reach them. Opening them to feminist and womanist and socio-ecological and underneath it all process theology is awfully hard work but on the whole it--works. Only a few then espouse process theology as such; but most proceed with a far weaker sense that Daddy will step in to fix things. And a much stronger sense of human responsibility for the shalom of the world. And to then announce that God insists but does not exist-well, back they would recoil in an instant, betrayed, to their old habits. Sometimes quite fundamentalist. Sometimes quite pragmatic, agnostic, confessional. They would not wait around for me to make the (rather scholastic) distinction between atheism and my position. Not just deconstructing the abusive God-symbolism of Christendom but actually constructing some helpful pushback against Him, in other words some alternative theism, is what I imagine God is insisting upon me, is how I make a bit of difference in the world. I need to be able to communicate with my folk. And of course I cannot communicate effectively unless I mean it. They can tell when we liberal theologians are lying to placate them, even if they cannot yet win the argument. This is part of the depression, indeed the possible doom, soon, of mainline Christianity, of course. So I go deeper-with my seminary students-into process theology. I know you know about this range of audiences. And I admit jubilantly that I use your What Would Jesus Deconstruct? in precisely this intro to theology required course.

The Weakness or The Insistence? Only in advanced seminars. Because whether or not they finally assent to a dogmatic form of God's Caputan inexistence, I think theological scholars need to meditate on "God insists but does not exist." Like a Zen koan. And it will not cease to haunt us.

And it will disturb the trope of God as "actual entity" in Whitehead. But delicately, for his point (political theologians take note) was to undermine the sovereign exceptionalism of divinity: God is here instantiation rather than exception of the "metaphysical categories"-that nothing exists outside of relationship; that existence is becoming. What did metaphysics mean for him-besides the risk of alienating most contemporary thinkers already in the 20's, including his student and co-author of the Principia Mathematica Bertrand Russell? It allows him to imagine, but to imagine philosophically, rigorously, transdisciplinarily, that which was silenced by both standard theology and standard science. Metaphysics is thus defined as "a series of metaphors mutely appealing for an intuitive leap." How scary is that?

God is "creativity's first creature" in Whitehead, it is because God only comes to be, only becomes, in and through interaction with a world. And there is in this view always some sort of universe, if not this one, so there is no ex nihilo of world-or God. So no, God in process theology does not exist in the classical sense of existence, or for that matter of essence, at all. The whole movement flows from Whitehead's deconstruction (as a mathematical cosmologist turned theistic philosopher, not as a theologian) of classical substance metaphysics. And so of the notion of any self-identically enduring existence, any subsistent existent. The pure possibilities may be eternal, but they remain abstract and inexistent apart from their actualizations in the bodies of actual creatures.

It is up to us to do God, I am saying these days, to put it simply. Of course God isn't simple. Classical simplicity is part of the problem, the notion of a noncomposite, ie., substantial and pure Oneness. For process theology the God which becomes comes to be out of all the unimaginably countless events composing the cosmos at any given moment and therefore giving God body. Charles Hartshorne, Whitehead's teaching assistant and another great philosopher ignored in most philosophy departments, articulated the metaphor of the "universe as the body of God." This would become the basis of some influential ecofeminist theology, Sallie McFague's Body of God and Ivone Gebara's "sacred body." The name of the little book in which he offers the trope is Omnipotence and Other Theological Mistakes. Punchy and teachable. So this fragile tradition that has evacuated theology of omnipotence yields an utterly embodied God, seeking materialization now in actions of planetary responsibility. Doing God. A new cosmopolitical theopoiesis.

I hear you saying, yes, nice, that is all very nice, surely better than the old alternatives, the old theism and the aging atheism. But it is not truly radical theology. As long as God is existing in any sense at all. And as long as you are doing, after all Catherine, metaphysics! "Wine without alcohol." (As you seem to dismiss the whole tradition of liberal and liberation theology, epitomized in a paragraph in Insistence by M L King. Who presumably would count as more "radical" if he had not occasionally presumed some existence of God, and if he had therefore shunned about 90% of the Black public and hung out drinking with the truly radical white guys?) So yes I admit to some reliance on thinking about God and cosmos that has called itself metaphysical. Though I can only use the term with irony (metaphysics meaning 'after the physics,' I do offer a metaphysics chapter on Deleuze and Whitehead immediately following my chapter on physics. Cloud. It is not my last chapter.) I admit that I do not think that "metaphysics" is a worthy opponent-whereas the guys in red dresses using metaphysics to burn other metaphysical thinkers, like Giordano Bruno and Marguerite de Porete, are worthy enemies indeed. As is racism, climate change denial, homophobia, neoliberal capitalism, and the versions of patrilineal authority, whether they do metaphysics and like the purveyors of value-free positivist technoscience, anti-metaphysics I do not think it is an opponent worthy of the Caputan brilliance. Which is undeniable, and crackles with hyperbolic satire.

It is just that I get a bit defensive when I realize that my involvement in a species of process theology might get me somehow mated with those guys who would have burnt all of us feminist theologians at the stake, if someone hadn't taken their matches away. But they are still going after Roman Catholic feminists such as Elizabeth Johnson and Ivone Gebara, those radical nuns whose work I depend upon. Johnson does not question God's existence, she just cashes it into a trinity of Sophias. Is that sheerly and explicitly metaphoric move less radical than saying He does not exist? Gebara differently, does question God's existence if is that of an entity rather than a relationship. Yet both of these thinkers are entangled in modes of process-linked, ontological relationalism which one can if one wishes dismiss as "metaphysical." They are victims, not victors, of the ongoing inquisition. Of a bully metaphysics-which is of course just what you mean to denounce. But you do generalize (cracklingly satirically, but not, thank the inexistent God, going up in the inquisition's flames) about metaphysics and about neoplatonism in ways that make me glad for the chance to raise these concerns. (I will try to avoid here a disquisition on the stunning radicality of so much of the tradition of negative theology, a tradition that you often love, including Bruno and Eckhart, as precisely and irrevocably dependent on aspects of neoplatonism; indeed on that strand lifted up by Plotinus, Proclus and the PsueduDionysius that was mesmerized by Plato's late dialogue Parmenedes, where as I read him he is deconstructing the Platonism to come. Where he eviscerates the logic of Being as The One. Much as Derrida finds him mid-way through the Timaeus soliciting khora.)

And I suspect the problem is still the guys in the gowns. You sense them sniffing for your scent. If I had your background I might feel as you do about "metaphysics." It might be for me then ruined by early and aggressive over-exposure to the scholastic brothers. Those metaphysical brothers and those magesterial fathers seem to be, well, it must be said, haunting you-but not in the appealing way of Es Spukt. But by the time I got into theology (fortified by a family background of unstable eclecticism with only vague hints and haunts of religion) it was in a Protestant context. And Protestantism, on its mainline side as also on its opposite, fundamentalist side, was thoroughly anti-metaphysical. In this it was all too true to the Reformation, which aggressively purged its churches of the whole tradition of scholastic rationalism as well as of cosmological imagination, indeed of most philosophy beyond a serviceably degraded Kantianism. No doubt much of Luther's brilliant hyperbolic satire was needed refreshment. And it was quickly consolidated into Protestant orthodoxies.

So I wonder if you can hear why for some of us the anti-metaphysical tone will never ring radical. It sounds not a call of liberation but au contraire the trumpet of retreat from exploration. It is not that "metaphysics" names (for me) liberation. It is that much of what does liberate gets dismissed as precisely metaphysical by the paternity of orthodox Protestantism. I am thinking not just of the relational alternative to the (unconsciously metaphysical habits of) independent substances and thereby of independent male egoes- a constituent and empowering relationality key to so much feminist theology. That relationality keeps me referring, citing, self-dissipating dangerously, no doubt sacrificing straight ahead coherence: so for instance Carter Heyward, another feminist relationalist and courageous pioneer of unstraight theology: her lesbian(ish) God perhaps exists. And she wrote Saving Jesus from those who are Right. It is lovely that you are also inverting the "Jesus saves" of the right. I want to spook you with these metaphysically dark precursors you would not count as radical.

Nor am I only thinking of the work of relational ontology on the front of ecological disaster and climate change, in the form of a half century of warnings from process theology. Nor am I thinking just of the interdependencies that undo the anthropocentrism to which deconstruction was so blithely indifferent until Derrida rather late (better late than ever) found a muse in his kitty cat. (That I am gladly haunted by the two of them is clear in my collaboration on Divinanimality.)

I am also thinking of the radical new insights into the material universe and how we are mysteriously, nonreductively entangled in its microcosmic and macrocosmic minuet. It was as I suggested Whitehead's attention in the 20's to the new physics that led him to metaphysics-that is, to the need to incorporate the insights of indeterminacy and interrelation radically, that is, into every level of existence. This was to bring down the detached subject-observer, into "the democracy of fellow creatures." It is to discern animation, experience, a rudimentary vitality in any event of materialization. The new materialists are getting there now; and the affect theorists are getting it in part from Whitehead, for whom "every actual entity has to house its actual world." A demanding hospitality! You, Jack, have come into this cosmic vicinity. I quote: "Even if human and animal bodies are not as old as the universe and even if they are in the cosmic scheme of things fortuitous short-timers, they are places in which the universe is curled up in curiously inventive and intense concentrations"

One can avoid the speculative edges of physics only by staying with a physics averting its gaze from nonbiological agency, from the consequences of the quantum observer effect, and certainly from the shockingly relational significance of what Einstein called "spooky action at a distance." He did not mean it as a complement. He was badly spooked by this implication of quantum theory, and tried with Rosen and Podolsky for the rest of his life to make it go away. He couldn't. It bothered him because it threatened the determinist and separative presumptions (that is to say, 17th century metaphysics) of classical physics, which relativity theory did not disturb. And it threatened it with something eerily like mysticism. Es spukt!

Let me offer this spooky action therefore as a gift of the chaosmos to your cosmopoetics. To put it in a nutshell (or a nucleus): take any particle of matter, like a photon, and combine it with another, then divide them. They will fly off in opposite directions, with the exact same angle of spin. If you measure twin A, it will respond (as quanta do) unpredictably, randomly, to your observation. That was no longer the shocker. This is it: twin B will respond-just as indeterminately-in exactly the same way. As though you had measured it, not just A. As though they were never separated at all. At any distance. Even if, physicists now infer, they are on opposite sides of the galaxy. This unfathomable relationality is why U.S. physicists who got interested in it were until this century told to "shut up and calculate." Don't think about the meaning of this.

The metaphysics. Most still obey. I tell the longer story in chapter 4 in the Cloud, the chapter that precedes the metaphysics of Deleuze/Whitehead. It is just the lowest register in the manifold of what I am tracing as "apophatic entanglement."

That low register, of the simplest particles, spooks from the bottom up. It suggests a universe cloudy, yes, even ghostly, woven of waves in a quantum void which is anything but "nothing." And in which from a certain perspective only emerging in this millennium, the insane magnitudes of the universe collapse into this utter proximity. Everything is in a certain sense haunted by everything? But the particular hauntings, the observations that "collapse the wave function" or that provoke your writing-they begin now to expose their unthinkable nonseparability from you. No wonder that independent old he-go had to work so hard to carve, write, smash or bomb out a territory for his substantial properties.

The radical interrelation of creatures in a boundless universe was perhaps first articulated as a theologoumenon by one of the guys in the gowns, old Nicholas of Cusa (my chapter 3). And it was his apophatic theology that led him right to it. Some readers are familiar only through your work with this ancient heritage of unsaying of all the idolatrous certainties of theology-such as that God is Father, Son and Holy Spirit, such as even that "God is a being, "or-- "God exists". It is a neoplatonic tradition, and as such could very precisely, from within, deconstruct the congealed things, beings, entities, of the fused Christian Platonic orthodoxy, the ontotheological heritage. Not because we cannot meaningfully say that God exists, etc, etc, but that we can them only to be unsay them again. It goes back a good millennium before Cusa. It allowed him, for instance, to say such impossibilities for orthodoxy as-God is not only mover but moved. And so not only creator but created. Indeed that it more true to say God is creatable than to say God is creator. And to acknowledge that none of this language is more than "conjecture." [De Visio Dei.]

More and more I have found this deconstruction avant la lettre indispensable. But these old monks could only have come to haunt me-rather graciously, calling for my hospitality, never imposing themselves-in cahoots with Derrida's attention to negative theology. Not that it is more radical than the monks, if you read them in context. And with of course your reading of Derrida. Indispensable for unsaying even the friendly feminist process entitativeness-or existence-of God. But this unsaying is a parasite hosted, as I think you would not disagree, by the saying. But then the saying will self-deconstruct, as you are also saying. And that is not just one more negation, no: it is a saying otherwise. A theopoetics. Which as some of us say flows from theopoiesis: 'becoming God' who is thereby becoming. Doing God who thereby undoes the dogmas. Bark bark. They were spelling god backward anyway.

In your perhaps I am unwaveringly with you, if not in the (backward) certainty of your "does not exist." And I just want to remind you that "God insists upon existing." Oh yes, just as you say-in us, through us, through the whole chaosmos of us. Not in and for Himself. Or just for his friends the Son and Bird. But if God insists upon existing, I know of no honest way to deny God that prerogative. In and through us. But this us so apophatically expanded through the "worlds without end" and so intimately entangled that something that will sound a lot like what you and I still nickname God will keep materializing. Whitehead's "consequent nature of God," strictly contingent upon the becomings of the world, is the only way that God exists in process theology-as then the "fellow sufferer who understands." Yes, an omni-haunted God. Spooked and spooky, impure and in need--and nonetheless holy for it, this spirit. "God, being merely infinitival, needs concrete finite bodies to conjugate this infinitive." The infinite entanglement Perhaps that metaphor (my favorite current nickname.) may be by now read as a "spectral effect" of the insistence with which you will persist in resisting His/Her/Its existence.

Yours with that b r *oken*

h

l

a

l

l

e

u

j

a

h

ck

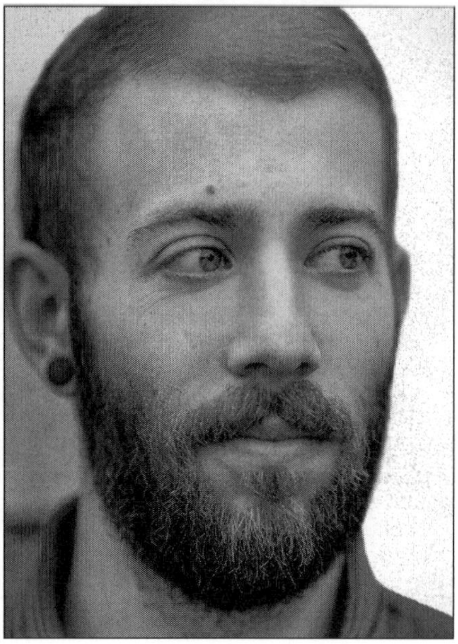

JOSHUA HARRIS

Sojourner

Observer

Réflecteur

THE FOLLOWING ARE THE MASKS JOSHUA HARRIS HAS BEEN KNOWN TO WEAR IN THE PUBLIC SPHERE:

He is a self taught artist and musician and has been working in varying aspects for years. After graduating with a B.A. in Religion from Kingswood University in New Brunswick, Canada, he spent several years exploring music while touring as the bass player in the band Atlantic. In that time he began to explore other mediums such as photography and graphic design. He now works in the creative arts department at Fountain Springs Church in Rapid City, SD and can be found all over social media at "/joshuaamharris".

HERE'S WHAT THIS CONTRIBUTOR WOULD SAY ABOUT HIMSELF:

I am a 29 year old artist and musician from Eastern Canada who likes to make and mix music, design and take photos of things, write, cook, and brew coffee. I would consider myself to be a "backslidden" conservative and a failed liberal. I am a reluctant creative but learning to accept it. I'm not tortured enough to be an artist (at least not until recently) or smart enough to be an intellectual. But I'm content to sit somewhere in the middle and try drink from both cups, enjoying them both equally. Those are the things about me, the things I do, and the people that I'm not - I'm hoping to someday figure out who I am. If I've learned one thing that I am through this adventure it is that I am unquestionably one thing - haunted.

In (the absence of)

Nine.
Nine days since his passing.
Nine days since the sickness finished its ravaging work.
Nine days since hell said "it is finished"

My father was 63, Lxiii. A teacher most of his life - in the classroom, in our home.
A tortured soul, I would say - never at peace, never at rest. He despised structures of hierarchy, looked upon the social class system with scorn, abhorred injustice with unbearable pain, and below the weathered frustration -
lay brokenness, lay sorrow, lay longing, lay a yearning.

I spent my life learning from him, but it was not until his death that something like scales fell from my eyes and I could make sense of what it was for which he pined.

I thought it was for a state of being, a dollar amount given, a number adopted, I was wrong. It wasn't for something he could touch... it was for a year. No wonder he couldn't face it, stand in it, live it... to continually be 49 (or 63) but never able to be 50, that would drive any of us crazy. To have your heart be continually and slowly severed from your body, its blood spilling unendingly but not seen by anyone-and then to finally stop, that's more than I could bear.

As I watched the cells slowly overwhelm his body, my wretched cries yielded no response. While the ghosts around me were silent, the melodies and harmonies filling the room spoke loudly. When no spirits stepped in offering help, trepid footsteps carried warm meals. When there were no healing hands waiting in the wings, the cold clammy hand I held in mine hinted at hope. As his subsistence was ripped from him, I saw another that might subsist. When there was no one in existence who could save him I realized... I must exist on h/His behalf.
A mere 29 years old, I must age 20 years in (the absence of) a heartbeat.

When the Gods cease to exist,
that
leaves
only
us.

Now I look.
Longingly,
East,
toward home
into the tragedies of the past, the remains from which I am attempting to emerge,
and the shadows threaten to overtake me.

I am saved by the dawn, at least for today, a ray of hope.

Another day in which to exist, to be existence, to try and age one more year.
"The existence of God is the companionship offered to the dying through the night,
God being there wherever two or three gather under the name of God."

HE does not exist.
Existence is not the business of the divine.
Existence is left up to us.
HE does not exist.
Existence is not the business of the divine.
Existence is left up to us.

Dare to hope

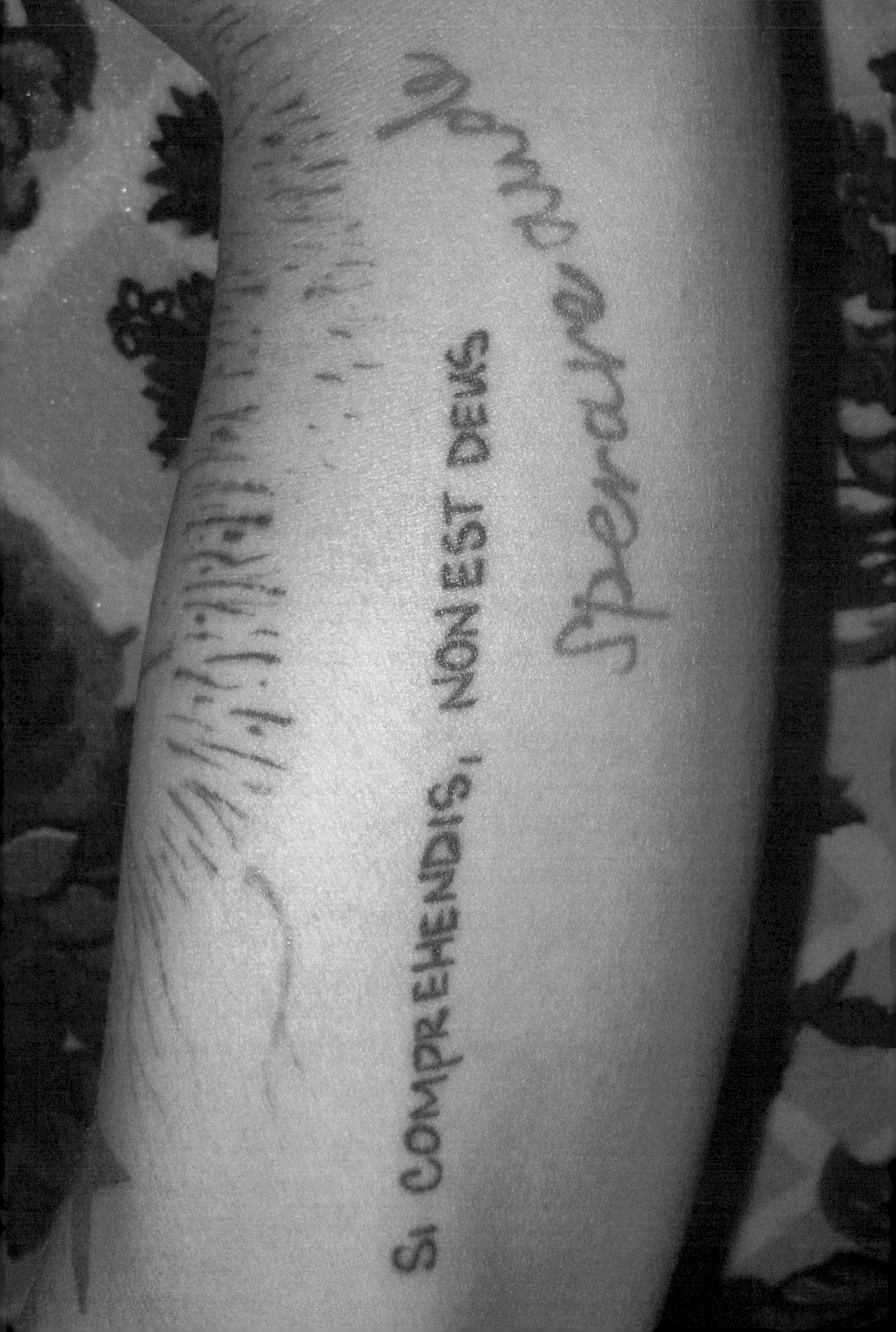

Dare to hope

The
End

Notes

Caputo

1. SoM: Jacques Derrida, Specters of Marx: The State of the Debt, the Work of Mourning, and the New International, trans. Peggy Kamuf (New York: Routledge, 1994). See my commentary on this text in The Prayers and Tears of Jacques Derrida: Religion without Religion (Bloomington:
Indiana University Press, 1997), 118-34.
2. John D. Caputo, Truth: Philosophy in Transit (London: Penguin Books, 2013), ch. 5.
3. See Immanuel Kant, "What is Enlightenment?" http://philosophy.eserver.org/kant/what-is-enlightenment.txt (accessed June, 2014).
4. Slavoj Žižek and John Milbank, edited by Creston Davis, The Monstrosity of Christ: Paradox or Dialectic (Cambridge: MIT Press, 2009). This debate revolves entirely around which of these positions is the true materialism. I have tried to settle the hash of both positions in The Insistence of God: A Theology of Perhaps (Bloomington: Indiana University Press, 2013), ch. 7.
5. Insistence of God, 97-103. I spell out my case in detail in "On Not Settling for an Abridged Edition of Postmodernism: Radical Hermeneutics as Radical Theology," in Reexamining Deconstruction and Determinate Religion: Toward a Religion with Religion, eds. J. Aaron Simmons and Stephen Minister (Pittsburgh: Duquesne University Press, 2012), 271-353.
6. See John D. Caputo, "The Weakness of the Flesh: Overcoming the Soft Gnosticism of Incarnational Christianity," in Intensities: Philosophy, Religion and the Affirmation of Life, eds. Steven Shakespeare and Katharine Sarah Moody (Surrey, England: Ashgate, 2012), 79-94.
7. Jacques Lacan, The Triumph of Religion preceded by Discourse to Catholics, trans. Bruce Fink (Cambridge: Polity Press, 2013), pp. 64.
8. I give a more nuanced account of the intertwining of confessional and radical theology in Insistence of God, ch. 4.
9. Jacques Derrida, "Circumfession: Fifty-nine Periods and Periphrases" in Geoffrey Bennington and Jacques Derrida, Jacques Derrida (Chicago: University of Chicago Press, 1993), 155.
10. Jacques Derrida, Rogues: Two Essays on Reason, trans. Pascale-Anne Brault and Michael Naas (Stanford: Stanford University Press, 2005), 110.
11. Johann Baptist Metz, Faith in History and Society, trans. D. Smith (New York: Crossroads, 1980), pp. 109-15.
12. This is one of the most famous lines to come out of the Monica Lewinsky impeachment hearings. Visit http://www.slate.com/articles/news_and_politics/chatterbox/1998/09/bill_clinton_and_the_meaning_of_is.html (accessed June, 2014).
13. http://poetry.rapgenius.com/Robert-frost-the-span-of-life-annotated#note-2172683 (accessed June, 2014).
14. For Levinas, the ethico-religious subject is not the agent subject of the "I am capable of" but the responsible subject, the "me," me voici, put in the accusative by the coming of the other. Emmanuel Levinas, Otherwise than Being or Beyond Essence, trans. Alphonso Lingis (The Hague: Nijhoff, 1981), 53-56.
15. I work out this dream in Insistence, ch. 2.
16. Hegel's Lectures on the Philosophy of Religion, One Volume Edition: The Lectures of 1827, ed. Peter Hodgson (Berkeley: University of California Press, 1988), 75-77.
17. Catherine Keller, The Face of the Deep: A Theology of Becoming (London: Routledge, 2003).
18. Martin Heidegger, "A Letter on Humanism," in Heidegger: Basic Writings, ed. by D. F. Krell, 2nd. ed. (New York: Harper & Row, 1993)
19. Paul Tillich, Theology of Culture, ed. Robert Kimball (Oxford: Oxford University Press, 1959), 25.
20. I elaborate this in Prayers and Tears, 26-41.
21. Derrida, Rogues, xiv. In Derrida, the "unconditionals," like justice, are always a weak force, without the "force of law."
22. The Complete Mystical Works of Meister Eckhart, trans and ed. Maurice O'C Walshe (New York: Crossroad, 2009), 83-90 ("Intravit Jesus in quoddam castellum").
23. For an insightful study of preaching and postmodernism, see Phil Snider, Preaching After God: Derrida, Caputo, and the Language of Postmodern Homiletics (Eugene, Oregon: Cascade Books, Wipf and Stock Publishers, 2012). See also Robert M. Price, Preaching Deconstruction, with a Foreword by Thomas J. J. Altizer (Mindvendor, 2014); Christopher D. Rodkey, Too Good to be True: Radical Christian Preaching, Year A, with Foreword by Peter Rollins and an Afterword by Thomas J. J. Altizer (UK: Christian Alternative, 2014).
24. Even someone as selfless as Louis Massignon (1883-1962), founder of Badalyia ("substitution"), a community of Christians in Egypt who were to be witness to Christ in the Islamic world, admitted that conversion to Catholicism may indeed be the object, or at least the result, of his work, but if it is to happen, it is to happen freely, without any pressure being applied on the part of the Christians. Cited by Derrida in Acts of Religion, ed. Gil Anidjar (New York and London: Routledge, 2002), 376n36.
25. Marguerite Porete, The Mirror of Simple Souls, trans. Ellen L. Babinsky (New York: Paulist Press, 1993), , 19 (101). See also 43 (122-23), 49-51 (127-29), 66 (142). I cite by chapter with the pagination in brackets.

DeLay

1. Jacob Taubes, To Carl Schmitt: Letters and Reflections, trans. Keith Tribe (New York: Columbia University Press, 2013), 26.
2.Luke Muehlhauser, "John Caputo—Postmodernism and Religion," http://commonsenseatheism.com/?p=9750.
3. Jacques Lacan discusses science, religion, and art as, respectively, psychotic, hysteric, and obsessionally neurotic expressions in The Ethics of Psychoanalysis 1959–1960: The Seminar of Jacques Lacan, Book VII, edited by Jacques-Alain Miller and translated by Dennis Porter (New York: W. W. Norton, 1997), 129-36.
4. Jacques Lacan, Écrits: The First Complete Edition in English, translated by Bruce Fink (New York: W. W. Norton, 1996), 742.
5. Jacques Lacan, The Triumph of Religion, translated by Bruce Fink (Malden: Polity, 2013), 64.
6. Abraham Joshua Heschel, God In Search of Man: A Philosophy of Judaism (New York: Farrar, Straus and Giroux, 1955), 10–1.
7. See Sigmund Freud, "Obsessive Actions and Religious Practices."
8. Jacques Lacan, The Ego in Freud's Theory and in the Technique of Psychoanalysis, 1954–1955: The Seminar of Jacques

Wilhelm Garbers

1. My thanks to Dr. Beth Bartlett who introduced me to A Chorus of Stones, and to the author of that text, Susan Griffin. Hers was the first truly haunted work that I read. This piece represents my continued attempt to try and let my writing become haunted. Susan Griffin, A Chorus of Stones: The Private Life of War (New York: Anchor Books, 1992).
2. Let me be clear here: I am aware that critiques can be levied at Beyoncé's work; however my lack of "critique" is meant to enact the way of doing theology that opens itself (see Caputo's essay).
3. This is one of the names that her ardent followers call her: #QueenBey.
4. For a great overall summary of the birth of this album, see: http://en.wikipedia.org/wiki/Beyoncé_(album).
5. Soraya McDonald, "Finally free of Sasha Fierce, Beyoncé is a 'Grown Woman,'" The Washington Post (December 28, 2013), http://www.washingtonpost.com/blogs/she-the-people/wp/2013/12/28/finally-free-of-sasha-fierce-beyonce-is-a-grown-woman/, retrieved October 25, 2014.
6. Sasha Frere-Jones, "The Death Drive," The New Yorker (December 16, 2013), http://www.newyorker.com/culture/sasha-frere-jones/the-death-drive, retrieved October 25, 2014. For a list of other reviews see: http://www.metacritic.com/music/beyonce/beyonce/critic-reviews.
7. Caputo, Final Draft of "Proclaiming the Year of Jubilee," 10.
8. Many womanist academics and cultural analysts have importantly pointed out the intersectionality of race, class, gender, sexual and other identities, and the colonization of feminist identity that white women have often enacted. Beyoncé has served as a point of reflection in this discussion. In instance, see: Mikki Kendall, "Beyoncé's new album should silence her feminist critics," The Guardian (December 13, 2013), http://www.theguardian.com/commentisfree/2013/dec/13/beyonce-album-flawless-feminism, accessed October 25, 2014.
9. "Grown Woman" refers to one of her songs from the album.
10. This piece is deeply influenced by and indebted to the work of Judith Butler, especially Giving an Account and Undoing Gender. Judith Butler, Giving an Account of Oneself (New York: Fordum, 2005) and Undoing Gender (New York: Routledge, 2004).
11. Sesali Bowen, "Beyoncé shows us what we really fear in 'Haunted' video," Feministing (December 18, 2013), http://feministing.com/2013/12/18/beyonce-shows-us-what-we-really-fear-in-haunted-video/, accessed October 25, 2014.
12. Butler, Undoing Gender, 74.
13. Butler, Undoing Gender, 219.
14. Martin Luther King, Jr. "A tough mind and a tender heartThe Man Who Was a Fool," in A testament of hope: The essential writings and speeches of Martin Luther King, JrStrength to Love, 65-74., ed. J.M. Washington, 491-497, (New York:Minneapolis, MN: Fortress Press, 2010), 69. HarperSanFrancisco, 1986).
15. Mary Lambert, "Secrets," Heart on My Sleeve, 2014 copyright by e (Capital Records, 2014).
16. Beetlejuice deals with a couple who comes back to haunt the new owners of their home. Tim Burton, Beetlejuice (Warner Brothers: March 30, 1988). Also, Bowen helpfully notes that the image of the black men with their faces painted recalls the critical 1995 film Dead Presidents that traces the life of a black man from the Bronx who fights in Vietnam and then stages a bank robbery. Albert Hughes and Allen Hughes, Dead Presidents (Buena Vista Pictures: October 6, 1995).
17. Caputo, 19.
18. Ibid., 35.
19. Lyrics to "Haunted" as they appear on the record: Beyoncé, "Haunted," Beyoncé, 2013 copyright by Parkwood Entertainment and Columbia Records. Lyrics obtained online: http://www.beyonce.com/album/beyonce/?media_view=songs, obtained October 25, 2014.

Crockett

1. Carl Raschke, "The Deconstruction of God," in Deconstruction and Theology (New York: Crossroad, 1982), pp. 1-33 (quote p. 3).
2. Charles E. Winquist, Desiring Theology, (Chicago: University of Chicago Press), p. ix.
3. Jeffrey W. Robbins, "Terror and the Postmodern Condition," in Religion and Violence in a Secular World, ed. Clayton Crockett (Charlottesville, University of Virginia Press, 2006), pp. 187-205 (quote p. 196).
4. Ibid., p. 197.
5. See Elizabeth Kolbert, The Sixth Extinction ().
6. Jacques Derrida, "Force of Law: The 'Mystical Foundation of Authority,'" trans. Mary Quintance, in Acts of Religion, ed. Gil Anidjar (London: Routledge, 2002), pp. 230-298 (quote p. 253).
7. Catherine Keller, Cloud of the Impossible (New York: Columbia University Press, 2014), p. 4.

Katharine Sarah Moody

1. See Thom Gunn, 'The Reassurance' in Collected Poems (London: Faber & Faber, 1994[1993]), p. 471.
2. See Ludwig Feuerbach, The Fiery Brook: Selected Writings of Ludwig Feuerbach, trans. ZawarHanfi (Garden City, New York: Doubleday, 1972), p. 153; and Ludwig Feuerbach, Lectures on the Essence of Religion (New York: Harper & Row, 1967), p. 23. See also Ludwig Feuerbach, The Essence of Christianity, trans. George Eliot (New York: Harper and Brothers, 1975).
3. See Karl Marx, 'Contribution to the Critique of Hegel's Philosophy of Right', in Karl Marx and Friedrich Engels, On Religion (Atlanta: Scholars Press, 1964).
4. Text in bold has been taken from John D. Caputo, 'Proclaiming the Year of Jubilee: Thoughts on a Spectral Life', published in this volume.
5. See Sigmund Freud, The Future of an Illusion, in The Standard Edition of the Complete Psychological Works of Sigmund Freud vol. XXI (London: Hogarth Press, 1953-74), p. 43; and Sigmund Freud, Civilization and Its Discontents, in The Standard Edition of the Complete Psychological Works of Sigmund Freudvol. XXI, p. 75. See also Brian R. Clack, Love, Drugs, Art, Religion: The Pains and Consolations of Existence (Farnham, Surrey: Ashgate, 2014), p. 84.
6. See Sigmund Freud and Josef Breuer, Studies on Hysteria, in The Standard Edition of the Complete Psychological Works of Sigmund Freudvol. II, p. 351.
7. See Freud, Civilization and Its Discontents, pp. 78-85.
8. See Freud, Civilization and Its Discontents, p. 75; Theodor Fontane, EffiBriest(London: Penguin, 2000), p. 212; and Clack, Love, Drugs, Art, Religion, p. 30.
9. See William James, The Varieties of Religious Experience (London: Collins, 1960), p. 158; Martin Heidegger, Being and Time (Oxford: Basil Blackwell, 1962), p. 233; and Freud, The Future of an Illusion, p. 17. See also Clack, Love, Drugs, Art, Religion, pp. 154-60.
10. See Freud, The Future of an Illusion, pp. 32-33 and 50.
11. See especially John D. Caputo, Radical Hermeneutics: Repetition, Deconstruction, and the Hermeneutic Project (Bloomington: Indiana University Press, 1987).
12. See John D. Caputo, The Insistence of God: A Theology of Perhaps (Bloomington: Indiana University Press, 2013), p. 41.
13. See Caputo, The Insistence of God, p. 224. See page 228 for Caputo's remarks on Paul as a ghost.
14. See Jacques Derrida, Learning to Live Finally: The Last Interview (Basingstoke: Palgrave Macmillan, 2007), especially pp. 26 and 51-2.
15. See Caputo, 'A Nihilism of Grace: Life, Death, and Resurrection', in The Insistence of God, pp. 223-45
16. See Grace Jantzen, Foundations of Violence I: Death and the Displacement of Beauty (London: Routledge, 2004), p. 4.
17. See Meister Eckhart, The Complete Mystical Works of Meister Eckhart, trans. and ed. Maurice O'C Walshe (New York: Crossroad, 2009), p. 10; cited by Caputo in The Insistence of God, p. 226.
18. See Clack, 'Religion Beyond Illusion', in Love, Drugs, Art, Religion, pp. 145-75.
19. See Michael Oakeshott, On Human Conduct (Oxford: Clarendon Press, 1975), p. 84 on the idea of religion as a reconciliation to nothingness.
20. See Jason Marc Harris, Folklore and the Fantastic in Nineteenth Century British Fiction (Farnham, Surrey: Ashgate, 2008) and Nicola Brown, Carolyn Burdett and Pamela Thurschwell, eds, TheVictorian Supernatural (Cambridge: Cambridge University Press, 2004). See also Martyn Jolly, Faces of the Living Dead: The Belief in Spirit Photography (London: The British Library, 2006). While we have surmounted 'primitive' modes of thought, such as the ghostly return of the dead, there are moments, Freud concludes, when – not yet feeling secure in our new modes of thought – weexperience the return of these repressed beliefs. Such is an experience of the uncanny (unheimlich). SeeSigmund Freud, 'The "Uncanny"', in The Standard Edition of the Complete Psychological Works of Sigmund Freud vol. XXI, pp. 217-56. See also Nicholas Royle, The Uncanny (Manchester: Manchester University Press, 2003).
21. See Mary Poovey, ed., The Financial System in Nineteenth-Century Britain (Oxford: Oxford University Press, 2003).
22. See Andrew Smith, The Ghost Story 1840-1920: A Cultural History (Manchester: Manchester University Press, 2010).
23. See Jacques Derrida, Specters of Marx: The State of the Debt, the Work of Mourning, and the New International (London: Routledge, 1994). See also Chris Baldick, 'Karl Marx's Vampires and Grave-diggers', in In Frankenstein's Shadow: Myth, Monstrosity and Nineteenth-Century Writing (Oxford: Clarendon Press, 1987), pp. 121-40; and Tricia Lootens, 'Fear of Furniture: Commodity Gothicism and the Teaching of Victorian Literature', in Diane Long Hoeveler and Tamar Heller, eds, Gothic Fiction: The British and American Traditions (New York: MLA, 2003), pp. 148-58. In The Ghost Story 1840-1920, Smith also draws attention to Peter Buse and Andrew Stott, eds., Ghosts: Deconstruction, Psychoanalysis, History (Basingstoke: Macmillan, 1999) and Julian Wolfreys, Victorian Hauntings: Spectrality, Gothic, the Uncanny and Literature (Basingstoke: Macmillan,

2001).
24. See Smith, The Ghost Story 1840-1920, pp. 32-48.
25. If ghosts represent an exploration of economically-understood subjectivity, this is perhaps part of the reason that both Miss Havisham (the imagined 'parent' of Pip's financial inheritance) and Magwitch (the second father who is the 'actual parent' of his expectations) are depicted as ghostly. The 'ghosts' in Great Expectations (1861) are figures of the tension between money and family that haunts Pip as he endeavours to negotiate subjectivity. See Crystal Downing, 'Finding Satisfaction in Great Expectations', in Charles Dickens, Great Expectations, ed. Jill Kriegel (San Francisco: Ignatius Press, 2010), pp. 599-613.
26. See Eugene Thacker, InThe Dust of This Planet: Horror of Philosophy, vol. 1 (Winchester: Zero Books 2011), especially pp. 98-132.
27. See Emmanuel Levinas, 'There is: Existence without Existents', in The Levinas Reader, trans. Seán Hand (London: Blackwell, 1990), p. 30; cited by Thacker, in In The Dust of This Planet, p. 129.
28. See Caputo, The Insistence of God, pp. 255-9.
29. See Thacker, In the Dust of This Planet, pp. 129-32.

Freeman

1. Yeshua is the historical Aramaic name for Jesus of Nazareth, which is translated as "Joshua" in English. However when translated from Hebrew into the Greek, the name Yeshua becomes Iēsous, which is how we arrive at the English name "Jesus." Throughout this text Jesus is called by his historical name "Yeshua" to de-familiarize him, and to make us think of him as a more anonymous or indeterminate historical figure - and thus to break the grip of the theological confessions of the Church which have always only interpret Yeshua as the Christ of faith. This distinction between the Jesus of history (Yeshua) and the Christ of faith (son of God, Logos made flesh, second person of the Trinity, etc.), while itself provisional and never able to stabilize into a settled structure, is the basic distinction underlying all contemporary New Testament research.
2. Mark 8:29
3. The one that Christians worship as the only begotten Son of God was an irreligious, irreverent, and impious peasant. He had sharp tongue, a volatile temper, was harsh to his mother and never even knew his biological father. Immediately after he began his meteoric public career he broke off relations with his family who thought he'd gone insane, and when he was rejected as a false prophet in his hometown he slipped away from his enemies after being almost thrown of the edge of a cliff... And while only the mentally deranged and demon possessed called him the son of God, he was considered a drunkard and a glutton who befriended whores, extortionists and alcoholics... or simply an agent of Satan by the more learned Jewish scribes. As a social deviant who avoided crowds and sought out solitude, he transgressed the purity regulations, and even dared to break the divine commandments of the Mosaic Law, while his baffled contemporaries even asked if he intended to commit suicide...
An eccentric teacher of poetic-paradox who spoke in strange riddles and razor-sharp aphorisms, this restless heretic proclaimed the already beginning reign of a Kingdom that was also soon to come, by invoking the most morally outrageous metaphors and the most obscene imagery. A fearless antagonist of the established order, he stirred up revolt against the rulers of his county, and sought to usher in his own anarchic Kingdom by inviting the most despicable and disaffected underbelly of society to the holy banquet... A shameless fool who exposed the hypocrisy of religious sincerity, he preached the break-up of the family and the love of ones enemies while his enigmatic message was constantly misunderstood, even by his closest followers. As the sheer single-minded lunacy of this bizarre mission without any human justification moved towards its inevitable climax, this blasphemous vagabond entered Jerusalem riding on a female donkey...
Walking into the Temple courtyards like a madman possessed, in a diabolical passion for a justice to come, he cracked a bullwhip and sent shock waves through the guardians of religious purity by turning over tables and chasing out the money changes. A rebellious outlaw exposing the sin of obedience, in a blessed rage for holy disarray he informed Jewish religious authorities that their own fathers killed the prophets and then threatened to tear down the Temple... In a murderous conspiracy at the highest levels of power, he was arrested in the dead of the night, given a mock trail and then brutally executed as a dangerous criminal for both treason against Rome and blasphemy against the God of Israel... while confessing, in his very last breath, that he was an atheist. Yeshua was never going to change the world, but at least he was willing to die trying......
4. While recent Catholic theology has only fuelled this scepticism by virtually dismissing the quest for the historical Yeshua as both historically impossible and theologically illegitimate, in recent decades popular culture has spawned a wide array of myth-busting conspiracy theories on the origins of Christianity, including: Dan Brown's fictional novel The Da Vinci Code; the widely debunked Zeitgeist film; as well as the New Age Gnostic that claim that Yeshua was originally an enlightened mystic who came from the East; and various scholars who argue that Christianity is an ancient mystery cult based on the "dying-and-rising god" motif found in various Pagan myths. The most credible of these contemporary "mythicist" scholars are Robert Price and Richard

Carrier.
5. The rest of Josephus' passage, which betrays signs of later Christian interpolation and editing, states: "He was the Christ. And when, upon the accusation of the principal men among us, Pilate had condemned him to a cross, those who had first come to love him did not cease. He appeared to them spending a third day restored to life, for the prophets of God had foretold these things and a thousand other marvels about him. And the tribe of the Christians, so called after him, has still to this day not disappeared." (Flavius Josephus: Antiquities of the Jews, Book 18:63-64)
6. See Meier's extensive discussion in "A Marginal Jew: Rethinking the Historical Jesus" (Doubleday, 1991), Vol. 1, pp. 57-88. Most intriguing here is Meier's conclusion that Josephus had access to a more direct or unfiltered witness to the historical Yeshua, i.e. an insight into the historical figure of Yeshua not seen even in the gospel traditions. Is it possible that Josephus knew something about Yeshua that his later apostles didn't...?
7. Other translations of the original Greek used by Josephus give us the following: Yeshua was a performer of paradoxical (astonishing, startling, or surprising) poetics (tricks, feats, works and deeds), a teacher of those who accept the abnormal (novel, truth, unusual and strange) with pleasure (gladly, delight).
8. The poetics of paradox (paradoxônergônpoiêtês) at the heart of the parables of Jesus is also a strikingly similar form of discourse to that which has recently been explored by Jack Caputo in "The Insistence of God: A Theo-poetics of Perhaps" (Indiana University Press 2013), as well as radical theologian Peter Rollins in "The Orthodox Heretic" (Paraclete Press 2009) and "The Fidelity of Betrayal" (Paraclete Press (2008).
9. Crossan, J. D. "In Parables: The Challenge of the Historical Jesus", (San Francisco 1973), p.13
10. When it comes to the historical Yeshua, there are just a handful of areas of fundamental scholarly consensus. Firstly, it is an uncontested historical fact that Yeshua is the one who proclaimed the kingdom of God. References to the "kingdom of God" are found over one hundred times in the gospel texts, as Perrin summarizes, "The central aspect of the teaching of Jesus was that concerning the Kingdom of God. Of this there can be no doubt and today no scholar does, in fact, doubt it. Jesus appeared as the one who proclaimed the Kingdom; all else in his message and ministry serves function in relation to that proclamation and derives it's meaning from it." (cited in Crossan 1973, p.23). Secondly, the historical figure of Yeshua gave voice to his experience of the kingdom of God primarily by way of parables. For instance, in the Gospel of Matthew we read: "All this Yeshua said to the crowds in parables; indeed he said nothing to them without a parable" (Matt. 13:34). A parable is a story, "drawn from nature or common life, arresting the hearer by its vividness or strangeness, and leaving the mind in sufficient doubt about its precise application to tease it into active thought."(Dodd, C. H. "The Parables of the Kingdom", Fontana 1961, p.16)
11. It's also important to note that none of the gospel authors were eyewitnesses to the public ministry or teachings of Yeshua. The gospel accounts of Yeshua that we have today are narratives that were developed within the oral language tradition and the socio-political situation of the early Christian communities: communities that first documented their experience of Yeshua approximately 30 to 60 years after his death. In other words, even that which claims to have originated with Yeshua himself will have been edited and reinterpreted through many years of oral and written transmission in the development of the early Church.
12. In this respect, perhaps the best advice comes from Crossan who offers a stern warning against constructing a picture of Jesus that we are comfortable and satisfied with, while also reminding Christians that if they "cannot believe in something produced by historical re-construction, then Christianity may have nothing left to believe in." (Crossan, "The Historical Jesus: the Life of a Mediterranean Jewish Peasant" (1991, p.426)
13. Luke 10:25-37 What has been overlooked in the historical development of Christianity since the 1st century is that Samaritans were the mortal enemies of the Jewish people and were looked down upon as a race of sub-human half-castes, ever since they split off from the rest of the nation of Israel during the reign of King David. In the context of this parable, then, Samaritan and Judean stand inconsiderable tension with each other, one a hated enemy of the beaten man and on the other God's specially chosen instruments of salvation.
14. Luke 15:11-32
15. Hultgren, A. J. "The Parables of Jesus: A Commentary". Cambridge, UK, William B. Eerdmans Publishing Company (2000), p.8-10
16. Matthew 20:1-16
17. Luke 18:10-14
18. Matthew 21:28-32
19. Luke 11:5-8
20. Luke 16:1-8
21. Luke 18: 2-8
22. Crossan, D. "The Good Samaritan: Towards a Generic Definition of Parable," Semeia 2 (1974), 82-107, esp. 98, 105.
23. Significantly, the parables of Yeshuaconstitute the very site of the revelation of the kingdom of God, as Ricoeur states: "the parables don't tell us what the kingdom of God is about, the kingdom of God is what

happens in the parables." (Ricoeur, P. "Figuring the Sacred: Religion, Narrative and Imagination", Minneapolis: Fortress 1995, p.165) Since the parables of Yeshuaconstitute the very site of the revelation of the kingdom of God, our ability to re-activate the dangerous memory of Yeshua and what he came to bring the human race is therefore intimately linked to the parables which reveal his own experience and understanding of the kingdom of God.

24. Significantly, the parables of Yeshuaconstitute the very site of the revelation of the kingdom of God, as Ricoeur states: "the parables don't tell us what the kingdom of God is about, the kingdom of God is what happens in the parables." (Ricoeur, P. "Figuring the Sacred: Religion, Narrative and Imagination", Minneapolis: Fortress 1995, p.165) Since the parables of Yeshuaconstitute the very site of the revelation of the kingdom of God, our ability to re-activate the dangerous memory of Yeshua and what he came to bring the human race is therefore intimately linked to the parables which reveal his own experience and understanding of the kingdom of God.

25. Crossan, D. "Cliffs of Fall: Paradox and Polyvalence in the Parables of Jesus", (New York, 1980), p. 9-10

26. Freeman, C. "Post-Metaphysics and the Paradoxical Teachings of Jesus: the Structure of the Real" (Peter Lang, 2010) -There are twenty one other parables in the synoptic gospels that also contain the spectral undecidability of radical paradox within their narrative structure. They are as follows. Unforgiving Slave (Matthew 18:23-35): an occasion for judgment is act of forgiveness, an occasion for forgiveness is an act of judgment. Rich Fool (Luke 12:16-21, Gospel of Thomas 63): the wisdom of working to secure ones future is foolish hoarding, the foolishness of an unsettled and uncertain future, is wisdom and security. Final Judgment (Matthew 25:31-46): those who know God's name are damned in never serving the poor, while those who serve the poor are saved even though they never knew God by name. Great Banquet (Luke 14: 16-24, Matthew 22:2-14, Gospel Thomas 64): the ones who to get in are the ones who are expected to be left out; while the ones who are left out are the ones who are expected to get in. Rich Man and Lazarus (Luke 16:19-31): the rich man who is glorified in this life is destitute and without hope in the afterlife, just as Lazarus who is destitute and without hope in this life is glorified in the afterlife. Wedding Feast (Matthew 22: 1-14): the outsiders are in, just as the insiders are out. Treasure in the Field (Matthew 13:44) finding is losing and losing is finding. Pear of Great Price (Matthew 13:45-46): looking through many is finding one, selling many is buying one. Father's Good Gifts (Matt 7:9-11, Luke 11:11-13): the suggestion of false gifts is an affirmation of good gifts, while the affirmation of good gifts is the suggestion false gifts (compared to the good gifts of the Father) Talents (Matthew 25:14-30): the risk of losing what has been given is to save one's life, to save what has been given is to risk of losing one's life. Slave at Duty (Luke 17:7-10): an occasion for grace is a demand for good works, while the occasion of good works is a confession of grace. Faithful and Wise Slave (Matthew 24:45-51, Luke 12:42-46): to be a slave in the master's absence is to possess all the riches in his presence, while to possess of all the master's riches in his absence, is to be a slave in his presence. Waiting Slaves (Mark 13:34-37, Luke 12:35-38): a promise is a threat as a threat is a promise. Wicked Tenants (Mark 12:1-12, Matthew 21:33-46, Luke 20:9-19, Thomas 65-66): a time for fruitfulness is an occasion of violence, while an occasion for violence is really the time for fruitfulness. Sower (Mark 4:3-8, Matthew 13: 3-8, Luke 8:5-8, Gospel of Thomas 9): just as abundant sowing leads to wide spread scarcity, the scarcity of a few seeds in good soil leads to wide spread abundance. Weeds and the Wheat (Matthew 13:24-30): a cause for division is a time for union, and what is a cause for union is a time for division. Barren Fig Tree (Luke 13:6-9): what is expected to be fruitful is judged to be barren, and a judgment of barren-ness is an opportunity for fruitfulness.SeedGrowing Secretly (Mark 4:26-29): manual labor is natural growth and natural growth is the manual labor. Lost Sheep (Luke 15:4-7) and the Lost Coin (Luke 15:8-10): the one that is lost is more valuable than the many that are saved. Children Playing (Matt 11:16-19, Luke 7:31-35): the funeral song is too sad for those that want to play the wedding dance, and the wedding song is too happy for those that want to sing the funeral dirge.

27. A small number (5) of parables do not conform to the paradoxical structure set out here, most likely because the paradoxical voice-print of the historical Yeshua was lost in translation through the oral transmission of the parable in the early Christian communities and obscured by the time they were written down in the gospel narratives. These five parables are: The Two Builders (Matt 7:24-27, Luke 6:47-49); the Demon Returning (Matt 12: 43-45, Luke 11:24-26); Parable of the Net (MATT 13:47-50); the Ten Virgins (Matt 25:1-13); and Landowner and King (Luke 14: 28-33).

28. See especially John Carroll's "The Existential Jesus" (Scribe 2007)

29. The Messianic secret is seen in: Yeshua'sCommands to silence demons who call him the son of God are found in Mark 1.34; 3.11-12; instructions not to make his healing-miracles public in 1.43-45; 5.43; 7.36; 8.26; teaching to the disciples in private are in 4.34; 7.17-23; 9.28; 8.31; 9.31; 10.32-34; 13.3; commands to silence disciples who called him Messiah in 8.30 and 9.9, and the parables as intended to obscure the message so that outsiders may not understand is in 4.10-13.

30. Mark 3:11-12

31. Mark 4:10-12

32. Yeshua spoke in parables not to give cryptic puzzles to be solved, and not simply to confound and confuse his audience - but to challenge us to think, to ask questions and to examine our fundamental biases and presuppositions. So when people asked Yeshua a question, instead of answering with a well-rehearsed theological doctrine, he usually fired another question straight back at them. He almost never gave a direct answer to anything!In other words, he spoke in these enigmatic paradoxes because he was encouraging his hearer's to be more sensitive to the tremulousness of their lives, to welcome the anonymous spook that cannot be silenced, and to be vulnerable to those unsettling questions that come over us "like a thief in the night…" and when we least expect.
33. Mark 8:27-33 (also see Matt. 16:13-16, 20-23; Luke 9:18-22)
34. Mark 8:29
35. While the gospel of Mark was the earliest gospel written - and therefore historically closer to the flesh and blood memory of Yeshua, Christian domestication on this passage begins in the later gospel of Matthew (and then Luke and John), where theological retrojection and embellishment begins to cover over the scandal of Yeshua's rebuke. While it is not possible to fully develop this point here, the author of Matthew's gospel invokes the natural/supernatural distinction in order to reify the Peter's confession into a 'higher' spiritual realm - and thus justify the early Christian communities proclamation of Yeshua's Messianic status as God's anointed one, where instead of the abrupt rebuke and subsequent silencing of Peter we see in Mark, we now find Yeshua saying "Blessed are you, Simon son of Jonah! For flesh and blood has not revealed this to you, but my Father in heaven…" (Matt 16:17) This Christological retrojection back onto the past is a reasonably straightforward case of theological obfuscation, for in the early Markan text we see Yeshua saying to Peter after this incident, precisely the opposite: "You do not have in mind the concerns of God, but merely human concerns." (Mark 8:33)
36. Mark 8:33, Matt 16:23 – The severity of this response that even suggests a hint of fear and trepidation in Yeshua himself about his impending death
37. The first (and only) one in Mark's narrative to see and enacted what it means for Yeshua to be the "anointed one" (i.e. Christ) was the anonymous spectre of the unnamed woman in Bethany at the house of an outcast, Simon the Leper. Understanding what Yeshua meant when he spoke of his impending death and recognizing that Yeshua is about to be crucified, she "anoints" (massages) his body with the entire content of a very expensive jar of perfume - a sign that she knew precisely what Yeshua was predicting, in preparing his body for death and burial... While onlookers were outraged by what they saw as a waste of precious oil, the first person ever to (literally) anoint Yeshua as the Christ (in Greek: "anointed one") was praised by Yeshua in unparalleled terms. "Truly I tell you, wherever the good news is proclaimed in the whole world, what she has done will be told in remembrance of her." (Mark 14:3-9)
38. For in all three synoptic gospel narratives, Jesus rarely refers to himself at all, and when he does he speaks of himself in cryptic sayings that interrupt his audiences expectations, he refers to himself only in ambiguous or spectral terms such as the homeless "Son of Man", an Old Testament name which simply means "human being", or one who is just like anyone else… e.g. "foxes have dens, and birds of the air have nests, but the Son of Man has no place to lay his head" (Matt 8:20; Luke 9:5; Gospel Thomas 86)
39. J. D. G. Dunn, (1970) "The Messianic Secret In Mark", Tyndale Bulletin, Volume:21
40. William Wrede, The Messianic Secret, trans. J. C. G. Grieg (Cambridge:James Clarke & Co., 1971) Wrede (1901) was the first to deal with this problem by arguing that Yeshua understood himself to be the pre-ordained son of God throughout his earthly ministry, but that he wanted to keep this secret until the resurrection, where all would be revealed…
41. M. J. Borg (Yeshua: A New Vision, 10): "Regarding Yeshua' own sense of identity, the growing historical skepticism produced a consensus. Whether Yeshua thought of himself as having a special exalted identity---as "Messiah" or "the Son of God"---we cannot know because of the very nature of the documents. When we do find such statements in the gospels... the careful historian (even if he or she is also a Christian) must suspect them as the post-Easter perspective of Yeshua's followers projected back into the ministry." Notable dissenters to this scholarly consensus include A. Schweitzer, M. Hengel and N. T. Wright (Jesus and the Victory of God, p. 488).
42. Also see Crossan, D. "The Dark Interval: Towards a Theology of Story" (Allen, TX: Argus Communications, 1975)
43. "… nothing is present without being haunted… nothing has Being unless it trembles with may-being… nothing is real unless it is destabilized by the irreal, that goes for God, for God above all… the most really real of all." Jack Caputo, "Proclaiming the Year of the Jubilee: Thoughts on a Spectral Life" (Shelter 50, 2014), p. 18
44. Mark 15:34 - these words are one example of only a handful of words in the Mark's gospel that were written in Yeshua own Aramaic tongue, which is therefore suggestive of a vivid historical memory...
45. Mark 1:26, 5:7
46. Moreover, if we look at the anatomy and physiology of Yeshua' death by crucifixion, it is likely that Yeshua died because of the shock and exhaustion led to increasing physiological demands on his heart, which eventually resulted in cardiac rupture. That is, the most probable medical cause of Yeshua's death on the cross is that his

heart exploded. In response to Jack Caputo's jarring question in The Insistence of God (2013), "could God, unawares, step on an explosive? Could God be blown to bits without so much as knowing what hit him?" Is it possible that in the Crucifixion, the very heart of God was literally blown to pieces...?

47. At the death of Yeshua, darkness came over the land, the bowls of the earth shook, tombs broke open and the Temple veil was ripped in two (Matt 27:52) in an ontological scandal (Zizek) that threw the very edifice of reality off the rails and exposing the sheer lack of anyrationalorder to the universe.

48. Mark 15:39

49. Jack Caputo, "Proclaiming the Year of the Jubilee: Thoughts on a Spectral Life" (Shelter 50, 2014), p. 35

50. "He comes to us as One unknown, without a name, as of old, by the lakeside. He came to those men who knew Him not. He speaks to us the same words: "Follow thou me!" and sets us to the tasks which He has to fulfill for our time. He commands. And to those who obey Him, whether they be wise or simple, He will reveal himself in the toils, the conflicts, the sufferings which they shall pass through in His fellowship, and, as an ineffable mystery, they shall learn in their own experience Who He is."⊠ Albert Schweitzer, The Quest of the Historical Jesus

51. Terry Eagleton Figures of Dissent: Critical Essays on Fish, Spivak, Žižek and Others, p.201

52. "The very structure of a specter, and therefore of a call, is that we cannot identify the provenance of the call or make out exactly who or what is calling or being called for, so that the responsibility falls upon me..." Jack Caputo, "Proclaiming the Year of the Jubilee: Thoughts on a Spectral Life" (Shelter 50, 2014), p. 33

Osinski

1. "In a theology of 'perhaps,' God does not exist; God insists, and it is our responsibility to bring about something that exists." Caputo, John D. The Insistence of God: A Theology of Perhaps. Bloomington: Indiana University Press, 2013. P 49

2. Kierkegaard, Søren. Discourses at the Communion on Fridays. Translated by Sylvia Walsh. Bloomington: Indiana University Press, 2011.

3. Caputo, John D. The Insistence of God: A Theology of Perhaps. Bloomington: Indiana University Press, 2013. P 84.

4. Francois Lyotard talks about "the Thing, that which preoccupies art and writing," and says that it "asks nothing of you. But there is this persistence of dread." This sounds like the "haunting" call of which Caputo speaks. It's something that commands, though it does not demand, a response. See Lyotard, Jean-Francois, "Anamnesis: Of the Visible," Theory, Culture & Society 21, no. 1 (2004): 107-119, 108.

5. Caputo,Insistence.

6. Caputo,Insistence.

7. Llewelyn, John. Margins of Religion: Between Kierkegaard and Derrida. Bloomington: Indiana University Press, 2008. P 10.

Higgins

1. Charles Dickens, A Christmas Carol, [Kindle iPad Version]. Retrieved from Amazon.com. (Stave One: Marley's Ghost, Location 296 of 1521)

2. "Anxiety." Merriam-Webster.com. Merriam-Webster, n.d. Web. 30 Sept. 2014. <http://www.merriam-webster.com/dictionary/anxiety>.

3. Genesis 1: 26-27, New International Version.

4. Exodus 3:13-14, New International Version.

5. http://newsfeed.time.com/2012/06/19/why-is-scary-music-scary-heres-the-science/. Accessed October 25, 2014

6. Dickens, Location 37 of 1521.

7. I John 4:12, New International Version.

Keller

1. John Caputo, The Insistence of God: A Theology of Perhaps (Bloomington: Indiana University Press, 2013).

2. Caputo, "Proclaiming the Year of the Jubilee: Thoughts on a Spectral Life," 17.

3. Catherine Keller, Cloud of the Impossible: Negative Theology and Planetary Entanglement (New York: Columbia University Press, 2014).

4. Caputo, 14.

5. Caputo, 17.

6 Caputo, 14.

7. Whitehead, Process and Reality

8. Whitehead, Adventures of Ideas

9. Whitehead, Process and Reality

10. Whitehead
Sallie McFague, The Body of God: An Ecological Theology (Minneapolis: Fortress Press, 1993). Ivone Gebara, Longing for Runing Water

11. Sallie McFague, The Body of God: An Ecological Theology (Minneapolis: Fortress Press, 1993). Ivone Gebara, Longing for Runing Water

12. Charles Hartshorne, Omnipotence and Other Theological Mistakes (Albany, NY: State University of New York, 1984).

13. Such feminist (not feminine) relationality ontologically radicalized was the subject of my first work, From a Broken Web: Separation, Sexism and Self. (Boston: Beacon), 1984.

14. Carter Heyward, Saving Jesus from Those Who Are Right: Rethinking What It Means to Be Christian (Minneapolis: Fortress Press, 1999).

15. Stephen D. Moore, Divinanimality: Animal Theory, Creaturely Theology (New York: Fordham University Press, 2014). Based on Transdisciplinary Theological Colloquium, Drew 2012??

16. I think especially of Jane Bennett and Karen Barad. Volume in process with Fordham Press, based on Entangled Worlds: Transdiscipinary Theological Colloquium, Drew 2014.

17. Whitehead, Process and Reality, 81.

18. Caputo, The Insistence, 212.

19. Mary Jane Rubenstein, Worlds Without End: the Many Lives of the Multiverse (NY: Columbia U Pr), 2014

9985656R00145

Printed in Great Britain
by Amazon.co.uk, Ltd.,
Marston Gate.